I'M THE
YORKSHIRE
RIPPER

I'M THE YORKSHIRE RIPPER

CONVERSATIONS WITH A KILLER

ROBIN PERRIE
& ALFIE JAMES

m
B

MIRROR BOOKS

m
B
MIRROR BOOKS

1

Published in Great Britain and Ireland in 2022 by
Mirror Books, a Reach PLC business,
5 St Paul's Square, Liverpool, L3 9SJ.

www.mirrorbooks.co.uk
@TheMirrorBooks

Print ISBN 9781913406905
eBook ISBN 9781913406912

Page design and typesetting by Danny Lyle.

Printed and bound in Great Britain by
CPI Group (UK) Ltd, Croydon, CR0 4YY.

Photos: Reach Plc, Alamy.

ABOUT THE AUTHORS

Robin Perrie

Robin developed a fascination with the Yorkshire Ripper case while growing up in the north of England in the 1970s. He studied law at Leeds University before starting his career in journalism, working on local newspapers in the city with reporters who had covered the story from day one, further firing his interest. He joined *The Sun* in 1995 as one of its northern reporters and covered countless stories about Sutcliffe, interviewing his family, victims' relatives, survivors and others close to him, which led to him securing unparalleled access to Sutcliffe via Alfie James.

Alfie James

Alfie has always had a passion for true crime and wrote to a number of high-profile offenders to understand the motives behind their actions. Peter Sutcliffe was the one who responded most readily and after communicating by letter and then weekly phone calls, he came to trust Alfie enough to place him on the list of people authorised to visit him at Broadmoor and then Frankland prison. Sutcliffe confided his innermost thoughts on every aspect of his life to Alfie, who diligently retained all of this material. Alfie James is a pseudonym.

CONTENTS

AUTHORS' NOTE

Peter Sutcliffe was known as 'Peter' or 'Pete' by his family and friends, or, in the Yorkshire vernacular, 'r Pete'.

That form is retained in this book during his earlier years to stay as close as possible to the events as they happened and to differentiate him from other male relatives.

As he grows older and begins committing crimes, 'Sutcliffe' is used.

It would be inappropriate to show him the respect of a first name when he failed to show any respect at all to so many others.

Why give him a voice at all?

There may be some who would argue that a murderer, especially one who brought so much devastation and misery to so many families, should never be heard and that view is totally understandable.

But everyone has an interest in somehow preventing the kind of crimes which Sutcliffe was responsible for.

If society has any hope of ever achieving that, it will only be by understanding why such offenders commit these crimes. We can only understand the perpetrator if we truly know them, and we can only ever really know them if we listen to them. This is not to lose sight of the appalling consequences of their actions or of their true nature.

As Elliott Leyton, a former president of the Canadian Sociology and Anthropology Association who is referred to as the 'father of serial killer research', says, real-life serial killers such as Sutcliffe bear no resemblance to the intelligent, engaging, master criminals of fiction.

More often than not they are "dull, unimaginative, socially defective, vengeful, self-absorbed and self-pitying humans".

Their acts profoundly damage many people, but they are not, in themselves, remarkable individuals and are certainly not to be glorified as evil geniuses.

In short, as Leyton makes clear, their only value, once captured, is as objects of study. This book is just the latest chapter in that long-running study.

Robin Perrie & Alfie James, 2022

CHAPTER 1

BETRAYAL

Bingley in 1969 was a tough Yorkshire mill town with no air or graces, so a handsome Italian businessman zipping through the streets in a Triumph Spitfire was bound to attract attention.

But it wasn't the exotic driver or his white convertible that caused Mick Sutcliffe to stop and stare while working on a road gang widening the carriageway between Bingley and Cottingley. It was the dark-haired woman in the passenger seat. His older brother Peter's girlfriend.

Mick and Sonia Szurma had never clicked, so there was no way he was going to delay passing on this juicy bit of gossip when he got home that night after work.

Peter and Sonia had been together for three years. They were engaged, he was madly in love and was convinced she felt the same way, so he refused to believe what he was now being told by his younger brother. He knew it couldn't have been Sonia in the sports car, but Mick insisted. It was her.

Peter asked around and quickly learnt the awful truth.

"I heard that Sonia was seeing an Italian ice-cream man who would pick her up from college and take her out at night," he said. "It depressed and upset me. I didn't want to lose her."

The revelation festered for a number of days as Peter wrestled with the fear that Sonia might view their relationship differently to him.

The insecurity grew and he couldn't shake the stark comparison between the exotic appeal of a good-looking foreigner in a Triumph Spitfire and what he could offer Sonia – a Morris 1000 and few career prospects. His labouring job at the water board was just the latest in a series of low-paid posts which never seemed to last.

But he wasn't prepared to give her up without a fight, and after mulling it over he settled on a plan. He would surprise her at the end of the day as she left the technical college in Bradford where she was doing an O Level course to enable her to go to teacher training college. He would confront her with what he had discovered and demand the truth from her own lips. He would also do everything in his power to win her back, sure in his own mind that he could persuade her they had a future together.

It didn't go to plan.

"I left work early and travelled on to Bradford," Sutcliffe said. "I caught her outside college and said: 'Are you surprised to see me?' She said: 'Yeah.'

"I said: 'Why, were you expecting somebody to pick you up?' I told her that Mick had seen her two or three days before, going through Bingley in a car. I was really having a go at her to find out what was going on and she wouldn't answer.

"I thought there's something fishy. She couldn't believe that I would doubt her because she expected me to trust her, which I did normally, but with Mick telling me that, I was a bit too eager to have a go at her."

As the confrontation in the street became more heated, Sutcliffe began to realise that he had pitched his approach all wrong. It was starting to feel like he might achieve the exact opposite of what he set out to do.

"I was like a bull in a china shop, I should have been a bit more casual about it."

The row escalated until he spat out a cruel remark, offering to buy the condoms himself to make things as easy as possible for her and the Italian.

He turned heel and stormed back towards his Morris 1000.

Seething with resentment, Sutcliffe now racked his brains for a way to settle the score. As he sped off an idea began forming in his mind which, to him, was the ideal response.

He considered that she had betrayed him, so he would do the same right back at her. An eye for an eye.

"I was so depressed. That's what led me to pick a prostitute up in the first place."

After driving around the streets for a few hours with no improvement in his mood, he found himself in Manningham, home to Bradford's red light district. A formerly grand suburb where merchants and bankers once lived in Gothic-style mansions when the city was the world leader in worsted wool products, the area had long since fallen on hard times.

Sutcliffe drove slowly along Manningham Lane until he spotted a woman and pulled up at the kerb.

After a quick conversation, the deal was sealed and she climbed into the passenger seat. He pulled away and she gave him directions to her sister's house, which she used as a place to take punters back to.

But, just like his confrontation with Sonia earlier in the day, this intended vengeance didn't go to plan either.

"I felt a bit silly taking her back to her place," he said. "We got there and there was a big fire going in her living room and a dog lying on the carpet. We went upstairs and she said, 'Can you help me take my dress off?'

"So I was unzipping it and I zipped it back up again.

"I thought: 'What the hell am I doing here with her?' I decided I didn't want 'owt to do with her. I said, 'Do you mind if we call this off, I've changed my mind, I don't want to go through with it'."

The woman shrugged, but reminded Sutcliffe he would still have to pay the £5 they had settled on. He agreed, but only had a ten pound note on him.

She didn't have a fiver, so she suggested they go back to a garage on Manningham Lane near to where he picked her up and where she could change his note.

Once there, Sutcliffe's day went from bad to worse.

"These two blokes come out," he remembered, "one with a big massive wrench, threatening to smash the car window, and another one walking her along, so I reckon they might have been her pimps."

Sutcliffe desperately tried to extricate himself from the rapidly worsening situation.

"I drove at them on the pavement, and they jumped over a wall and smashed through a greenhouse; they probably cut themselves badly.

"I drove off. I thought that'll teach them, but that was what started it off. Everything went wrong from then on."

His mood darkened as he made his way home to Bingley.

"I felt more resentful than ever. I hadn't solved the situation, I was intending just to have sex with somebody, so I wouldn't be blaming Sonia all the time.

"That was what started it off. Jealousy can be so negative and destructive.

"I got back home and I got depression again. Then the voice came for the second time.

"It had been saying good things for about two years, but this time it was giving me advice that wasn't really good... saying that they're the problem in society... 'don't you realise why you've had the good advice for two years... it's all been leading up to this, you've got a mission to go on and get rid of these people'."

The voice in his head wouldn't stop as his depression deepened over the following days and weeks.

The situation with Sonia was no better and he couldn't get the memory of his clumsy attempt at revenge with that woman out of his mind.

BETRAYAL

As the summer moved into August, he began to realise that something had to give until one night when he was with his best friend Trevor Birdsall cruising the city streets as they did on most of their evenings together.

Nothing remarkable ever happened on these nights. Sutcliffe would gawp at the working girls, make crass jokes about them to Trevor and sometimes shout snide remarks from a half-opened window as they drove past.

They would stop for an odd pint here and there, grab something to eat and then head home. Another dull evening under their belt.

Tonight it was a game of pool and then food.

They visited a local fish and chip shop, bought a fish supper each and climbed back into Trevor's Reliant Robin.

He parked up in St Paul's Road, just off Manningham Lane, so they could eat their meal. As they tucked in, relishing the greasy yet satisfying taste, Sutcliffe suddenly sprang into life without warning.

Trevor glanced up and saw a lone woman walking past as Sutcliffe put his fish and chips to one side and opened the passenger door.

The woman walked down the street and disappeared into the darkness, with Sutcliffe following closely behind as she made her way home.

Thoughts of vengeance and a new willingness to obey the voices were swirling around his head while in his pocket his hand tightly gripped a home-made weapon. A sock filled with pebbles.

The Yorkshire Ripper was about to commit his first ever attack.

CHAPTER 2

LOVE AND HATRED

Before the horror, there was neglect and abuse but also love and affection.

Peter Sutcliffe was the eldest of six children who grew up in a raucous household embraced by a devoted, selfless mother but also within arm's reach of a violent father capable of lashing out with belt and fist, often for no apparent reason.

Luckily for the children, he spent the majority of his time out of the house. When he wasn't at work in the mill, he was more interested in pursuing his hobbies of sport and amateur dramatics than spending time with his children.

"I hated him," recalled Peter many decades later. "When we were growing up, none of us were close to Dad, we were much closer to our mother.

"He was never in. He had musical union, amateur dramatics, rugby, football, cricket, he played them all. He never had a spare minute from coming home from work, he was back out again. Ignored the family, really. My mum brought us up."

John, a renowned womaniser, was selfish with his money as well as his time and would keep more than half of his weekly wages to spend on himself, often in the pub.

"He could be really nasty and drunk. He used to beat my brothers up when they were little. He never beat me up, he hit me with a belt a few times, but never beat me up with his fists and his feet, but he set about them with his feet and fists."

6

As well as the violence, Peter's memory was of a cruel, insensitive man.

Even when his father tried to do the right thing, it seemed to go wrong.

On Christmas Eve, 1952, he arranged for a neighbour to shout that he had seen Father Christmas landing on the Sutcliffes' roof to add to the children's growing anticipation of the big day. Peter was so excited he couldn't sleep and a short time later was convinced he could hear Santa approaching his bedroom to deliver his presents. But in one shattering moment he came to learn that Santa didn't exist as his own father clumsily staggered into the room, chatting to his wife as he laid the presents at the foot of Peter's bed.

"All the magic went," he said seven decades later as he recalled the story in such detail it felt as if it was only yesterday. "It's magic when you believe in Santa Claus. I never believed after that. He spoiled it."

Another incident a few years later also stuck in Peter's mind for the rest of his life. He was never a sporty child, but he did enjoy a kick around on the local recreation ground.

One day in early September, in the run-up to his younger brother Mick's birthday, the ground was wet and muddy and Pete returned home with a dirty football.

The ball, given to him by his parents on his own birthday three months earlier, was his most cherished possession and he made sure he looked after it.

"I scrubbed it in the sink and ran the hot tap on it and got some soap on it, scrubbed it clean and put it in the cupboard," he said with pride.

A short time later the ball vanished, much to Peter's puzzlement. He looked for it everywhere but it was nowhere to be found until, on the morning of September 6, he watched in silent devastation as Mick excitedly opened his presents, including a sparklingly clean football.

"My dad gave him it for his birthday," he said as he recalled the event many years later in a phone call from Broadmoor, the handset nestled against his greying beard and pudgy face as his soft, high-pitched voice floated down the line.

There was a sense of his shoulders sagging as he recounted the tale, and his voice trailed away as he struggled to find the words to explain what the ball had meant to him.

"And he'd given me it for my birthday first, you see…"

Peter's relationship with his mother was the polar opposite. They had a particularly strong bond which developed in the early years when, as the firstborn and with his father largely absent, he was the sole target of his mother's love and affection. It was a bond that lasted far beyond childhood.

"Nobody could have had a better mother," he said.

John Sutcliffe and Kathleen Coonan met, like so many couples of that generation, at a dance.

Kathleen loved dancing. She would often spend her nights at a village or church hall around the Bingley area as part of the crowd looking for a brief respite from the darkness of war by losing themselves in dances such as the *Chrysanthemum Waltz, The Dashing White Sergeant* and the Latin American sensuality of the tango.

With the passion she showed on the dance floor, the attractive, dark-haired young woman was never in short supply of men asking to take her out.

Handsome John, a skilled ballroom dancer himself thanks to the tutelage of his father, was the one who finally won her hand and in 1941, shortly before he left to join the Merchant Navy, they were engaged.

Their romance blossomed despite him spending most of the war stationed in Gibraltar and, while he was home on a month's leave, they married in 1945 at Bingley's Catholic Church, St Joseph's, with a reception at the local St John's Ambulance Hall and a week's honeymoon in Morecambe over on England's north west coast.

The birth rate around the world rocketed when peace broke out as millions of servicemen and women returned home and the Sutcliffes played their part in the population explosion when, just a few months after their wedding, Kathleen found herself expecting.

John was demobbed in the April and two months later, on June 2, 1946, on a ward in the Bingley and Shipley Maternity hospital, Kathleen, exhausted but overjoyed, gave birth to the first of her seven children, the one who, in another 35 years, would ensure that their family name would be known all around the world.

A second son, Tommy, arrived the following year but died soon after birth due to a congenital heart condition.

But before the tragedy of Tommy, there was the disappointment of Peter.

John's hopes of a strong Yorkshire lad who would grow up in his image were shattered right from the start. When he visited the maternity ward (fathers were not allowed at the birth then) he found what, to his mind, was a 5lb weakling.

The doctors assured him that his son, although small, was fit and healthy, but John refused to be persuaded.

When Peter learnt to walk, it was by holding on to his mother's skirt as she moved around their home doing the constant housework. It was an image that John, dismissive of any sort of 'mummy's boy' traits, couldn't shake and became one of the most abiding memories of his firstborn's early years, although it was a version of his childhood that Peter hated.

"I was only two years old, what did he expect of a two-year-old?"

Over the next 11 years another two sons and three daughters came along to make for a noisy, chaotic family home.

After a couple of moves up and down the valley, the family finally settled in a house in Cornwall Road – or Corny Road as they called it – on the Ferncliffe estate which sits above Bingley town centre.

Bingley lies along the foot of the Airedale valley not far from Bradford, although it dances to a different beat than its big city neighbour. The road through Bradford heading towards Bingley passes by the Al-Falah Supermarket, Manningham Halal Butchers and Javid Arshad and Co Solicitors, but once it arrives in the slower-paced market town it's the Yorkshire Gift shop, Suzy's tea room and Inghams Property Residential and Letting.

Life there was hard after the war with the lack of food being the most common complaint – cheese powder instead of cheese, spam with almost every meal and the resignation that even bread rationing was around the corner.

Kathleen struggled to feed her growing brood in the best way she could, although her eldest remembered the period with a misty-eyed romanticism.

"We had dripping sandwiches with salt on as kids. Thought they were delicious. It was all from cooking the meat, and it used to solidify and you used to put it in a cold place on a stone shelf in the pantry to go solid and then spread it on bread and put salt on it. Like a thick grey paste. It was really tasty."

There was no central heating and the house always felt cold, especially when the harsh Yorkshire winters came down from the moors and blew through the valley, unless you could grab a sought after spot in front of the open fire.

"We all used to sit around the fire," remembered Pete. "They had a fire guard in front of it and my mum had a diamond on her legs from the heat where the wire of the fire guard had made the pattern. I said: 'Mum you shouldn't sit so close to the fire guard'.

"She said: 'Oh well, it's a cold house.' I said: 'You'll suffer for it in later life' and she got all varicose veins and phlebitis and that in her legs. I'm sure it was due to that, sitting too close to the fire. It's bound to damage your blood vessels isn't it?"

Kathleen's determination to educate her children in her own Roman Catholic faith meant Peter's first school was St Joseph's RC Infants and Junior school, not far from the family home. The school was attached to the Sacred Heart church, where Peter would later serve as an altar boy.

Perhaps it was being separated from his mother for the first time or his inability to mix with other children, a trait which remained throughout his childhood, but Peter hated school.

He was smaller than the other children and was shy and withdrawn. The skinny-legged lad just didn't fit in, but the weekly trips to Bingley baths for swimming lessons on Tuesday afternoons were a high point for him and a rare occasion when he felt part of the crowd.

"They'd give us a blue token which we handed to the bus conductor which covered our 4d fares. Then all the lads would sing out in the changing closets: *'There was an old man called Michael Finnegan, he grew whiskers on his chin-a-gen, the wind came up and blew them in again, poor old Michael Finnegan – begin again!'*"

On other occasions it would be wild swimming.

"We'd go swimming in the River Aire at Seven Arches where the canal viaduct takes it over the river in Bingley. We'd swing out on a rope tied to a high tree branch and let go when we got into the middle of the river."

It was an age of innocence when children enjoyed far more freedom than they do now. Stranger danger was something for the future, explained Sutcliffe, without any hint of irony.

"When I was a kid there used to be no fears about these weirdos, paedophiles and stuff. We used to go out anywhere we wanted, from morning till night. We'd come back for our dinner, back out again straight afterwards. My mother wouldn't see us all day. There was no fear of anything happening."

He remained a withdrawn, unremarkable child when he moved to the big school, Cottingley Manor, and although bright, was never destined to excel academically.

One incident, though, did put him right at the centre of the playground gossip. His stature and quiet nature meant he had always been a target for bullies, but when yet another decided to pick on him, the way he reacted revealed a previously hidden violent streak. And a calculating one at that.

The bullying became so bad he started "wagging off" school. He would make a noisy exit from the house each day, so his parents thought he was heading to lessons, only to then creep silently back up the stairs to climb into the loft where he would spend the day reading comics by torchlight.

He wasn't just spending his time in the loft reading his comics, though. He was plotting his revenge. When a local education authority official called to inquire why he hadn't been attending classes his parents made sure he was dressed and ready to go the next morning.

As he walked through the school gates he wasn't tortured by anxiety at the thought of facing his tormentor. Instead, he had revenge in his heart.

"I really psyched myself up. I went back to school and kicked the seven shades of shit out of that bully. I had enough of it and I went back to school as angry as anybody could be. I kicked him and smacked him in the face. He fell over and I kicked him again."

Teachers rushed to deal with the incident, but Peter's anger hadn't abated.

"The headmaster wanted to know what it was all about, and I said: 'That's why I've been wagging school, for that prat. I'm not putting up with it any longer'. He kept clear of me after that."

Not clear enough. Peter may have had his revenge but he never forgot the ordeal his tormentor had put him through.

"The lad who bullied me got his comeuppance when I bumped into him years later. I gave him such a pasting. I punched him hard in the face. He looked at me, asking what was that for and who was I? Before laying into him I said, 'you'll find out'."

As he reached his teenage years, he developed an interest which would eventually open up a route to male friendship as well as a means to explore beyond the confines of Bingley, to the surrounding towns and cities, and eventually to their red light areas. Engines.

First motorbikes and later cars, but anything with an engine now sparked Pete's interest. The bedroom he shared with Mick came to resemble a mechanic's garage with the floor constantly littered with engine parts. He even kept an entire Norton 600 engine under his bed.

"I was happy swapping engines or stripping them down. I used to do all that sort of work on my own cars and other people's. I did spray painting and everything. I'd do my own cars first and learn the process, and I got pretty good at it. I could do a flawless spray paint job."

His school days drifted to an end and he left without any qualifications, although there was no shortage of manual labour jobs in the mills and engineering works along the valley in the early 1960s. That was fortunate because he never seemed to be able to hold down a job.

A failed fitter's apprenticeship, a stint at the mill where his dad worked and a job chopping up rags and asbestos all came and went in quick succession, with workmates developing a similar view to earlier classmates. He was a "queer bugger", commented one.

After he passed his 16th birthday, Peter finally realised his dream of owning a motorbike, despite objections from his worried mum.

"My mother didn't want me to have my first motorcycle, but I got one. From then on there was no stopping me. I had lots of different bikes after that."

He swapped bikes more often than he swapped jobs, but the bikes were more fun and took him into a world where he was finally part of a group of like-minded men, a local motorbike gang known as the Rebels.

Peter had finally left behind the puny, thin-limbed physique of his early years thanks to puberty and regular body-building sessions. He bought a Bullworker and would spend at least an hour each night in his bedroom pushing the spring-loaded cylinders together as well as lifting weights with home-made equipment.

"I used to train with railway wheels fitted to metal bars. I could lift a 15 stone man straight above my head, which I did on more than one occasion."

The bulked-up Peter proved useful on more than one occasion now that he had friends who might need protection in the tough Yorkshire of the 1960s.

"There was one big fella picking on a mate of mine once and I grabbed hold of him and lifted him right up over my head. He said: 'Put me down, put me down'. He was like a little kid. He was amazed I could do that."

On another occasion he took on an entire group of youths single-handedly during a night at a local fair.

"This gang, there were about four or five of them, had been bullying a friend of mine. He pointed him out on the waltzer, I went up to the biggest one and said, 'lay off him', he said 'or else what?' So I cracked him right under the jaw. He went right over the rails and fell on the ground below the waltzer. The others all beat it."

He was spending more and more time with his new friends in the Rebels, which he joined in 1964.

"We got fantastic enjoyment out of our motorbikes and we used to do the ton, but never ridiculous speeds like 160 or 170. You can't stop in time if you're doing speeds like that.

"Our bikes were faster than the cop cars, well most of them anyway.

"We'd ride to the Majestic Ballroom in Barnoldswick, near Colne, on a Saturday night and go to the Lakes, all over the place.

"Sometimes we took girlfriends with us. One or two had their own bikes, but some would just ride on the pillion."

Peter was unlikely to have been one of those with a girlfriend on the back for he remained crippled with shyness and awkwardness around members of the opposite sex.

He was, though, obsessive about his looks and spent forever in front of the bathroom mirror grooming his hair and carefully manicuring his sideburns and, later, a full beard.

"You're better off with a safety razor. Wilkinson was my favourite, they always give the best shave. You can't go wrong with Wilkinson. I tried different styles, I had a goatee with long sideboards and side-whiskers. I had a full beard, then a shaved beard, different types."

Peter turned 18 in 1964. Over the next two years a series of unconnected events occurred which would resonate through the rest of his life. They helped to create both stability and chaos as an aimless youth began the change into a committed family man while also taking the first steps on a road that would see that man turn into a monster.

Until then, he remained a devoted grandson to Grandma Coonan, who had moved in with her daughter Kathleen and her lively brood and inattentive husband.

The children loved her, although it did make for an even more crowded house now that the front room had been converted into her bedroom.

An added challenge was that Grandma Coonan wasn't a well woman. She had breathing difficulties and wore a built-up shoe thanks to a deformed foot. She wasn't great on her feet and the family always had to be ready to give her a hand if she was ever attempting any steps.

One day, a few weeks before Peter's 18th birthday, she steadied herself at the top of the stairs ready to descend as the family's two new pet kittens played with each other down below.

As she neared the bottom step, Pete watched with dawning horror as he realised what was about to happen.

"She was nearly at the bottom, I shouted: 'Grandma be careful… there's a kitten'… she still kept coming down."

His warnings came too late.

"She stepped on one and all blood came spouting out of its mouth."

Grandma was heartbroken while Peter was furious with her, shouting and swearing in shocked anger, the one and only time anyone could remember him speaking to her like that.

The incident had a terrible effect on both of them. She never forgave herself and just days later suffered a stroke which left her paralysed and bedridden. She never left the house again and on May 10, 1964 – around ten days after the kitten's death – the family gathered around her bed to say their final farewell.

Peter blamed himself for her demise and regretted the way he shouted at her for the rest of his life. He also blamed the incident for triggering a decline in his mental health.

"For quite a while I was suffering a sort of depression," he said, "blaming myself for my grandmother's death. I was depressed because I shouted. I never raised my voice to her in my life, but it was a shock when I saw her foot come down on the kitten and crush it.

"I never forgave myself for shouting at her like that."

Around this time Peter started yet another new job, but this one would take on a huge significance in his life.

He earned £7 for a 44-hour week as a gravedigger at Bingley Cemetery and for the first time in his life enjoyed a sense of camaraderie with a group of workmates. Just like everywhere else he had worked, Peter was seen as a bit different, but the cemetery boys soon treated him as one of their own and, for the first time outside the confines of his family, he became ''r Pete'.

"We used to have a few laughs," he said. "We called it the 'Dead centre of Bingley' – though it was just on the outskirts. We had to have a bit of fun as the job was a sad one, really. We didn't have any digging machines, we had to do it all with a pick and shovel.

"It was hard graft grave digging, especially when it had to be 9ft 6in deep for four people."

Peter began leading the practical jokes, hiding under a shroud in the Chapel of Rest until a cleaner or a workmate walked past when he would make just enough movement to scare the living daylights out of them.

But his clowning around also took on a darker edge. One day he hit a colleague over the head with a mallet and another time he was seen to hurl a rock at a coffin as he said: "That'll waken you."

While developing solid friendships with work colleagues, his bond with the Rebels motorbike gang was also growing and was about to be cemented even further – there's nothing like a mass brawl to really anchor a brotherhood.

Dick Hudsons has been famous round Bingley way for as long as anyone can remember for its great beer, warm welcome and views to die for, stretching across the valley.

It has had various names and numerous landlords since it began life as a refreshment stop on an ancient packhorse route between Shipley and Ilkley, but Dick Hudson proved to be the most popular when he took over in 1850. By the time he served his last pint in 1878 the sign outside may have still read The Fleece, but anyone worth passing the time of day with at the bar only ever referred to it as Dick Hudsons.

In the mid-1960s it was the place where Peter and his motor-bike gang would stop on summer evenings on Nortons, BSAs and Triumphs after attempting the ton along the country lanes which snake over the moor. They would chat to girls, swap boasts about how their bike was performing and eye with suspicion any other groups of men who happened to be there.

The stand-offs sometimes developed beyond hard stares – "we did get into the odd scrap or two" – as it did one night in 1965 when a group of engineers from Hepworth and Grandage, a pistons manufacturer in Bradford, called in during a coach trip.

"A coach load of them were there, and they came out and started knocking our bikes over," remembered Peter, who was 19 at the time, "so we came out and a scrap developed."

After the fighting had subsided the engineers climbed aboard their coach and left. A short time later Peter, clad in his biker's leathers, climbed onto his BSA and a friend, Donald Sumner, got on the back.

With the adrenalin from the fight still pumping, Peter roared out of the car park, opened the throttle and headed down the valley.

He could handle bikes, but tonight something didn't feel right. As he took the various bends heading down into the valley towards Eldwick Beck Bottom it dawned on him that there was something wrong with the way the bike was handling.

He approached the last sharp turn and tried to accelerate up the other side of the dip, but the front tyre gave up its grip on the road.

"I went down a sharp dip where the stream goes under the road and it shoots up at the other side.

"The front wheel, with a flat tyre, couldn't steer and I went straight into a telegraph pole.

"The tyre was let down before I set off. One of them must have let some air out of my front tyre and I didn't notice until I got to Eldwick Beck Bottom."

Donald landed safely in a shocked but uninjured pile, but Peter slammed into the telegraph pole. He was knocked out cold. More than half a century later the dent in his skull was still noticeable to the touch and he would happily let friends visiting him in prison feel it.

He also kept his damaged helmet for years.

"It broke in two, it was a reminder of how lucky I was to have survived. Looking back, maybe it wasn't so lucky… look what happened."

He was convinced the head injury played a role in future events, although others treated it less seriously.

"Two or three days later I woke up… I came round eventually and I thought it was the next morning", he said, shocked his mother had not called for medical help.

"I couldn't believe she hadn't called a doctor. She thought I was just sleeping it off and had too much to drink, but I hadn't drunk much that night. I was fully in control of the motorcycle, it was just because they'd let air out of the front tyre."

Extensive research into Traumatic Brain Injury (TMI) is yet to agree on whether it is a cause of schizophrenia, the condition that Peter would be diagnosed with many years later, but he was convinced.

"I really believe my problems were because of the bike accident, the head injury."

As well as Dick Hudsons, he was also becoming a regular at a number of pubs in Bingley and Bradford with his friends from work, particularly the Royal Standard on Manningham Lane.

They christened their favourite spot 'Gravediggers corner'. It was in a room which had been transformed into a disco called Fisherman's Cove, with a smattering of fishing nets and corks hanging from walls to give it a veneer of authenticity.

"We drew on the walls in the discotheque, gravestones and skulls and crossbones and stuff and wrote the Gravediggers Union and all our names in translucent, bright green," he said.

They rarely missed the weekly disco, including in 1966 when two girls who Peter had never seen before walked in.

The fact that Marianne Szurma and her younger sister Sonia even contemplated going to the disco at the Royal Standard is testament to the power of teenage rebellion.

Their father, Bohdan, an intelligent and cultured man, would never have allowed it.

The Polish-born university graduate and his Ukrainian wife Maria had arrived in England from Czechoslovakia in 1947, just two of many thousands of refugees being spat out of Eastern Europe during the turmoil brought on by the advance of communism after the Second World War.

Following a period in a transit camp near York, they moved to Bradford, where they were given the keys to a council house that would become their long-term home in Tanton Crescent.

Bohdan would not allow his daughters to attend a city centre disco in a pub, especially with Sonia being so young. Marianne was a year older, but even she wasn't legally allowed to drink as she hadn't turned 18 yet.

As they sat down and took in the sights and sounds of the disco, they caught the eye of a striking looking man with sideburns (the full beard would come later) and thick black hair, although it wasn't the younger of the two sisters who Peter chatted up first.

"I sat with Marianne and I was talking to her for a while," he said. "Then she had to go to the toilet and one of my mates moved up on the seat, so I was left near Sonia. I started talking to her and when Marianne came back from the toilet me and Sonia were snogging away. Never looked back."

As they talked, Sonia came clean about the subterfuge she and Marianne had employed with their strict father.

"I said to Sonia, 'how come you were in a place like that when you're underage?' She said they should have gone to the opera, and they showed their dad the tickets so he let them go out. They didn't go, they went round the pubs and discotheque instead. He would have been upset if he'd known they'd gone to a disco. He only let them out once a week, and then they had to go somewhere where he knew they had tickets, really strict they were."

Sonia was different to the other girls in the Fisherman's Cove. The absence of thick make-up, her unconventional hairstyle and the drab, home-made clothes marked her out in a way that might not appeal to most of the traditional Yorkshire teenage lads who went to the Cove. But Peter, who had shown no serious interest with any girl or woman previously, was smitten right from the off.

On the surface it seemed an unlikely romance between the shy young man from a rough and tumble Yorkshire family and the serious schoolgirl daughter of newly immigrated Eastern European parents determined she would grow up to be well-mannered and cultured.

But perhaps it wasn't that unlikely. Both, in their own ways, were considered different by their wider peer group. Sonia would go on to suffer crippling mental health issues and Peter would claim the same. They both felt they had found their soulmate and Peter soon came to view the early stages of their union as a magical period in his life.

"The time I met Sonia was around the best time of my life on reflection," he would say later, looking back on the first weeks and months of his first proper romance. "I know what makes her tick and we have a similar sense of humour. I loved her right from the start more or less.

"We used to go all over the place, we met regularly every few days."

Their trips took them across the wild moors above Bingley or as far as the coast, with Morecambe a regular haunt.

"We went for walks, there was a good place with a very large reservoir where we'd go up past Clayton Heights. We'd drive there and go for a long walk between Queensbury and Halifax. Other times we'd walk over the tops from Queensbury to Haworth, Bronte land.

"We used to go swimming in the sea and she'd swim right out as far as I could see, till I couldn't see her anymore. I told her not to get swept away by the tides, but she always managed to find her way back. I used to call her Sunny Sea Lion because she swam out so far."

He would go to hers for tea every Saturday, with Sonia visiting Corny Road for a meal on Sundays, followed by a stint in front of the television.

He grew close to her parents and would later teach her mother to drive. At Corny Road, however, relations between Sonia and her boyfriend's family never warmed.

His family couldn't fathom the intense quietness which enveloped Sonia, complaining that she would sit on a seat at the back of the room, beyond the edges of the circle of chat which she rarely joined in with.

"She just doesn't have any conversation," said his dad John, who also accused her of possessing an air of superiority.

Whether Peter was aware of the developing disapproval of his family or not, he wasn't going to let it get in the way of this developing romance. Sonia was fast becoming the most important woman in his life, alongside his mother.

Shortly after their first meeting in the Fisherman's Cove, Peter was hard at work one day in the cemetery. Rain-heavy clouds darkened the Bingley skies as he stood chest-deep in a freshly dug grave when he heard a strange voice.

At first he was convinced it was his workmates engaging in yet more banter.

"I thought some of the lads were having a bit of fun. I got up and looked around, I couldn't see anybody, nobody hiding in the bushes or behind any gravestones."

The sound was impossible to pin down, and he quickly realised it was something beyond the latest practical joke. He put down his shovel and climbed out of the grave.

As rain began to fall, he walked towards the noise, which seemed to be coming from a grand-looking headstone in the Catholic section of the cemetery, a cross adorned with a crucified Jesus atop a three-tiered white plinth at the head of a neatly tended grave. It was the final resting place of Bronislaw Zapolski, a Polish man who had died on June 19, 1965. As Peter stared at it, he barely believed what he was hearing.

"It was like a wonderland, like a miracle happening. I was awestruck. It was like an echo voice, superimposed upon itself like a double echo, so I wasn't able to distinguish the words."

He tried to work out exactly where the voice was coming from.

"It appeared to be coming from the top of the cross. It repeated itself some two or three times, and it was direct from the stone itself."

The grave is engraved with the words: "Treasured memories of a dear husband Bronislaw Zapolski" and three Polish words – Pokoj Jego Duszy – which translate as RIP.

But to Sutcliffe they meant something else. He thought they meant "We be echo".

Whether he did hear the voice in the way he claimed would be the subject of fierce debate years later, but he insisted that in the following weeks and months, the "echo" happened again and again and began giving him advice on dealing with major life events.

"After a few weeks and months it got really clear. Like when I was blaming myself for my grandma's death. Lots of good advice on that, saying 'don't blame yourself, it wasn't your fault, she was elderly and not well'."

When the echo had shifted into focus, he understood it to be a voice delivering messages. His belief about where they were coming from also came into sharp focus.

"I decided it was some kind of message from God. I couldn't confide in anybody, my mother or Sonia or anybody. It was between me and God."

He was under no doubt that he had to keep it a secret, even from Sonia as their relationship developed and strengthened.

Peter had got to the stage where he was now in awe of her. She may have had simple tastes influenced by her austere Eastern European parents – "She wasn't fussy about clothes and neither was I – we'd just throw any old thing on most of the time," – but Peter had her on a pedestal, taking delight in her different talents. It was a hero-worship that lasted throughout his life.

"Sonia speaks loads of languages really fluently," he said years later, "but she's always going abroad anyway to refresh them.

"Last time she went to Germany, she said she didn't speak a word of English all the time she was there. Same when she goes to Spain or anywhere.

"She just speaks the language of the country she's visiting."

By 1968 he was convinced she was the one.

"I proposed in the Midland Hotel in Bingley," he said, "but I didn't have an engagement ring at the time, so we went on to Keighley to buy that after she chose one she liked."

Peter was deliriously in love and couldn't imagine anything getting in the way of their future happiness. He was convinced that Sonia felt the same way.

CHAPTER 3

ON A MISSION

"That's when I started on the first attack, with a sock and a load of pebbles in it, and I hit one on the head."

The row with Sonia over the Italian and Sutcliffe's humiliating attempt at revenge with the prostitute in the summer of 1969 had brought him to a pivotal moment in his life.

In the build-up to his latest night out with Trevor Birdsall he had made the decision to finally act on what had been building in his head for weeks, preparing himself by taking along a home-made weapon of a sock full of pebbles and gravel.

Whether it was down to the depression triggered by his grandma killing the kitten, a brain injury caused by the motorbike crash or his growing faith in the voices, Sutcliffe was ready to take the first step into the next stage of his life which would cause untold tragedy and heartache and leave countless lives changed forever.

Luckily for his very first victim, he staged a clumsy assault.

"I was trying to kill her, but I didn't know it wasn't going to be effective," he said. "It split apart and the pebbles went all over the cars, and she wasn't injured. It was a clumsy attack, proving it was my first attempt. It didn't really injure her.

"After that, the voice told me I needed to find a better way of dealing with them."

As the woman fled, Sutcliffe returned to the car, flushed and mumbling about what he had done.

"He looked a bit excited and was not breathing normally. It looked as if he had possibly been running," said Birdsall, who was soon left in no doubt about what had just happened.

"I told him that I'd hit a prostitute over the head," said Sutcliffe.

It appears oddly reckless to commit his first attack while with someone and then admit it to them, even if it was a loyal friend. But whatever drivers were at play, the compulsion to act had overcome any concerns about being caught.

"I just had the urge to attack, it didn't matter if someone was with me or not. I was on the mission. I saw that she was a prostitute and attacked her."

He told Trevor to drive away, suddenly concerned that some-one might have witnessed the assault.

He was right to be worried, although he was about to enjoy the first in a long series of close-calls and near-misses.

"Somebody took the number of [Trevor's] car. They told the police and they went to his house. He told them my name and address.

"They came to see me and said: 'Does a Peter William Sutcliffe live here?' My mum said: 'Two policemen to see you, Pete.' I said: 'Oh right, you go in the room, don't worry, it's nothing.'

"I took them in the dining room and we talked there. They said: 'You know what we've come about?' I said: 'Yeah, I guess I do, it's that attack with that prostitute on the head with the sock with pebbles.' They said that I could be in serious trouble and I said, 'Yeah, I realise that.' They said: 'You don't look bothered.' I told them that I wasn't, I think I was even laughing as we were talking. But you see, I felt protected by God.

"They said: 'You might be surprised to know but the woman is not pressing charges,' and this is what made me even more certain that it was God that was directing it.

"They added: 'Because her husband's in prison for doing exactly the same thing to somebody else.'

"It's weird that, isn't it? She didn't press charges because her husband had done the same thing to another prostitute. I thought this was God's intervention."

The case was dropped. Sutcliffe's second lucky escape came a month later when he was back in the Manningham area again, this time alone.

On September 29, 1969, he was armed with more serious weapons than a handful of pebbles in a sock.

A passing police officer spotted a Morris by the side of the road, its engine idling and passenger door open. As he inspected it, he discovered a man hiding behind a privet hedge in a nearby garden, holding a hammer.

Sutcliffe had managed to hide the knife that he also had with him.

"I was going on a mission and the hubcap came off," he said, "so I backed up, picked the hubcap up, tapped it back on and the police car pulled in behind me.

"They said that I was going equipped for theft, the bloody idiots. It wasn't that at all, but I didn't complain. I couldn't tell them I was on the mission."

Relieved that no-one had cottoned on to his true motives, he readily pleaded guilty at court and was issued with a £25 fine, to be paid off at £2 a week.

* * *

The Bankfield Hotel is the kind of place that families in Bingley book for "summat special", their weddings, 21st birthday parties and funeral wakes. Sitting at the foot of Bingley, where the A650 does a left turn towards Bradford, it has always been thought of as a grand place and a sign next to the front door gives a clue as to its importance in the local community: "The Rotary Club of Bingley meets here Friday 12.30pm." Inside the wood-panelled reception area is a board with the hand-painted names of local Rotary

Presidents going back to 1931. A man with the good Yorkshire name of R M Illingworth held the 12-month post in 1969 and around this time the Bankfield witnessed one of the oddest incidents in its long and illustrious history.

A crisis had been brewing in the Sutcliffe household for some time and was about to reach breaking point. John and Kathleen's marriage was teetering on the edge, although John, unsurprisingly, had no idea.

He had never changed his drinking, womanising ways and hardly ever paid Kathleen any attention. Despite her strong Catholic faith, the end result was inevitable.

She began spending time with a neighbour, a married police sergeant called Albert, who lived a few streets away.

John was unaware until one day when he phoned her at the bookmakers where she had a cleaning job to let her know he would be late home from work. They rarely spoke on the phone and he had recently had false teeth fitted, meaning his voice sounded different so Kathleen didn't recognise him.

She asked who it was and John, making light of it, replied: "Who do you think it is?"

Kathleen made the fatal mistake of assuming it was the other man in her life as she replied: "Is that you, Albert?"

John was stunned, but quickly continued the conversation pretending to be Albert, only to hear his wife ask: "When can I see you again?"

He was horrified and rang off on the pretext that someone was coming. As the truth slowly dawned on him, he began making plans to expose her adultery.

He called her again, still pretending to be Albert, and told her he had booked a romantic meal for two at the Bankfield for the following Saturday night.

He didn't allow the hypocrisy of his plan, given his own adultery, to divert him and alerted the older children to an impromptu family gathering, ordering Peter to take them in his car.

The family group were sat around a table at 7.30pm in the hotel with everyone but John in the dark as to what this strange gathering was all about.

When Kathleen arrived John leapt to his feet, marched outside and tapped her on the shoulder. The blood drained from her face. In a state of shock, Kathleen allowed herself to be led inside to be greeted by a still-puzzled array of familiar faces.

As the bigger picture began to dawn on the rest of the family, their sympathy flowed only one way.

"Poor thing," said Peter. "You should have seen the expression on her face when she saw us all there and he confronted her.

"My dad drove her to seeing that copper with all his antics. My mum was suffering all that time and he didn't give a toss. He drove her into the arms of somebody else who fancied her. He just drove her to it. She wasn't getting no love, no affection or anything; he was a right cold fish.

"He showed her up in public in front of her kids. Horrible man."

John struggled to cope with the idea of his wife being with someone else and soon embarked on his own extra-marital relationship. He moved out for a while but after a number of months returned home, happy he had made his point.

He might have been happy, but the hotel humiliation and the stress of the brief marital split, piled onto decades of hard, daily graft, was doing nothing for Kathleen's health.

* * *

Shortly before the hotel confrontation, Peter and Sonia had managed to steer their own relationship back to calmer waters.

By the start of 1970 her friendship with the Italian was over and they were looking forward to the next stage of their lives which, for Sonia, involved a huge transition. She got a place at the Rachel McMillan Teachers' Training College in Deptford, south east London, to study on a three-year course with painting as her speciality, later changing it to pottery.

Peter visited her regularly, but she struggled to fit in.

In the autumn of 1971, shortly after Sonia started her second year, Peter received a telegram from her.

"She sent a telegram saying: 'Meet me at King's Cross station – Sonia'. It didn't say what day, what time or anything, so I thought: 'There's something wrong here'. I took the telegram to them [her parents] knowing something must be wrong and her father went straight to London where she'd been admitted to hospital. He discharged her and took her home to Bradford, where she was treated for a nervous breakdown at Lynfield Mount Hospital."

It wasn't just a nervous breakdown. Sonia had suffered a total mental collapse. She exhibited aggressive and restless behaviour, undressed at inappropriate times, heard voices and suffered delusions that she was the second Christ.

Doctors diagnosed it as schizophrenia, the same diagnosis that, almost a decade later, would form a central part of Sutcliffe's murder trial.

Sonia was discharged from hospital after 22 days, but her recovery was long and slow. Peter helped nurse her back to full health. They went for long walks across the moors as he became a central part of the family, playing chess with Bohdan and ferrying Maria to the shops and her job at a nursing home.

It took four years for Sonia to make a full recovery and resume full-time teacher training.

In 1974, when she was well on the way to recovery, her parents gave their blessing to marry her devoted boyfriend, who they now held in the highest regard.

By then, it had been five years since he had attacked anyone. The absence of any attacks between 1969 and 1975 – at least none that Sutcliffe admitted to or was ever charged with – remains an enduring mystery.

He claimed it was down to him resisting the voices, even making major life choices to avoid the demands they were placing on him. After quitting Bairds TV in 1973, he got a job at Anderton International on the canal side in Bingley, where he worked in the heat treatment section to strengthen metal clips.

This move was made in part, he said, because it involved him working the night shift, meaning he couldn't be prowling the streets after dark looking for women to attack.

"At first I was arguing with God, telling him that I didn't want to do it, asking him why me? That he should pick someone else more worthy, like a priest or a vicar.

"I even tried to avoid doing the mission. I applied to do night time work for three and a half years to make it more difficult for me to attack anyone. You see, I hadn't killed at that stage and I knew that's what it was gonna end up as, the first killing.

"So I went on nights to avoid it because I knew what I was leading up to, I knew what the purpose of the mission was."

On another occasion he explained: "I knew it was building up to me killing after the sock attack which resulted only in injury. The voice was now telling me to find a more effective way to deal with them, to find a better weapon. That's why I started working at night at Anderton."

Sonia Szurma became Sonia Sutcliffe on her 24th birthday on August 10 1974 as the warm summer sun shone down on the Baptist Church in the village of Clayton, six miles south of Bingley.

The stag do was the night before, a pub crawl around Manningham with Peter wearing a pristine, white suit. It was one of the few occasions in his life when he got completely plastered.

"They'd been spiking my drinks. I didn't know how much I had, I must have had a lot more than I thought I had because they were spiking lager and beer, putting double Pernods in without me knowing.

"I went to the toilet and I slipped and it was all wet and filthy on the floor with piss and that. My white suit was covered in black water. It was badly stained and I had to send it to the cleaners."

As for the day itself, Peter left the arrangement to his intended and his future mother-in-law.

"Her mother and Sonia did it, sorted it out, the reception and everything at the pub down the road," he said.

It went off without a hitch. The Rev William Nelson married the happy couple and after exchanging vows they stepped outside for photographs before the 40 guests retired to the nearby Quarry Arms pub for a cold buffet lunch.

For their first song, the couple chose a foot-tapping rock'n'roll number.

"We danced to *I ran all the way home* by the Royal Showband. One of our favourite songs."

Peter remembered the day with fondness, but for his family, who still hadn't warmed to Sonia, it registered as yet another disappointment.

"After the speeches it just seemed to dissolve," said his dad John, who along with the rest of the family would have enjoyed a good knees-up. "They went off and we went home."

The couple travelled to Paris for a short honeymoon where Sonia, schooled in the more cultural aspects of life to a greater degree than her new husband, took him to museums and art galleries. One day they visited the Louvre to view the Mona Lisa.

They strolled through the Parisian streets hand in hand, making plans for the future, but even in the beautiful setting of one of the world's most romantic cities, whatever was inside Sutcliffe was continuing to build, distorting his view of what was around him.

On one day, they passed a woman who appeared to be a street prostitute.

"A girl came up to me while I was with Sonia and spoke to me in French. I said sorry, but I can't speak much French. She was wearing hot-pants and a crop-top, she was a prostitute, as if I'd go with a prostitute on my honeymoon."

On another day a man approached Sonia and said something. To Sutcliffe's twisted thinking, the brief exchange could only have meant one thing.

"I must have thought that the man thought Sonia was a prostitute, rather than Sonia saying something to him. From that time we stayed glued together."

First dingy pubs and backstreets in Bradford and now tree-lined Parisian boulevards. To Sutcliffe, they were one and the same, afflicted by the same ills which dogged society as a whole and which had a common cause.

The rage inside him was growing.

* * *

It took a million bricks to build the Ritz cinema in Keighley. At least that's what proud locals used to boast when the town's only art deco building was opened in 1938. The 'super-cinema', as it was known, could seat 1,500, had a resident organist and in an early nod to health and safety was even guaranteed to be "absolutely fireproof".

A downturn in cinema audiences meant it had been turned into a bingo hall by the time that 42-year-old Irish divorcee Anna Rogulskyj was found in the alleyway behind it in the summer of 1975, with three head wounds and slash wounds to her abdomen.

Of Polish extraction but born in the small town of Tralee in County Kerry, on the south west coast of Ireland, Anna moved to England as a young woman.

She left school at 15 and followed her sister from Ireland to Keighley where she got a job at Woolworth's, met her future husband, got married and then divorced.

By July 4, 1975, she was living alone in Highfield Lane, Keighley, a short walk from the town centre. Her relationship with her boyfriend Geoffrey Hughes was difficult, though, and after yet another argument she went out on her own that Friday evening to Bradford city centre.

She got a lift home in the early hours and, tipsy and unhappy, she put on her favourite record, *Crying in the Chapel* by Elvis Presley, before deciding to go and see Geoffrey.

She left her home shortly before 2am and headed towards his house, around the same time that Peter Sutcliffe was in town looking for a prostitute to attack, having been told in a throwaway remark by a work colleague that Keighley was teeming with working girls.

Geoff wasn't in, so Anna headed home.

Sutcliffe was urinating in a doorway near the Ritz with voices bouncing around his head when he saw her.

"They kept reminding me that I had a mission... I was told again that this was the night to go."

He waited for her to pass before asking her if she fancied him.

"Not on your life," she replied but, undeterred, he fell in step with her, trying to chat her up as they headed towards the bingo hall.

As they walked down the alley behind it, he raised the hammer he was carrying and hit her on the head three times. As she slumped unconscious to the ground, he knelt down, lifted her top and slashed at her abdomen with a knife.

"I think I intended to kill her, but as it turned out I didn't," he said.

A local resident heard a noise and shouted out into the dark to find out what was going on.

Sutcliffe fled and an hour later Anna was found lying unconscious and covered in blood.

Her life was saved in a 12-hour operation at Leeds General Infirmary.

Dr Michael Green, a Home Office forensic pathologist, examined her a few hours later and made a note of the unusual wounds she had suffered.

She suffered no permanent brain damage but had no memory of the assault and could not provide a description of her attacker.

Her blonde hair had been shaved for the operation and when it grew back it was steel grey.

As the days passed and nothing appeared in the news about a murder in Keighley, it was obvious to Sutcliffe that she had survived. He had failed in his mission, but it would not be long before he tried again.

On the night of Friday, August 15, 1975 – five days after Peter and Sonia's first wedding anniversary – Olive Smelt was following her established routine.

The 46-year-old mother-of-three always went out with her friend Muriel Falkingham on a Friday night, leaving her husband Harry at home to look after their youngest child Stephen, aged nine. Their daughters were 15 and 25 and old enough to look after themselves.

As Harry settled down to watch a *Kojak* movie starring Telly Savalas, his wife and Muriel were having their usual good-spirited night in the White Horse pub in Halifax, a welcome distraction from her domestic chores and her evening cleaning job at three different firms.

They parted company shortly before closing time and Olive moved on to the Royal Oak pub for one more drink, reminding herself to collect a fish supper on the way home to share with Harry.

While in the Oak, she popped to the ladies, passing by Sutcliffe, who was sitting with Trevor Birdsall at a nearby table.

Sutcliffe had been scanning the pub and when he saw Olive he said to his friend quietly: "I bet she's on the game."

When she passed by them, Sutcliffe commented about her being a prostitute and Olive, being no shrinking violent, delivered a quick and effective put down.

As the loud pub chatter swirled around the Royal Oak, noises of a more sinister kind were inside Sutcliffe's head.

"I knew it was my mission. I heard voices – echoes. Sometimes it was the voice, sometimes an echo, sometimes it was very clear, sometimes not."

At 11.30pm Olive left the pub with two friends who gave her a lift to the top of her street. She said her goodbyes and walked in the direction of home.

She was 400 yards and two minutes' walk from the safety of her front door when Sutcliffe and Trevor drove past.

Sutcliffe quickly pulled over to the kerb side, told Trevor he was going to see someone and leapt out, leaving his friend alone.

Olive realised someone was at her right-hand side, but either emboldened by the drinks she had consumed or put at ease by the man's easy charm, she wasn't concerned.

"A man approached me saying: 'Weather's letting us down, isn't it'," she remembered later.

"'Yes it is' I replied. I was struck by his lovely thick, dark hair and Yorkshire accent. He wasn't frightening, so I wasn't anxious."

It was the last thing she remembered before waking up in the intensive care unit at Leeds General Infirmary.

Sutcliffe had slowed his pace and Olive thought he had wandered off, but he was still behind her and was clutching a hammer he used to smash her twice over the head.

As she fell to the ground, he pulled out a knife, lifted her top and pulled down her skirt and drew the blade across the small of her back, making two wounds in the shape of a cross.

"I was going to kill her. I had the knife with me at that time. I was going to kill her, but I did not get the chance."

Her life was saved when a car passed by, disturbing Sutcliffe, who headed back to his Ford Capri, where he had left Trevor in the passenger seat.

This time he didn't tell his friend what he had done, but Trevor read a report in Bradford's local paper, *The Telegraph and Argus,* about an attack on a woman near to where they had been.

In his heart he knew it was the same woman, but he didn't go to the police. It would take the murders of 13 women before he spoke up.

Olive had a similar operation to save her life at Leeds General Infirmary as Anna five weeks earlier.

Dr Green, later Professor Green, also examined Olive and was immediately struck by the similarities of the two sets of wounds.

They were so obvious that in his report to Dick Holland, the detective then in charge of Halifax CID, he wrote: "It might be interesting to look again at the case of Mrs Rogulskyj."

Olive was lucky to survive, but the incident took a terrible toll on her. She suffered depression and the attack placed a strain on her marriage.

Twelve days after he attacked Olive, Sutcliffe was driving around the countryside north of Bingley on a pleasant summer's evening on August 27, 1975.

That evening, 14-year-old Tracy Browne and her twin sister Mandy had been visiting friends down in the small town of Silsden.

They had been allowed to stay out later than normal, past 10pm, as it was still the summer holidays, but on their walk home up the hill towards their farm they became separated because Tracy had spent longer chatting to friends.

She walked alone along Bradley Lane, which turns into Horn Lane and which would have taken her safely home if Sutcliffe had not parked his Ford Capri further up the hill.

Tracy was tired and stopped to take off her platform sandals to make it easier to walk when she spotted the stranger coming towards her.

"Mandy was totally out of sight and I just remember looking up and happened to see this chap walking towards me and I fell into step with him," said Tracy.

"He asked me my name and we were making conversation, but he kept hanging back to tie his shoelace and each time he would hang back I would stop and wait for him.

"On the third time he hung back just a few yards from the actual gateway to the farm itself and I went to turn round to thank him for his company. I didn't even get to turn before he was hitting me, all these hammer blows rained on my head, about five hammer blows, with a ball pein hammer.

"I could feel him grunting with the sheer impact of the blows.

"I remember this car came down and it obviously frightened him off, so he picked me up and threw me over a fence and ran off.

"He had black or very dark brown Afro hair, a full beard, almost black eyes, you couldn't mistake him… he was an ordinary bloke with extraordinary features."

Sutcliffe contradicted Tracy in one aspect.

"She's got it wrong, I never hit her with a hammer, it was with a stick," he said.

Sutcliffe would always claim he was acting on the direction of God ordering him to kill prostitutes. By now he had a vast knowledge of the red light areas, he knew where the sex workers were based and how they interacted with potential punters.

Yet here he was, in a deserted country lane a long way from the city, assaulting a teenage girl who was clearly not a sex worker.

He would later explain this contradiction by claiming that on a previous trip through Silsden with a friend they picked up a couple of hitch-hikers who he became convinced were prostitutes.

"They said they were really grateful for the lift and would see us right, also they knew a place we could go," he said.

"My friend and I looked at each other and said: 'No thanks, we haven't got time.' We dropped them off and went on our way.

"At a later date when I was on my own, I felt the urge to carry on with my mission, I went to the usual red light district but couldn't find a prostitute. It was then that I remembered the two girls I'd given a lift to, so I made my way to the Silsden location."

Sutcliffe placed the responsibility for the glaring mistake of assuming Tracy was a prostitute on the voice, which corrected itself halfway through the attack.

"I thought she was a prostitute at first, walking slowly and looking round.

"As I was walking with her, I dropped back to blow my nose. I then picked up a piece of wood off the ground and started hitting her over the head with it a few times.

"But for some reason, something in my head was telling me to stop, something isn't right.

"I heard the voice saying: 'No, no, it's a mistake... stop, stop.' I said to her: 'You'll be okay, I'm going', because I realised that she wasn't a prostitute.

"I picked her up and put her over a fence."

There then followed that close escape when a car drove past.

"I then jumped over the fence as there was a car approaching and I didn't want them to be able to identify me."

He said of the attack: "I never intended to kill her."

Tracy contradicts him on this point and insists his intention was to kill her. The severity of her injuries leaves little doubt that she is right in that assertion.

He had struck her with such force that bone fragments from her fractured skull were driven into her brain. She was able to stagger home and had to undergo emergency brain surgery.

She provided an excellent description of her attacker, which was accurate enough to produce a photofit, along with some vital personal detail.

"I remember he kept blowing his nose because he had hay fever," she said.

The police now had a good description and some decent leads but, frustratingly, detectives ruled that Tracy's attacker was not the same as the man who had assaulted Anna and Olive.

She had not been stabbed, the location of her attack – country-side rather than town centre – didn't tally and detectives were sceptical generally of eyewitness testimony from victims who had suffered head injuries.

An opportunity to link all the attacks and close the net at an early stage had been missed.

After three non-fatal attacks in six weeks, Peter Sutcliffe had still not yet achieved what he set out to do – to kill.

But it would not be long.

CHAPTER 4

FIRST VICTIM

Leeds sits on a map like a dart board. The circle of trebles is the inner ring road which loops around the city centre with arterial routes spreading out in all directions towards the outer ring road of doubles.

The road that heads up in the direction of double top is Scott Hall Road, a wide open dual carriageway which skirts the edge of Chapeltown.

Not far out of the city centre, a small road called Scott Hall Avenue veers off the main road and scoops round for a few hundred yards before rejoining it. The houses on the left of the street enjoy fabulous views over the adjacent Prince Philip Playing Fields and across the city.

Wilma McCann was too busy bringing up four children as a single mother with very little money in her purse to enjoy the view most days.

She grew up one of 11 in Inverness in the far north of Scotland. After leaving school she got a job at a hotel in Perth, 100 miles down the road. She was a single mum before her teens were out, having given birth to a daughter whose dad didn't stick around.

She then met Gerry McCann, a joiner from Northern Ireland, and, with them both looking for a better life, they decided to follow a number of her brothers who had already moved south to Yorkshire.

The marriage was a violent, unhappy union, which didn't last, and by October 1975 she was bringing up the children on her own in a semi without carpets or heating on Scott Hall Avenue.

On the evening of Wednesday, October 29, 1975, she dressed in a pair of white flared trousers and pink blouse, combed her dyed strawberry blonde hair and did her make-up in a broken piece of mirror which lived above the kitchen sink, holding it in one hand as she applied her blue eye shadow with the other.

She had put the kids to bed early so she could get ready. She wasn't a completely neglectful mother and often did arrange for a babysitter to look after the children, but tonight she left them alone.

She grabbed her jacket and plastic purse which her eldest daughter Sonia had written MUMIY on and slipped out the back door so neighbours wouldn't see her go, hurrying down the alleyway between the houses and the playing fields.

By 1am, after visiting various pubs, she was ready for home. Clutching a white plastic takeaway tray containing her favourite meal of chips and curry sauce, she set her inner compass north, up towards double top, and headed for home.

She never made it.

* * *

"The first one I killed was Wilma McCann in 1975," Sutcliffe would remark many years later, as offhandedly as if he was talking about women he had dated.

Following those three failed efforts in the summer, he set out on that autumn night determined to kill for the first time.

"I was driving through Leeds late at night, I'd been somewhere to have a couple of pints. I saw this woman thumbing a lift. I stopped and asked how far she was going. She said: 'Not far, thanks for stopping' and she jumped in."

She gave him directions and as they drove, Sutcliffe later told police, they agreed a price of £5 for sex.

Wilma had no convictions or cautions for soliciting and her family contest the idea that she was a sex worker, but Sutcliffe claimed: "I realised shortly after she had got into the car that she was a prostitute because she asked me if I wanted business and the evil chain of events went from there."

She directed him to park near the Prince Philip Playing Fields, not far from her home.

"We sat there for a minute talking, then all of a sudden her tone changed and she said: 'Well, what are we waiting for, let's get on with it.'

"I was a bit surprised. I was expecting it to be a bit romantic. I couldn't have intercourse in a split second. I had to be aroused."

Wilma got out, slammed the door and stormed off shouting: "You're fucking useless."

Sutcliffe leapt out and urged her to come back, but Wilma's response of "You can fucking manage it now, can you?" only served to stoke his raging fire.

Sutcliffe suggested they have intercourse on the grass next to his car as the Capri was too cramped.

Wilma wasn't happy at his suggested location, so walked a short distance away up the slope.

With her back turned, Sutcliffe opened his boot and collected a hammer before laying his coat on the grass for her to sit on.

She began unfastening her trousers and told him: "Come on then, get it over with."

"Don't worry," replied Sutcliffe, "I will," as he brought the hammer down on the top of her head with all the force he could muster.

He repeated the blow and Wilma slumped backwards.

He returned to his car, collected a knife and stabbed her 15 times to the chest, neck and abdomen, carrying out the assault with a more determined violence than the previous assaults.

"I knew she was dead, I made sure of that before I left," he said.

Sutcliffe drove through Leeds back to his in-laws' house in Bradford, where he and Sonia were still living.

A short time later Alan Routledge woke early, just as he always did on the days he was working on his milk round.

His ten-year-old brother Paul was going with him and they headed across to Scott Hall to start their established daily routine, which on this day would kick-start the biggest murder investigation Britain had ever seen.

Around the same time, Sonia McCann was shaking her brother Richard awake, whispering so as to not disturb the younger two: "Mum's still not home."

It was 5.25am, dark and cold, but Sonia, in charge because she was seven and around a year older than Richard, who had a week to go until his sixth birthday, decided they would get dressed and go looking for mummy.

They left by the back door as Sonia tried to reassure Richard, and herself, that she had probably just popped to the shops.

After checking nearby streets and the closest bus stop, they returned home. Sonia went to check on her younger sisters, Donna and Angela, while Richard prepared breakfast, bowls of cereal with powdered milk. They couldn't afford the fresh stuff.

It was now 7.41am and Alan Routledge pulled into the car park of the Prince Philip Centre, just behind Scott Hall Avenue, to deliver milk when he spotted what he thought was a pile of rags or a discarded Guy, Bonfire Night being just a few days away.

He was suspicious enough to go and investigate, together with his younger brother, and they walked through the early morning mist, trying to figure out what the shape was.

It was Paul who first exclaimed: "It's a body, it's a body."

Alan ran to a nearby caretaker's bungalow to phone the police.

His call went through to Brotherton House, the former headquarters of a chemicals firm at the Westgate end of the Headrow in the middle of Leeds, which was now the Leeds Area HQ.

His information quickly went up the chain of command and less than half an hour after Wilma's body was found Detective

Chief Superintendent Dennis Hoban, the head of Leeds CID, was being woken by the telephone at the side of his bed.

He quickly got ready and drove to the scene, where he saw that officers had laid wooden boards across the grass to provide a walkway to the body and protect the area from contamination.

Hoban carefully walked over and completed the first and often the most important task in a long list which any murder investigation demands – the visual inspection of the body.

There was no doubt that they were dealing with a murder, the grass behind her head being stained dark with blood.

Professor David Gee, a Home Office forensic pathologist, arrived soon after and following a quick update he drew a sketch of the scene on his notepad and used Sellotape to take samples from the victim.

He placed plastic bags over her head and hands to protect any evidence and wrapped her in a large plastic sheet to transport her to the mortuary.

As the first police officers were gathering, Wilma's son Richard was told by his sister Sonia to go to the front gate to check again if he could see their mum.

He did as he was told and immediately realised something was happening.

"I could see that there was some sort of commotion going on at the end of Scott Hall Avenue," he said years later. "A couple of police cars were parked there, and their blue flashing lights were attracting a crowd of onlookers, just a few yards from the route Sonia and I had walked earlier. I went back in and told Sonia that something was happening in the street."

They knew they had to investigate further. They left their younger siblings in the house and walked along the street. As they approached the growing throng, a uniformed officer spotted the two nervous-looking children. He inquired who they were and what they were doing, to which Richard replied: "Our mum hasn't come home. We are looking for her."

The children were taken back home and gently questioned by police officers, who quickly realised that they had a strong potential identification for the murder victim.

Journalists also quickly got to know and a few hours later, in the first ever newspaper report of a Ripper murder, the *Yorkshire Evening Post* declared on its front page: "Murder in fog". A sub-heading summed up the unbearable tragedy of what Wilma's children had already endured in the short time since her death: "Heartbreak of 5am search by children".

The police drove the bewildered siblings away from their house and took them to a nearby children's home. All they wanted was for their mum to come home and the fuss to be over, but their lives would never be the same again.

Richard grew up to be a successful author and motivational speaker, but Sonia never came to terms with the early childhood trauma she had suffered.

She battled depression for many years, turned to drink and drugs in an effort to cope, fell into abusive relationships and in December 2007, 32 years after her mum was murdered, she hanged herself at her home in Armley, Leeds.

"She had a very difficult life," Richard said after her inquest.

* * *

As Prof Gee was beginning the first post-mortem of a case that would dominate his career for the next five years (he conducted post-mortems for all 11 Ripper victims killed in West Yorkshire), a 137-strong team of police officers was gathering to trace Wilma's killer, headed by Hoban, who launched himself in to a punishing schedule of 15-hours days.

A determined, tenacious man, Hoban was considered a legend among Leeds detectives. Up until the morning he received the early call to head to Prince Philip Playing Fields, he had investigated around 50 murders and none were languishing in the unsolved file.

In the January before Wilma was killed, a firebomb had been placed in a packed Woolworths store in Leeds city centre. The bomb squad was alerted, but they were based at Catterick Garrison in North Yorkshire and were an hour away.

Fearing the bomb was about to explode, Hoban decided there was only one course of action and made it safe, earning himself the Queen's Commendation for Bravery.

Hoban knew the value of publicity to a murder inquiry, especially in its early stages, and within three hours of Wilma's death he held his first press briefing.

The details about Wilma's head injuries were kept from the press, Hoban using it as his 'elimination information', a specific detail which only the killer could know and which helps eliminate those who confess to crimes they haven't done.

Later that day, Hoban also gave his first briefing to the murder squad at Brotherton House, where the incident room had been established.

Teams of detectives were tasked with various lines of enquiries such as interviewing her neighbours and friends and attempting to trace the men listed in an address book which had been found in her house, men that Hoban tactfully described as 'boyfriends' to the press.

Despite Hoban's own professionalism and determination, some aspects of the inquiry had a distinctly amateurish feel right from the off, which was down to a lack of resources.

Detectives didn't have their own personal radios at the time and the established rule was for them to ring in to the incident room every 90 minutes from a payphone to check if there were any new instructions for them to follow.

There were so many officers working on the case – detectives had been pulled in from other areas of the city to assist – that a lack of transport also proved to be a problem.

They worked in pairs on 12-hour shifts, with one car shared between eight officers. Four detectives would set off at the start of the shift to conduct their enquiries, returning to the station four hours later for a meal and to hand over the car to another four officers.

The first group were unlikely to see the vehicle again for another four hours and would have to spend that time completing paperwork or conducting inquiries by foot.

Exactly a week after the murder, road blocks were set up on Wilma's route home in the hope of speaking to drivers who weren't local but who might pass through Leeds for work on a seven-day cycle.

Drivers and staff from a total of 483 haulage companies were spoken to as part of the exercise, without any breakthrough.

Police spoke to 29 male friends of Wilma's, but all were discounted. Her purse with MUMIY written on it was never found.

Over the next 12 weeks, 53,000 police hours were spent knocking on more than 5,000 doors and taking 538 statements.

All of these inquiries were logged on index cards and filed in a system that would eventually grow into a monster.

As for Sutcliffe, he felt a sense of elation that he had finally begun what was now his life's sickening purpose. But he was also worried that the police might be closing in on Wilma's killer.

In characteristic fashion, his thoughts quickly became dominated only by worries about his own plight, a self-absorption present throughout his life.

"I felt I'd finally started the mission, but after killing her, my thoughts immediately turned to me, what about me? What's gonna happen to me now? I was reading all the newspapers and watching the TV about the murder, I was constantly looking out of the window, waiting for the police to knock on my door, but there was nothing."

He needn't have worried. By the evening of January 20, 1976, a few hours after Wilma had been laid to rest and as Emily Jackson, a 42-year-old mother, was looking for business in Chapeltown, detectives were no closer to finding the killer.

CHAPTER 5

COMPULSION

Smiler. It was the perfect nickname for such a happy, popular character at the mill where Emily Jackson worked after leaving school.

She was always ready with a laugh and a joke to help lighten the mood on those long, hard shifts at the weaving looms.

Yet there was another side to her character, a determination to acquire a better life for her and her family than the cramped and damp two-up two-down back-to-back in Armley, Leeds.

Her husband Sid was more cautious, not wanting them to get ideas above their station and overreach themselves.

She reminded him he wasn't just a roofer. He was a businessman. They now ran their own business, S & E Jackson, and the success of the firm would help them acquire the necessary funding to purchase the posh, new house in Churwell, on the edge of the market town of Morley.

It was only a few miles away, but the house was a step up from the inner city life they had always known, with its ceiling to floor windows and glass-panelled doors.

Sid worried about keeping up the mortgage payments while Emily made plans for the new home. After they moved in, he tried to push these money worries out of his mind as Emily proudly showed off their tiled bathroom and mod cons such as the immersion heater to visiting relatives.

But times were always hard. They couldn't afford new furniture so they had brought the old stuff from their previous home, including a second-hand sofa which dated from the 1940s, and Emily spent the first few weeks at her sewing machine knocking up curtains for the boys' bedrooms.

When the feared money concerns became a reality they found themselves contemplating a desperate route out of debt, one which countless women the world over had followed before.

Perhaps the choices they made, which would later shock family, friends and neighbours when they got to find out, were less difficult to stomach for Sid and Emily because of the unimaginable family tragedy they had previously endured.

It arrived out of nowhere one day in 1969 blowing in on a draft that swept through the house when both front and back doors were open at the same time. Their eldest son Derek was holding onto the back door with its large glass pane when his mum and dad returned home, their opening of the front door causing the gust that slammed the back door shut shattering the glass into razor sharp shards, one of which severed the brachial artery under his arm causing a fatal blood loss.

One immediate effect was on the business, such a tragedy hardly being conducive to the profitable running of a small family firm.

In time the business recovered, but it was always precarious. They had to work hard through the summer, knowing that the winter months and the bad weather would bring a drop in trade.

By January 1976 the red bills were piling up, sparking rows between the couple until Emily finally settled on a way of making ends meet that was a closely guarded secret from everyone apart from Sid.

On the evening of January 20 she stood in front of a mirror, carefully applied her red lipstick in readiness for a "night out" and blotted it with a tissue. Her earrings and mascara were already in place, and this was the final flourish.

Her youngest two, Chris and Angela, were glued to the television watching *Bugs Bunny*. Neil, who was 17, was babysitting and was keen for mum and dad to leave so he could get the kids off to bed and have the TV all to himself for *Columbo* and then the golf.

Wearing a blue and white horizontal striped dress, over which she threw a white cardigan, she applied a couple of drops of Coty L'Aimant perfume behind her ears and on each wrist as a finishing touch.

Sid was going with her, heading to the pub while Emily was "playing bingo".

She said her final goodbyes to the three kids, put on her slingback shoes, grabbed her blue, green and red checked overcoat, delivered one last reminder that bedtime for the young ones was 7.30pm and left the house, for the final time.

She climbed behind the wheel of their battered blue Commer van, with its front bumper hanging off, and headed down Churwell Hill, the pink fluffy dice swinging from the rearview mirror as she did a left at the bottom of the hill towards Holbeck, round Armley Gyratory and on to Leeds city centre and Chapeltown beyond.

They reached the Gaiety around 6pm. Now long demolished, it was renowned at the time as an entertainment bar with strip shows and topless waitresses.

It was a Tuesday and still early, but they were met by clouds of cigarette smoke and a packed, lively atmosphere when they entered. They ordered drinks and chatted for around 20 minutes before Emily headed out on to the street, leaving Sid to drink alone.

Around 7pm, she was chatting with a 19-year-old prostitute called Maria when a man in a Land Rover, aged around 50 and with a ginger beard, pulled up beside her. After a brief negotiation, during which Emily ignored the ring on his wedding finger, she climbed in and they drove to a quiet location.

After they had completed their business, she was dropped back off near to the Gaiety and began looking for her next punter.

It wasn't long before a lime green Ford Capri pulled over to the kerb as she loitered near some phone boxes and the driver asked how much.

"Five pounds," she replied, and climbed into the front seat.

Peter Sutcliffe had no intention of having sex with her.

He had come straight from his driving shift collecting tyres from Pudsey and was wearing his work clothes and Wellington boots. The next day would take him to the Pirelli depot at Burton-on-Trent, but before then Sutcliffe, determined and focussed, had his mind on something else.

"I felt an inner compulsion to kill a prostitute," he said.

He pulled away from the kerb and followed her directions to the derelict Manor Street Industrial Estate less than half a mile away.

He parked near a cobblestone cul-de-sac, next to Enfield Terrace, cut the engine and then turned the ignition back on one click, so the dashboard lights came on, part of his planned ruse to trick Emily into thinking he had engine trouble.

He told her he needed to check under the bonnet. Emily, ever friendly and helpful, offered to hold a cigarette lighter so he could see in the dark. As he got out of the car, Sutcliffe reached down and took hold of the hammer and Phillips screwdriver which were concealed in the driver's footwell.

They walked round to the front of the car, Sutcliffe popped the bonnet and they leant in. Sutcliffe then took a step back.

"She was holding her lighter… I took a couple of steps back and I hit her over the head with the hammer," he said. "I think I hit her twice and she fell down onto the road. I took hold of her hands or wrists and pulled her into a yard which had rubbish in it."

He dragged her down a litter-strewn cul-de-sac next to a burnt-out building, where he launched a frenzied assault, using the screwdriver to stab her again and again. He paused briefly four times before re-starting the attack, leaving a pattern of 52 stab wounds in five distinct areas.

It was revenge rather than gratification, he insisted to police later, which drove him on to pick up a piece of wood around three feet in length, measuring 3in by 1in, and thrust it between her legs before throwing it to one side.

At one stage of the attack he stood on her thigh, leaving a muddy footprint – "I didn't do it on purpose, I don't think my boot print would've been on her thigh, it wasn't intentional" – but the filthy, wind-swept nature of the area ensured very few other clues were left behind.

He did, though, benefit from yet another narrow escape.

"Another car pulled up, but turned their lights off quick," he said. "That's what people done when they had prostitutes with them. If they had them on longer, they could have seen my car and registration number, then that could have been it, stopped at the very beginning of everything."

The driver of the other car was too busy with his own liaison to take much notice of Sutcliffe, who was able to drive away without raising any undue suspicion.

He checked his clothes as he drove away and found that despite the frenzied assault, he had no blood on him.

"I'd hit them on the head, then everything was done on the ground so I never had any blood on me," he said.

Sutcliffe headed back to Bradford, where he spent the rest of the evening calmly chatting with his wife Sonia and her parents Bohdan and Maria, as if he didn't have a care in the world.

As the evening wore on, Sid finished his final drink in the Gaiety and walked out to the car park where he and Emily had arranged to meet at 10.30pm.

There was no sign of her and, never having learned to drive himself (Emily drove him to all his roofing jobs) and having no way of contacting her, he assumed she was with a client and caught a taxi home.

A workman found her body the following morning at 8.05am. Dennis Hoban arrived shortly after, followed by Prof Gee.

As they gathered their thoughts at this fresh murder scene, they were conscious that they were standing less than two miles from where Wilma had died. They were also struck by what a pitiful place it was to die, filthy and wet, with piles of rubbish littering the deserted streets outside unwanted buildings.

Once he arrived at the mortuary at Leeds General Infirmary, Prof Gee donned his heavy yellow apron, gum boots, surgical cap and gloves and began repeating the same slow, methodical inspection of Emily's body that he had carried out with Wilma.

Prof Gee paid particular attention to the mark on Emily's right thigh, where Sutcliffe had accidentally stepped on her in his boots. It was similar to a footprint found in sandy soil at the murder scene, which had already been preserved with a plaster cast.

The boot was later identified as being a Dunlop Warwick and was likely a size seven, although they had to be cautious as boots can give a misleading guide of a person's shoe size.

Noting the double head wound and large number of puncture stab wounds, Hoban was convinced they were dealing with the same man who had killed Wilma.

At the first press conference called after the murder, he said: "I believe the man we are looking for is the type who could kill again," and said he was also confident of the killer's motivation: "We are quite certain the man we are looking for hates prostitutes."

What he didn't say publicly, but what his copper's gut instinct had told him after Wilma's death, was that the killer could be a long-distance lorry driver.

He had tools with him, she had been killed on a route which lorry drivers use to get from the A1 to the M62 (it was long before the A1-M1 link road was built which now allows drivers to bypass the city) and there was no indication that the killer was connected to Wilma's own circle of acquaintances, strongly suggesting it was a stranger attack by someone passing through the area.

Peter Sutcliffe hadn't actually started work as a long-distance lorry driver by then, but he was a delivery driver and his long-term dream of passing his HGV test would be realised 12 months after he killed Wilma.

Hoban's instinct was red-hot. He just didn't have a name.

* * *

As detectives poured over the Commer van, which was still parked at the Gaiety with ladders on the roof ready for that day's job, other officers headed to Churwell.

Sid opened the door to a detective and two local uniformed officers; one of them, PC Palmer, was a friend.

After taking the youngest two children to a neighbour to be looked after, Sid and Neil went into the front room, where the officers broke the news.

The rest of what the officer said barely registered. Words such as "murder" and "frenzied attack" floated past their heads, with Neil especially refusing to accept what he was hearing.

"No, Mum's not dead," he cried out, insisting that the only reason the van wasn't parked outside the house in its usual spot was because it had been playing up and mum had taken it to the garage.

Father and son were taken to the mortuary to identify the body, but Sid was almost paralysed with shock. Barely able to talk, he slumped onto a wooden bench in the ante-room at the mortuary as the pathologists made the final preparations for the body to be viewed. Failing to respond to the detectives' gentle but insistent demands that the body had to be identified, they turned to Neil instead to perform the gruesome task. At the last moment, as Neil stood before the sheet-clad body, Sid stepped forward, finding an inner resolve from somewhere, and said: "I'll do it."

He nodded in the affirmative when the sheet was lifted back and he was asked if the lifeless body before him was Emily.

They were then taken to Millgarth Police Station and were split up to be interviewed separately.

Sid was reluctant to reveal every aspect of their personal lives to begin with, which strengthened the finger of suspicion which had already begun pointing at him, although that didn't last long once Hoban was convinced the same man had murdered Wilma and Emily.

As the shock of Emily's murder – and the revelations that she had worked as a prostitute – reverberated through the family and the local community, the police followed a similar publicity campaign as they had with Wilma.

Announcements were made at football and rugby matches, large posters were printed up with Emily's photo and the words "Have You Seen This Woman" in the hope of eliciting details of her final movements.

Acting on the information about Emily getting into a Land Rover with a man with a ginger beard, 1,294 such vehicles were traced in the West Yorkshire area, but none of the drivers proved significant.

A potential suspect was traced to Essex. He admitted to being in Leeds on business, admitted to using prostitutes in the past but denied paying anyone for sex that night or picking up Emily. He had a cast-iron alibi, so he was put down as NFA – No Further Action – and his details were placed along with 6,400 others in the growing index card system.

Over the next 12 months, the murder squad clocked up 64,000 hours, conducted 3,700 house-to-house inquiries and took 830 statements.

But the contradiction in what would become such a large, unwieldy investigation was that the more work that was done, the less efficient the incident room became.

A paper-led system could be a very blunt tool.

One example – thanks to the description of the man with a ginger beard who Emily had been with before Sutcliffe, an index was created for men with ginger beards to cross-reference with any other relevant information which might come in about a potential suspect at a later date.

But no index was created just for men with beards of any colour meaning that if someone like Sutcliffe, with his black beard, crossed paths with the inquiry – as he would do, again and again – the fact that he had a black beard would not sync with another piece of relevant information to create a red flag.

Yet another growing problem, which would come back to haunt West Yorkshire Police long into the future, was the early focus on the killer's apparent hatred of prostitutes. There was little sympathy among the public at the time for the reasons why a woman might be forced into sex work, meaning this focus hampered the flow of information. "They've only got themselves to blame," was not an uncommon opinion.

It also allowed anyone who wasn't a sex worker to wrongly assume they were not at risk.

The murder squad chased every lead, spoke to every witness, tracked every potential suspect but, as with Wilma's murder, the trail soon went cold.

* * *

Peter Sutcliffe was keeping a lot of balls in the air. In the space of just over six months he had murdered two women and tried to kill three others while, in his other life, he was working hard to show he was a devoted husband and the perfect son-in-law and was pressing on with his ambition of becoming a long-distance lorry driver.

He and Sonia were still living with her parents in Tanton Crescent following their wedding as they were saving up for their own place and, as Sonia improved and got stronger following her breakdown, she was also able to contribute to the family purse.

She took a job working one night a week as a nursing auxiliary at Sherrington nursing home, where her mother also worked, before taking up her first post as a supply teacher at Holmefield First School. She had always dreamed of being a teacher, and it proved as satisfying a career as she had hoped.

"She really enjoyed it," said Sutcliffe. "We used to go shopping on a Saturday and many a time a little kid's voice would say 'Mrs Sutcliffe, oh it's Mrs Sutcliffe', and you could tell how fond they were of her. They'd shout out when they were shopping with their mothers. I mean it's a really rewarding job, and they complain that teachers don't get paid enough, I don't think they do."

In February 1975, five months before he attacked Anna Rogulskyj, Sutcliffe took a £400 voluntary redundancy package from Anderton and used part of it to pursue his dream. The money bought him 30 hours of HGV driving lessons with the Apex Driving School in Cullingworth, near Keighley, and he said: "The lessons and Class 1 test cost about £250 at the time, a good investment."

He passed his HGV test Class 1 at Steeton driving school on June 4 that year, two days after his 29th birthday, meaning he was now allowed to get behind the wheel of the biggest trucks on the road.

He was chuffed to bits, but his next job wasn't quite what he had hoped for, although it was a step closer to where he dreamed of ending up. In September, he started working for the Common Road Tyre Company, and although he wasn't driving a big artic – it was a rigid-bodied truck – he was getting there. The job could take him anywhere around the North and Midlands collecting and delivering tyres to garages, but the work soon became a drag for him.

"I didn't like it," he moaned. "My worst HGV job because you used to load the tyres onto a trailer by hand, and they were full of water. When you slung them up onto the trailer you'd get soaked from head to foot, summer and winter. You'd get all the filthy water sloshing over you as you threw them up onto the truck. Big lorry tyres, most of them. Kept you fit, but you were always soaking wet and it wasn't even clean water; it was the filthy rainwater that had collected inside the tyres."

He did achieve something during his short stint at the company – he rapidly improved his knowledge of the road network across the region. The daily routine of driving around towns and cities meant he was developing a mental map of the quickest routes and the little rat-runs to avoid heavy traffic.

It was another job that was short-lived, but it wasn't poor timekeeping that saw him leave this time. Instead, he was caught enjoying one of the 'perks' of the job, taking home tyres which had literally fallen off the back of a lorry.

"We had a whole truck full, and we threw a couple off near the depot where we worked and somebody, a beady-eyed person from one of the big houses, saw us," he said. "He rang the firm because the phone number was on the truck. Me and another lad, and we got done a fiver a piece at court in Dewsbury.

"Sixpence, that's all it was worth, a tyre. The gaffer said: 'You should've asked, you could've had as many as you like, they're only sixpence each. They're worthless to us really, they're just scrap tyres.'

"We knew they were worth nothing but they just looked to be decent tyres, that's all, good tread on them. But they were all scrap.

"It's pathetic really. It was the bloke in the office, the clerk, who wanted us taken to court. He was one of these prim and proper charlies and if it wasn't for him insisting on going to court, calling the police… it wasn't worth it, the court case must've cost a lot more than a fiver or sixpence for the tyre. Stupid really, even the gaffer said it's a pathetic waste of time."

A theft conviction, however minor, meant he was once more looking for work.

There followed a period of unemployment, but Sonia and her parents were reassured by the number of posts he was applying for and he eventually came home armed with some good news. He had finally landed the big one.

Tom Clark and his son Willie had agreed to take him on at their engineering and haulage firm, T & W H Clark, on the Canal Road industrial estate between Bradford and Shipley.

At first, they thought he was quiet and shy compared to the average lorry driver they employed, but they were soon delighted with their new recruit.

Sutcliffe kept his vehicles immaculate, his record-keeping was meticulous, he was polite, smartly turned out and happily headed off on long trips all over England and up to Scotland without a word of complaint.

After a few months behind the wheel of the four and six-ton 'big rigids', he got his reward when he was handed the keys to one of only two, 32-tonne articulated lorries the firm owned, which had been christened 'Wee Willie' although not, as has commonly been reported before, by Sutcliffe himself.

"Willie Clark named it that, I didn't name it. He named it after himself. He had it printed on the cab. It was the biggest truck in the fleet, so he called it 'Wee Willie' after himself."

The £213,450 Ford Transcontinental was 'King of the Road' as far as truckers in the UK were concerned when it was first introduced in 1975.

It was fitted out with cutting-edge technology for the time and the cab itself was higher than that of others in its field, meaning that truckers behind the wheel of a Ford Transcontinental looked down on everyone else, both literally and figuratively.

Sutcliffe couldn't have been happier and spent hours cleaning and polishing it. He got a £9.50-a-night accommodation allowance by the firm for long trips, although his truck had a bunk bed in the cab, but with him and Sonia saving up for their own place, he pocketed the cash instead of booking into a B&B. Workmates reckoned that he loved 'Wee Willie' so much he would happily have slept in it, even without a financial incentive.

"I really did enjoy my job long-distance lorry driving," he said. "I had a good geographical knowledge of the country and could easily find most places without a map.

"Most of the time, I carried truck drive axles, steering axles and gearboxes to Volvo, Caterpillar, JCB, you name it.

"It was great, you're your own boss. You could arrange for your own return loads, look in the *Trucker Magazine* for places where you could get return loads, and you'd get extra bonuses."

After his disappointing stint at the tyre firm, he was loving his time at Clark's and was fast becoming a model employee. His managers thought him hard-working, diligent and, most importantly for him, honest.

It was an anomaly that was difficult to explain. Despite committing multiple murders, he was always desperate to be seen as an honest person.

While at Clark's, all the drivers were sacked at one stage in a widespread cull after they were accused of stealing from their loads. All apart from Sutcliffe.

"They'd been weighing in a lot of castings at the scrapyard instead of delivering them to various firms in and around Birmingham as rejects," he said.

"But I was too honest and wouldn't get involved, so I ended up being the only driver until they set a new crew on. It was daft to risk losing a good job for a few hundred squid."

The management liked him so much, he was chosen to appear in a promotional brochure for the firm as he sat in the cab of 'Wee Willie'.

"I'd been loaded up with axles, ready to go to Irvine in Scotland the next day. I was just driving into the yard when I noticed Clark and a guy with a camera; he just took the photo."

An enlarged print of the photo was hung in the reception area of the firm's offices.

But the quiet, polite, clean, do-anything-for-anyone, softly-spoken young man was only one side of Sutcliffe's character.

He exhibited another when he was in the red light districts, driving past the street girls and shouting insults and crude comments at them.

The Barker brothers, Ronnie and David, who he became friendly with because they lived next to Sonia's family in Tanton Crescent, also witnessed it.

"We used to drive to places like Manchester, York, Leeds and Bradford," said Ronnie. "He seemed fascinated by the red light districts and he used to tour them with his car window wound down, shouting things at the girls on the pavement."

One night, he drove down Lumb Lane and told the brothers: "This is Ripper country."

On other occasions he would drop them off at home at the end of the night, but instead of getting out himself and going inside to see Sonia, he would drive off into the night.

Sutcliffe's friends were never sure whether he actually used prostitutes himself.

"I never saw him actually pick a girl up," said Ronnie.

Trevor was the same.

"He said he got VD off prostitutes. That was before I met him, so I don't know whether that was true or not," he said. "When he was with me, he never actually went with a prostitute, so I didn't know whether he did or not."

Sutcliffe himself vehemently denied it: "I never used a prostitute, though, never actually used one."

One night he approached his old mate Keith Sugden in the Ferrands pub in Bingley and told him about the sensitive issue, which he later also mentioned to Trevor.

"I think I've got a dose," he said to Keith. "It don't look right."

"I went to the toilet with him and he showed me an' he were right, it didn't," said Keith. "It had all gone white at the end, bloody white an' flaky. So I told him: 'You'd better get up to 'ospital.'"

When he was asked where he thought he picked up the infection, he replied: "Off one of them mucky bitches."

Perhaps the perfect son-in-law wasn't so perfect after all.

CHAPTER 6

WORST YEAR

Jimmy Savile had one of the best views in Leeds. The high profile and much-loved (in those days) television personality lived at the top of an exclusive apartment block at the end of West Avenue, in Roundhay, north Leeds, the kind of suburb which gets described as leafy. West Avenue, which cuts into Roundhay Park, was among the leafiest. It is only two miles from Spencer Place in Chapeltown, the heart of the red light district at the time which is also tree-lined, but was never described as leafy in 1977.

At the end of West Avenue is Lake View Court, which enjoys uninterrupted views over Soldiers Field and the sports pitches one way, open park land to another, and down to the lake on yet another.

Inside Savile's apartment, a set of powerful binoculars were close to hand on the window sill, innocent enough perhaps, given the view. Perhaps less so, given the later revelations which elevated Savile to Britain's worst sex offender.

If he had used the binoculars on the morning of February 6, 1977, to look down and to the left, towards Soldiers Field, he would have seen a 46-year-old accountant called John Bolton jog into the park. He had left his home in Gledhow Lane a short time earlier for his early morning run and headed towards the park.

Moments later, Savile would have seen John suddenly depart from his intended route and run over to the sports pavilion, where the local football teams get changed.

He had seen somebody lying on the grass and, keen to help, jogged over to inquire if they were okay.

"Hello," he said to the prostrate figure. "What's the matter?"

There was no response, so he got closer, leaned down and moved the woman's shoulder-length, brown hair away from her face, quickly realising there would be no reply.

"I saw the blood on her neck and her eyes were glazed and staring. She was obviously dead," he said.

* * *

The murder of Irene Richardson was the second attack in Roundhay Park by Sutcliffe in the space of nine months.

The previous summer, on the evening of Saturday, May 9, 1976, Marcella Claxton, a 20-year-old native of St Kitts in the Caribbean, was leaving a party on Spencer Place when Sutcliffe pulled up alongside her in his Ford Corsair.

It was past 4am and she'd had a good night. She didn't live far away, but it had been a long night as well as a good one, so she was delighted with the prospect of a lift home. Sutcliffe had less innocent intentions in mind when he offered to drive her the short distance back to hers.

He was convinced she was a sex worker.

"Oh, she definitely was a prostitute, definitely," he said.

She wasn't, and answered in the negative when he asked if she was doing business and tried to give her a fiver.

As he drove away from Spencer Place, it quickly became apparent to Marcella that they weren't heading towards her home. Instead, he drove towards Roundhay Park. Now terrified and desperate to extricate herself from the situation, Marcella, a mother of two who was four months pregnant with her third child, said she needed to urinate and ran to some bushes where she hid.

She emerged after a short time when she thought he had gone, but moments later she was struck over the head from behind a number of times with a heavy metal implement she thought was a spanner.

She slumped to the ground, seriously injured but alive and conscious. Sutcliffe went back to his car and drove away as Marcella crawled to a nearby phone box to call 999.

It remained a mystery why he didn't continue the attack until she was dead, like he had done with other recent victims. Even he couldn't explain it.

"I just couldn't bring myself to hit her again," he said. "I went back to the car in a stupefied state of mind. I was acutely depressed."

The mission was over for tonight.

Marcella was taken to Leeds General Infirmary and treated for eight severe lacerations to her head, which required 54 stitches. She also lost her unborn baby. She was allowed home after six days, but once she had left the care of the NHS she got a pretty rough deal from the rest of the authorities.

She had a low IQ of 50 and was described at the time as being educationally subnormal.

The detectives who interviewed her tried to get her to say she had been attacked by a black man, despite her insisting he was white.

The police insisted he was black. She said white. They never could agree.

She produced a photofit which bore a striking resemblance to the one created by Tracy Browne – and to Sutcliffe – but it wasn't made public because the police concluded there was no link between her attack and the rest of the series.

She suffered depression, was scared to go out and was vilified by neighbours and even her own family who assumed that, as she had likely been attacked by the Ripper, she must have been working as a prostitute.

More than 40 years later, she was still suffering from blackouts and headaches.

The gap between the attempted murder of Marcella and the next attack was the longest in the entire Ripper series, save for a period in 1978-79 which coincided with the death of Sutcliffe's mother, a diverting event in his life.

But when he did strike again, back in Roundhay Park at the start of February 1977, it led to the bloodiest of years.

It was, in his own words, "my worst year... that's just how it happened."

By the end of the Queen's Silver Jubilee year, which the rest of the country had spent enjoying street parties and waving at Her Majesty as she toured her nation, four more women would be dead by Sutcliffe's hand and a further two would be left alive, but changed forever.

It began with Irene Richardson, the woman who at first glance to jogger John Bolton had appeared asleep when he saw her lying prone in Soldiers Field.

It was a brutal end to a sad, chaotic life for Irene, who had fallen just about as low as it was possible to fall even before she had the misfortune of crossing Sutcliffe's path.

She had been born in Scotland but moved south to try and make a life for herself. Irene came from a large Glaswegian family – seven girls, three boys – and left home at 17 for London, where she had two children to two different men and lost touch with her own family while she was there.

She wasn't much more than a child herself and struggled with her own offspring, who were eventually taken into care. She rebuilt bridges with her family and for a while stayed with her sister Helen in Blackpool, enjoying a period of relative stability.

She got a job at the local Pontins holiday camp, met and fell in love with a plasterer called George Richardson, and married in 1971.

She had two children with him, but her fourth pregnancy triggered another bout of depression. One day she left home without telling anyone where she was going. George contacted the police to report her missing and she finally got in touch a few months later to say she was back in London.

They got back together briefly, but it didn't last and in April 1976 she vanished again, this time for Leeds with a new boyfriend, Stephen Bray, who was on the run from Lancaster Prison.

They moved into a boarding house in Chapeltown. Irene got a number of jobs as a chambermaid at various city centre hotels and as a cleaner at a YMCA in Chapel Allerton, while Bray found work as a bouncer at Tiffany's, the popular nightclub in the Merrion Centre in Leeds city centre.

In January 1977 they decided to marry, even though they were both still married to someone else. Ignoring that little hurdle, they fixed a date and on Saturday, January 22, were booked in at Leeds Register Office. Neither turned up. Neither told the other they wouldn't be turning up.

Irene began missing work and then asked for an advance on her wages to help her make the break from Bray. She was still desperately trying to achieve some sort of normality in her life and applied for a job as a nanny with a family in Roundhay, not far from the park.

But everything was stacked against her. At one stage a man, thought to have been Bray, turned up at one of her jobs and collected her wages for her, but kept them for himself.

A generous landlord allowed her to stay in a bedsit in Chapeltown rent-free, but that couldn't last forever. The rent was normally £5-a-week, the price of a trick for the girls who worked the nearby streets.

Irene was now at rock bottom, yet she still had a rung or two to fall. She took to sleeping rough and in the last two weeks of her life, home was a block of public toilets on Roundhay Road.

She had never worked as a prostitute, but was so desperate she began hanging around the streets of Chapeltown after dark.

Just before midnight on Saturday, February 5, Sutcliffe was driving through the red light district looking for a victim because, as he told it, God was telling him to clear the streets of prostitutes.

"I drove to Leeds to find a prostitute to make it one less. I saw a girl and she got in without a word."

He drove to Roundhay Park and pulled into West Avenue, Jimmy Savile's street.

Bordered by large detached houses with their high gates and long drives on one side and parkland on another, it was quiet and dark. The moon was bright, but it was still discrete enough.

Irene got out and went to spend a penny on the grass before they had the sex that she assumed was about to take place, with no idea that Sutcliffe had something else in mind.

"As she was crouching down, I hit her on the head at least two or three times. She fell down, and I lifted up her clothes and slashed her lower abdomen and throat."

He had smashed her over the head with a ball-pein hammer – the type with the rounded end rather than a claw hammer, most often used for hammering out sheet metal, in leather work or by plumbers – with such force that it drove a "punched out" disc of bone into her brain. He dragged her a short distance over the grass, cut her throat and stabbed at her body three times, leaving one seven-inch wound to the left side of her abdomen which was so deep and gaping that several coils of intestines spilled out.

Sutcliffe rearranged her clothing before walking back to his car. He drove out of West Avenue, south through Leeds and then west to Bradford. It was Saturday night, when Sonia and her mother worked the night shift at the nursing home. He was able to arrive home, compose himself, wash his hands, change out of his clothes and go to bed. All before Sonia returned around breakfast time.

* * *

Dennis Hoban had been promoted to Deputy Assistant Chief Constable (Crime) and his old friend and colleague Jim Hobson was now the Detective Chief Superintendent heading up the Eastern Area CID. Hobson would be Senior Investigating Officer on this latest case, but Hoban, with the other two unsolved murders still in his mind and living only a short drive away, couldn't resist turning up at the crime scene.

He looked dapper as ever in his suit, shirt and tie and full length mac as he wandered across the wet grass deep in thought. Next to him was Hobson, clad in a leather, fur-collared coat popular in the 1970s, inspecting the brief notes he had already made in his notebook as they discussed the obvious – was this number three?

Prof David Gee arrived later, as 20 uniformed members of the Task Force walked slowly across Soldiers Field, staring intently at the ground looking for clues.

Other officers were on hand to alert the arriving Sunday morning footballers that there would be no matches that day.

Prof Gee began his usual careful examination of the woman, who measured 5ft 7in and was lying on her front with her head turned to the left. There was clear blood staining on her head and the surrounding area.

Her long, brown leather boots had been carefully placed along the length of her legs from her thighs down to her calves, in what appeared to be an oddly purposeful manner, leading some to wonder if it was a ritualistic signature.

Sutcliffe explained that there was a simpler, more practical reason – he didn't want to get caught.

There had been a full moon two nights before the attack, on Thursday, February 3, and by Saturday, when he killed her, it had passed into the waning gibbous phase. Waning, but still very bright.

"It was nothing to do with religion or to shock people that found the body. I was surprised how illuminated her legs were from the light of the moon, I couldn't leave her laying there like that as I needed to get away.

"I placed her coat on top of her legs and her boots to hide her legs, plus her things were only placed on top of her so I could move her and everything in one go."

More than a hundred officers were soon making inquiries in Roundhay and Chapeltown.

Steven Bray was traced and eliminated, although he was returned to prison to complete his sentence for theft.

One of those interviewed as part of the house-to-house inquiries was Jimmy Savile.

He hadn't been at home at the time of the attack, but when told about it by a neighbour he said: "This is terrible. It is a ghastly thing to happen practically in your own front garden."

Prof Gee was certain this murder was connected with the previous two.

Hobson issued warnings to the "good time girls" of Chapeltown not to get into strangers' cars.

When that was largely ignored, the police instead mounted a crackdown on prostitution in the area. Scores of women were arrested or issued with cautions to try and clear the streets of potential Ripper victims, a policy which attracted criticism.

The murder of Irene did throw up one solid clue – tyre tracks on the grass close to her body.

Casts using plaster of paris were taken and compared against approximately 250 varieties of tyre which were then available on the open market. The tyres were found to be two India Autoway tyres on the front and an Esso 1110 and a Pneumant, which was made in East Germany, on the rear. All were cross-ply and the front two were worn.

This line of inquiry was one of the most complex of the whole investigation as it involved detailed measurements and the analysis of huge amounts of technical data.

The distance between the wheels was measured, which narrowed the list of potential vehicles down to 100, later whittled down to 51 thanks to the input of a tyre expert from Dunlop.

It was a mammoth task, but the murder squad set to work on what became known as the Vehicle Tracking Inquiry, checking any car they came across after dark in Chapeltown that was on the list to see if it had the correct formation of tyres.

Scrap yards, vehicle breakers and auctioneers were also checked. When the Chapeltown trawl failed to find the car, it was extended across West Yorkshire and the Harrogate district of North Yorkshire, due to its proximity to north Leeds where the red light area was. There were 53,000 potential vehicles to discount, including a white Ford Capri, registration number KWT 721D, registered owner Peter Sutcliffe.

The monotonous task of checking thousands of tyres had fallen to already exhausted detectives. It was morale-sapping work and the sheer number of checks meant it descended into chaos.

It was the best clue so far and couldn't be ignored, but there was an obvious weakness to it – people change their cars and replace their tyres.

Sutcliffe, in particular, was constantly getting new vehicles.

"After one of my attacks, Irene Richardson, the police were looking for a certain type of car," he said.

"At that point I'd sold it and bought another one, so I was okay. I didn't sell it because of the attack, I just got a different one. I just happened to change cars."

The operation was done in secret to prevent the killer simply changing his tyres to avoid detection. But, of course, Sutcliffe claimed to have an extra layer of divine protection.

"This was why I felt God was protecting me," he said, "because I always seemed to get away with things without really trying."

To compound matters, the police were guilty of a glaring, naïve error.

The index card system recorded only the details of the vehicle, not the owner, a baffling oversight given that it was the driver who was murdering women, not his car.

If owners had also been recorded, then the killer's name would be in the index card files, even if he had got rid of his car or swapped one or more tyres. It wouldn't convict him for Irene's murder at this stage, but it could prove significant if another murder threw up more clues which were linked to him.

In short, it would have meant that the name Peter Sutcliffe would now be in the system.

* * *

While Irene's attack was being linked with the murders of Wilma and Emily, the murder squad was also taking another look at a killing further afield.

Joan Harrison was a mother of two who had fallen on hard times by the time she was kicked to death in a disused garage in Preston, Lancashire, in November 1975, less than a month after Wilma was murdered.

She had been married twice, had struggled to hold down jobs as a machinist and shop assistant and was an alcoholic who was also addicted to cough mixtures due to the small amount of morphine they contained. She had never been convicted of prostitution but was known to have sex with men for money to earn enough to fund her habits.

On the day she was murdered, she spent the afternoon drinking in a number of pubs before wandering back to a homeless hostel where staff allowed her to sleep for a few hours. By 10pm she was sober enough to return to her own home, where she rowed with the man she was living with when he refused to give her money. She stormed out and was never seen alive again.

She was found in a derelict garage three days later. Her clothing had been displaced in a manner which appeared similar to the Ripper murders. She had suffered a wound to the back of her head which had possibly been caused by a hammer, although the heel of a shoe was also possible.

Her handbag was missing, suggesting that robbery was a motive, her killer had likely had sex with her and there were no stab wounds, all of which contradicted the attacks over the Pennines.

Hobson was not confident that the murder was linked, a view shared by Detective Chief Superintendent Wilf Brooks, head of Lancashire CID. But there were enough similarities for Brooks to make the journey across the Pennines to share information with his Yorkshire colleagues following Irene's murder.

What was potentially significant – and which would take on far greater importance later on in the Ripper investigation – was that Joan's likely killer had left a couple of significant clues.

Samples of semen recovered during the post-mortem revealed that the man who had sex with her before she was killed was a secretor in the rare blood group B. Only ten per cent of the population has blood group B, 80% of whom are secretors. A secretor is someone whose blood antigens (molecules on the surface of red blood cells which determine blood type) are present not only in their blood but also in other bodily fluids such as saliva, tears, mucus and semen.

This meant that the person who had sex with Joan shortly before she died, and was very possibly her killer, was confined to just 8% of the population. Joan had also suffered a bite to her left breast, which revealed that the person who inflicted it had a gap between their front teeth measuring an eighth of an inch. That detail was kept from the public.

For now, detectives on both sides of the Pennines maintained a holding pattern in respect of whether the murders were linked or not.

CHAPTER 7

INNOCENCE

Tina didn't have anything to worry about. Yes, she worked the streets, but she didn't work *on* the streets. Well, she did now and then, but she also had a place to take the men back to, a ground floor bedsit on Oak Avenue, in Manningham.

This meant she was different to a lot of the other girls in Bradford, who used punters' cars for business or the shadows of Southfield Square. The men she took back could be anyone, but Tina wasn't worried. Leeds, and the maniac who was attacking the women over there, was a million miles away, so Tina felt safe and tonight, on Saturday, April 23, 1977, she was in the mood for a party. Or rather today. Tina had been out drinking most of the day in her favourite spot, the Carlisle Hotel.

Her love of a good party had left men behind in the past, notably her husband Ramen Mitram. Patricia Atkinson was only 16 and working in a mill when she met Ramen in a dance hall in Bradford. Ramen was known as Ray, Patricia preferred Tina.

They hit it off and, risking the wrath of some in his community at the time, Ray started dating a white girl.

At first her wild ways proved irresistible to Ray, who had been raised in the more conservative traditions of the Pakistani community. After a short engagement, they married in 1961 – on April Fool's Day – and went on to have three daughters.

But Tina wasn't made for marriage and motherhood and by the early 1970s she was a regular in the pubs along Lumb Lane

– the Perseverance (known as the Percy), The Queens, the Flying Dutchman and her favourite, the Carlisle.

Ray couldn't keep up. He didn't want to, not with three girls to look after.

The inevitable happened and after their split Ray took custody of the girls, finally divorcing Tina in September 1976.

Tina moved on and by 1977 the boyfriend who kept her company on her nights out was Robert Henderson.

Halfway through April she had taken possession of the keys to the bedsit, which was small and sparsely furnished. Tina was delighted with her new place.

She was busy these days but had a rule of "never on a Sunday". Thursday was pay day in the local factories, so she was available from then until late on Saturday, but after her last client left on a Saturday night she locked her door and closed her curtains and was done, only emerging after a long Sunday lie-in.

On Saturday, April 23, she got dressed in her usual attire of blue jeans, a blue shirt, and a short, black leather jacket and headed for the Percy.

She became noticeably the worse for wear before leaving the Percy and heading to the Carlisle. At 10.15pm, she announced loudly that she was leaving and walked out into the night. The last time she was seen alive was 11.10pm, shortly before a white Ford Corsair pulled up alongside, looking like any other kerb crawler.

* * *

"That was her idea [to go to her flat]," said Sutcliffe. "Do you know what, if she hadn't closed the curtains I wouldn't have killed her. I had to think of saving the mission at all times, so if she hadn't done that, I'd have later found someone else and killed them… it's a strange thing, fate."

In the characteristically offhand way he discussed the murders, Sutcliffe explained what happened after he picked up Tina near St Paul's Road, the street where he had committed that first attack while out with Trevor Birdsall in the summer of 1969.

He saw her up ahead, apparently drunk and involved in an altercation with the driver of a white Mini.

"I pulled up to her and stopped, and without me asking, she jumped into the car. She said: 'I've got a flat, we can go there.'

"She told me she lived alone. I parked up outside her flat and she got out and went in. I picked up a hammer as I got out of the car. I remember this was a claw hammer that I had bought at the Clayton hardware shop. I followed her into the flat, she closed the curtains and I hung my coat on the hook on the back of the door… the hammer was in the jacket pocket. The reason I took the coat off was so she wouldn't see the hammer."

As she sat on her bed with her back towards him, he hit her over the head with it.

It was the only attack which Sutcliffe ever conducted inside a property. All the others were outside in darkened parks or dimly lit, deserted backstreets. Now, under the glare of electric light, he was struck for the first time at the sight of blood.

"This was the first time I had noticed the red blood, before it had always been dark, but this time in the light I saw lots of blood on the bed and on the floor."

He lifted her clothing and mutilated her body with the claw end of the hammer.

* * *

Robert knew not to disturb Tina too early on a Sunday when she liked a lie-in, so he didn't bother her until just before opening time that evening.

He rang her bell and when there was no answer he tried the front door. It wasn't locked, so he entered and walked into a blood-soaked scene of horror.

It was immediately apparent to the first officers at the scene that the attack bore a striking resemblance to those murders over in Leeds and when a detective chief inspector contacted John Domaille, the newly appointed head of Bradford CID, he simply said: "Boss, we've got one."

Domaille, just two months into his new post, was in no doubt what his colleague was referring to.

As soon as he saw the body, he knew his DCI was right due to the massive head injuries and the tell-tale assault to the body.

As was now routine, Prof Gee arrived and began his work in the sparsely furnished room where two wooden dining chairs sat either side of a chest of drawers with a wide mirror on top, the type that Tina would have used to do her make-up before a night out.

Her white cotton pants had been pulled down, leaving her buttocks exposed, a departure from the previous murders where underwear had not been interfered with. It led to Domaille telling reporters that a sex attack had not been ruled out. The newspapers were now calling the killer Jack the Ripper, an echo of the similarities between the wounds being inflicted on these latest victims and those on the five women murdered by the 19th century serial killer.

During the attack on Tina, Sutcliffe had left a bloody impression of a footprint on the bedsheets, the second murder scene where such a clue had been found. But, unlike at the Emily Jackson murder scene in Leeds, the imprint in Tina's flat was too indistinct due to the material it was on to say whether it had been left by the same man.

Fifty officers were soon working on the murder inquiry (which would rise to 90) with door-to-door inquiries and a fingertip search of nearby woodland to look for the murder weapon the early priorities.

It was clear right from the off that the Leeds killer was also responsible for this latest attack, but senior officers insisted that the

Atkinson inquiry would be run separately from an incident room in Bradford.

Just like Wilma, Tina had an address book which contained the names of a number of men, in her case 50, and officers set about tracing them.

A theory had been building among the police that the attacker might be a taxi driver due to knowledge of red light areas and having a legitimate reason to be driving around them late at night.

Tina was a regular user of taxis and all of Bradford's 1,200 registered drivers were spoken to. Officers also knocked on 2,300 doors appealing for information, but every lead eventually ran into its own dead end.

* * *

It took the brutal murder of a sweet 16-year-old to change everything.

Up until June 1977 there was a widespread belief that the Yorkshire Ripper targeted only prostitutes and "good time girls". The police appeals were heavily based towards this premise, leading to women who didn't class themselves as either wrongly assuming they were still safe to walk the streets after dark.

That was until the mutilated body of Jayne MacDonald, who worked in the shoe department of the Grandways Supermarket on Roundhay Road, was discovered next to a children's play area just off Chapeltown Road.

Jayne was a typical teenager. A keen fan of the Bay City Rollers, she had recently split with a boyfriend because it was getting too serious and was looking forward to having fun as she got ready at the family home in Scott Hall Avenue, Leeds, six doors up from where Wilma McCann had lived.

Concerns about a killer stalking the nearby streets was the last thing on her mind as she decided what to wear for her Saturday night in the city centre, finally settling on a blue and white halter-neck sun top before going downstairs to say goodbye to her parents, Wilfred and Irene.

They were a close family and Jayne always told her parents where she was going and when she would be back. Like many families at the time they didn't have a phone, but there was an arrangement in place for her to ring their neighbours, the Bransbergs, who did have one so she could leave a message that she was going to be late. Wilf and his wife Irene, a waitress, were popular with their neighbours, as was Jayne – "She was a lovely girl and really pretty, just like a film star but unspoilt," said one who lived across the road.

As she was leaving, Jayne bent down and kissed her father and said: "I won't be late tonight, Dad." A silver cup inscribed "For the world's best dad", a present from her and her brother Ian, was nearby on the sideboard.

It seemed to Wilf like no time at all since she was a young child and, in truth, it wasn't. One of her favourite dolls, a wind-up toy that played *Raindrops keep falling on my head*, still took pride of place in her bedroom.

But she was growing up fast. She had a busy social life with friends, but Saturday was the only night of the week she stayed out late and that night she ended up at the Hofbrauhaus, the Munich bierkeller-themed bar in the Merrion Centre where the music was provided by a 'German' band made up of a Geordie, a Scouser and two Yorkshire lads dressed in lederhosen and Tyrolean hats.

Beer was 32p a pint, tunes like *The Happy Wanderer* blasted out and everyone had a great time in one of the first themed pubs in the city.

Jayne spent the night dancing with a boy called Mark Jones, who she had just met. They had taken a fancy to each other and after leaving the bar at 10.30pm they walked through the city streets.

She was peckish, so they bought a bag of chips and, realising she had missed her last bus home, they sat on a bench outside C&A on Boar Lane to eat them, around the same time that Peter Sutcliffe was also buying chips, with a side order of fish, in Bradford.

After a day spent viewing a house with Sonia he had been out with the Barker brothers, but the friends had a minor fall-out at the end of the night when Peter failed to get the last round in, and they headed home in silence.

He dropped them off at the end of Tanton Crescent, but instead of parking up and going in to his in-laws he drove to Leeds.

Shortly before midnight, Jayne and Mark had finished their chips and started walking home, having forgotten to ring the Bransbergs to let her parents know she would be late.

They eventually parted company around 1.30am and Jayne tried to ring for a taxi from a kiosk at the Dock Green pub by the junction of Beckett Street and Harehills Road. None were available, but she wasn't far from where she worked and had walked home plenty of times from here before.

She walked along Bayswater Mount at 1.45am and threaded her way through the terraced streets before popping out on to Chapeltown Road, where her route would take her a few hundred yards north through another couple of streets and into her own road and home.

As she crossed over Chapeltown Road close to the Hayfield Pub, a Ford Corsair cruised past and pulled into the pub car park.

Sutcliffe would never waver from his conviction that he believed every woman he attacked was a prostitute. In reality, all it took to persuade himself that that was the case was for a woman to be on her own on a street late at night.

"At this time the urge to kill prostitutes was very strong and I had gone out of my mind," said Sutcliffe.

"This is what I believed was the voice of God saying it was the prostitutes who were responsible for all these problems. It kept saying I had to go on with a mission and it had a purpose. It was to remove the prostitutes. To get rid of them.

"I saw this lass walking along quite slowly. I anticipated that she was going to walk up one of the streets up past the Hayfield. I drove my car into the Hayfield pub car park and got out.

"I took my hammer out of the car, I think it was the claw hammer. I also had a knife with me; that time it was a kitchen-type knife with a black ebonite handle and thin blade."

Jayne was now just half a mile and ten minutes' walk from home, but as she turned onto Reginald Street, Sutcliffe slipped out of the darkness.

He fell in behind her along the barely-lit street – the street lights automatically switched off at 11.30pm – and before she had time to realise she was at risk, he struck her over the head from behind.

He dragged her unconscious body onto a patch of litter-strewn, derelict land next to the playground between Reginald Street and Reginald Terrace. A dirty, discarded mattress and roll of carpet lay nearby.

He struck her twice more to the head, then pulled up her jacket and stabbed at her body. He thrust a blade into one wound repeatedly, as many as 20 times, a motion which would take on great significance at his trial.

Satisfied she was dead, Sutcliffe walked back to his Corsair in the pub car park. As he climbed in, he saw a group of people walking down Reginald Street, passing within yards of where Jayne's body lay without noticing anything. A few minutes earlier and they would have seen either his initial assault on her or possibly heard the murderous assault that followed. Another close shave.

He drove home and went to bed on his own as Sonia was working another night shift at the nursing home with her mother.

As well as Sutcliffe's claim he was being driven to kill by voices from God, he also told police after his arrest that the attacks were based in part around his wife's shift pattern.

"I have remembered that my wife started doing some Friday and Saturday nights at Sherrington Private Nursing home in Bradford," he said. "That is why I have done a lot of my attacks on a Saturday night."

* * *

So far, a different senior investigating officer had been in charge of each of the four previous murders, but it had already been decided that should there be a fifth, then one man would take overall control. That man was George Oldfield.

The ruddy-faced Yorkshireman had been promoted to Assistant Chief Constable (Crime) the previous year, the culmination of a police career which started just after the Second World War, during which he served with the Royal Navy.

He joined the West Riding Police in 1947 and by 1974, the year before the first Ripper murder, was appointed head of CID for West Yorkshire Police.

Oldfield was considered brusque and unapproachable by junior officers, who felt him dismissive of ideas that didn't chime with his own way of doing things. A short fuse could also give rise to memorable outbursts.

"George was a blunt Yorkshireman," said Frank Morritt, a retired detective superintendent who worked closely with him. "If he wanted to tell you it was X, it was X, no argument. I think he listened yes, and at the end of the day he came to his own opinion and having come to that opinion, that was it. Get on with it."

Yet those closest to him had unswerving loyalty. Dick Holland, a detective superintendent who joined the Ripper inquiry at the same time that Oldfield took overall charge, said: "He was a bloody good commander."

His passion for hard work and long hours was sustained by whisky and Craven A cigarettes. When the 11am tea and coffee tray went round, the only drink on there for Oldfield was a glass of water to accompany his Scotch.

Now, on the morning of Sunday, June 26, he was about to take charge of a case that would define his entire career. It would also come to dominate his life and, some would say, end it.

On Sunday morning, Oldfield left his home in a village near Huddersfield and drove to Chapeltown.

Holland, the deputy head of CID for the western area of the force, arrived shortly after. He would now be Oldfield's right-hand man on the growing series of murders.

Prof Gee also arrived and they began a careful examination of the scene. It was clear that the victim had been dragged around 20 yards to the position where she now lay face down, still fully clothed.

A degree of blood staining was apparent around her head and left hand, and on her clothing. Two wounds to her head were visible. She was carefully turned over and two things became clear – firstly, there were larger areas of blood staining under where her head and stomach had been, indicating more severe wounds, and secondly, she looked so young.

A four-hour post-mortem revealed head wounds that were typical of the other attacks.

While Prof Gee was detailing the precise injuries, Oldfield's officers were setting up an incident room on the fourth floor at Millgarth, the new police station in the centre of Leeds.

Following the decision to bring all the murder inquiries under one roof, all the paperwork relating to the four previous attacks was also brought together. That paperwork was about to explode.

The established way of investigating murders in the old Leeds city force was all about legwork. Hit the doors and the pubs and speak to all your contacts, and hopefully you'll get a name.

But that was considered old-fashioned and inefficient.

The West Riding method, of which Oldfield was a keen adherent, was a more considered, paper-work based approach.

At the heart of it lay a reliance on the index card system where all potentially relevant information from numerous interviews was noted down on a card and filed, along with other paperwork, in dozens of filing cabinets placed around the outer edge of the room. Five maps were pinned up on the walls with coloured pins showing the locations of attacks.

Two superintendents – Holland and Jack Slater – shared an office with Oldfield at Millgarth and it was their job to keep an overall check on the inquiries being done by the murder squad. They oversaw a team of around 20 personnel whose job it was to analyse the mass of information coming into the inquiry before filing it onto index cards. They also advised on which interviews should be followed up on, and which new lines of enquiry to explore, while making sure Oldfield was kept appraised on significant developments.

To help drive the flow of information from the public, Oldfield began giving daily press conferences, immediately becoming the public face of the Ripper inquiry.

A large map was created in the incident room showing the sightings of cars and people who needed to be traced and eliminated. It quickly amounted to 200, which included individuals and groups of people as well as vehicles, divided into three charts relating to 1am to 2am, 2am to 3am and 3am to 4am.

A mobile police station with a large radio mast and humming generator was set up in Reginald Street as a base for officers, but also to build bridges with the community and to make it easier for local people to pass on information.

Oldfield stressed in his public comments that Jayne wasn't a sex worker and referred to her as the first "innocent" to fall victim to the man stalking the red light district which sent shock waves through the city.

This divide between sex workers and "innocent" women, with the former seen as bringing it on themselves while the latter were more deserving of sympathy, would bring huge criticism for the police and see them accused of victim shaming long before the phrase was invented.

The media at the time reflected the messages that were coming out of the police.

The *Yorkshire Evening Post* carried an open letter to the killer. Addressed to "The Ripper" it read: "You have killed five times now. Your motive, it is believed, is a dreadful hatred of prostitutes, a hate that drives you to slash and bludgeon your victims.

"But inevitably, that twisted passion went terribly wrong on Sunday night. An innocent sixteen-year-old lass, a happy respectable, working class girl from a decent Leeds family, crossed your path. How did you feel yesterday when you learned that your blood stained crusade had gone so horribly wrong? That your vengeful knife had found so innocent a target?"

Oldfield needed to stress that both groups of women were now at risk.

"We now have a clear picture in our mind of the type of man we are looking for, and obviously no woman is really safe until he is found," said Oldfield.

The different tone of the police appeals, the press coverage and the public reaction all reflected the step change in the case. The police and media pushed the message that the threat was bigger now, and the public received it loud and clear.

Even the picture of Jayne issued to the media underlined it. She was the only one of the victims so far who, at the time her photo was taken, looked like she was actually enjoying life.

The others had their various struggles – drugs, alcoholism, soliciting convictions, poverty, parenting challenges, abusive relationships – writ large across their tired, worn faces.

By contrast Jayne was bright-eyed and fresh-faced with a wide smile which revealed a row of perfect, gleaming teeth.

The killing of a young woman who wasn't a prostitute had changed the community's views about who was at risk, but the one person it had no effect on was the killer himself.

"It didn't change for me," said Sutcliffe, looking back on that pivotal moment in the series of murders. "I didn't know at the time how old she was, I didn't see her face. It was around 2am, she was walking through an area used by prostitutes, plus the way she was dressed, I thought she was one."

Reflecting the matter-of-fact way in which he discussed all of his attacks, without any emotion or remorse, he added: "As she walked past me, I stepped out and hit her on the head."

He didn't think of his victims as human beings, viewing them instead as faceless examples of a group which he claimed God had instructed him to exterminate.

"I didn't remember a lot of their faces at the time, it was only when their photos appeared in the paper, I then knew what they looked like."

Neither did he pause to consider the devastated communities and families left in his wake, either at the time or years later, because the only thing he cared about was the voice in his head and to him there was no doubt over its authenticity.

"The voice seemed so real," he said nonchalantly, as if that belief alone was enough to explain and excuse his actions.

Twelve days after the attack, police released an artist's impression of a bearded man they wanted to speak to. He was the man who had been seen speaking to Emily Jackson shortly before she was killed, and police investigating Jayne's murder also had reports of a similar looking man in the area on the night of her murder.

The same man was thought to have been involved in an incident with a prostitute in Manningham in March 1975, ten months before Emily was killed. The description was detailed – aged between 35-40, 5ft 8in tall, stocky build, full beard, wearing overalls with a deformed or badly burned left hand and a tattoo on his arm.

Sadly, his beard was ginger.

Police received 117 tips of men who bore a resemblance, 56 of whom were traced and eliminated. The rest were never found and 'Ginger', as he was now nicknamed by the murder squad, remained a strong person of interest, but tantalisingly untraceable. Two weeks after Sutcliffe killed Jayne, with hundreds of officers continuing to interview people all over Leeds in the desperate hope of a breakthrough, he struck again.

CHAPTER 8

SURVIVAL

A detective leaned in towards Maureen Long's hospital bed and gently asked her another question. He had been warned by medical staff that she was still very poorly and he wouldn't be able to talk to her for long.

She was about to be taken to theatre for a life-saving, three-hour neurosurgical operation and after ten minutes she was exhausted and the officer had to call it a day.

Her memory was hazy, but she was able to say her attacker's car may have been white. The information was passed back to the Ripper incident room where senior officers were already convinced, due to her wounds, that he had claimed another victim. The difference this time was that she had survived. All four of the women who had previously survived an attack were still on the list of 'maybes' or 'definitely nots'. As far as the murder squad was concerned, Maureen was their only surviving confirmed Ripper victim and was, therefore, a vital witness.

She had spent the early part of the evening of Saturday, July 9, at home in her terraced stone house in Donald Street, Farsley, getting ready to go out for a night of drinking and dancing. Farsley is on the western edge of Leeds but is closer to Bradford city centre than Leeds and Maureen often travelled there for her nights out.

She was living with a new partner but remained on good terms with her former husband and was due to meet him for a drink before going dancing at the Bali Hai ballroom on Manningham Lane.

Maureen said goodbye to her ten-year-old daughter, the only one of her three children who lived with her, and headed into Bradford.

After a couple of drinks with her husband, she moved on and eventually made her way to the Bali Hai, the club inside Tiffany's that used to be the Mecca and which featured in the film *Billy Liar*.

Maureen didn't work due to a nervous condition and survived on £13-a-week social security payments, although she made sure she lived life to the full.

She emerged from the Bali Hai around 2am and walked along Manningham Lane aiming to get a taxi, but as she walked past the burger stand a white Ford Corsair pulled up and the driver asked her: "Are you going far?"

"Are you giving me a lift?" she replied.

She climbed in and directed Peter Sutcliffe to her ex-husband's home, where she was staying the night.

She banged on his front door for a few minutes and when there was no answer she got back in his car and directed him to "a place where we could go".

They drove a short distance to a darkened patch of land on Birkshall Lane, just off Bowling Back Alley, in Laisterdyke, a couple of miles to the south east of Bradford city centre. Bowling Back Alley is a desolate road peppered with scrap yards, small industrial units and car body shops, the kind of place sought out by fly tippers. A travellers' site, unofficial in 1977, is now official with fixed accommodation. A series of dead-ends lead off the main road, most of which feel like the kind of end-of-the-world wasteland that were designed for the activities Sutcliffe had in mind.

As he killed the engine, Maureen got out to urinate.

"I had my hammer ready and I also had a knife. I think it was the same knife I had at MacDonald. I got out of the car while she was having a piss and as she was crouching down I hit her on the head with the hammer," he said.

He dragged her further into the darkness and stabbed her five times with such force she suffered three broken ribs.

It was 3.15am. A guard dog at a nearby factory began barking and the security guard went to investigate. He looked out into the night just in time to see what he was convinced was a white Ford Cortina Mark II speed off.

Sutcliffe arrived home and went to bed alone, Sonia being on another Saturday evening night shift. As he slipped into an untroubled sleep Maureen Long was lying on the patch of wasteland, still alive, but only just.

She was only 5ft 1in and had suffered terrible injuries, but she showed enormous reserves of strength and hours later, as the travellers' site was waking up, she was able to issue a weak cry for help. At 8.45am, two women in a caravan heard her cries and found her, seriously injured and also now suffering from hypothermia.

She was rushed to hospital in Bradford where, as soon as it became apparent she had been attacked by the Ripper, she was placed under round-the-clock police guard.

Prof Gee examined her injuries to confirm it was indeed the same man who had killed five other women. Her wounds were so serious that he considered her very lucky not to be number six.

The detectives' early delight that a victim had survived quickly vanished. She hadn't suffered permanent brain damage, but her memory of the attack was almost nil and it never returned.

Sutcliffe was shocked to read that his latest victim had survived and worried she would be able to identify him, a concern that was quickly replaced by a calm relief when the feared knock on his door failed to materialise.

"I wondered if she recognised me," he said, but quickly added, "I didn't show any signs of nervousness because I knew God was in control you see. I was very calm about things.

"I believed that I was being looked after by God, you see, and everything was all right."

A couple of years later Sutcliffe, to his horror, walked straight past Maureen at the Arndale Centre in Bradford while he was shopping with Sonia.

He immediately recognised her, but quickly realised she hadn't recognised him.

"She didn't even remember me. I saw her in town when I was shopping with Sonia, we walked right past her and I looked her in the face, but she didn't show any sign of recognition. She didn't even remember who I was."

Before the full extent of Maureen's memory loss was apparent, Oldfield expressed the police's optimism at a press conference two days after the attack.

"The investigation is beginning to bubble," he said. "I feel we are getting nearer to the man I am looking for."

Oldfield's use of the first-person singular – "... the man *I* am looking for..." rather than "we" which would have included the 300-plus officers searching for the killer, further personalised the hunt as if it was a game of cat and mouse involving just two men, him and the Ripper.

Just two cases into his tenure in charge of the investigation and his personal obsession with the case was building.

The early optimism quickly evaporated, and the only significant, long-term consequence of it was a negative one.

The Vehicle Tracking Inquiry, which was launched after tyre tracks were left at the Irene Richardson murder scene, was still ongoing.

More than 30,000 of the potential 53,000 vehicles which could have left the tracks had been eliminated but the long, laborious task was slowing down and now there was another problem.

The white Ford Cortina which the security guard insisted he had seen driving away after Maureen's attack was not on the list of potential vehicles at Irene's murder scene.

He was adamant about which car he had seen and due to his conviction and the lack of manpower – "If you were warm and breathing, you were on the bloody Ripper case," said Dick Holland – the decision was made to end the Vehicle Tracking Inquiry.

Instead, the focus switched to Cortinas and a list of owners living in West Yorkshire was drawn up. It numbered around 5,000, of which approximately 3,000 were traced and discounted, but there was a fatal flaw in this latest line of inquiry.

The security guard had been mistaken. He hadn't seen a Ford Cortina, it was a Ford Corsair.

Just over 20,000 cars were still to be checked in the tracking inquiry when it was scrapped. Sutcliffe's Ford Corsair was one of them.

A Freefone line that went straight through to a white telephone and answer phone was set up in the incident room, for those who might have crucial information but who wanted to remain anonymous.

There was also a red telephone, which was staffed round the clock for those happy to speak to someone. The response in the immediate aftermath of Jayne's murder was huge. Hundreds of phone calls were received each day, but it drifted away over time without any call providing a significant breakthrough.

Oldfield continued his daily appeals for help, although they began to feel desperate and took on a tone of him blaming the public for failing to solve the crime.

"The public have the power to decide what sort of society they want. If they want murder and violence, then they will keep quiet. If they want a law-abiding society in which their womenfolk can move freely without fear of attack from the likes of the individual we are seeking, then they must give us their help," he said.

Officers trawled previous attacks on women to see if they might be linked and looked again at the assault on Anna Rogulskyj, attacked two years earlier in Keighley, although her case was still not officially included. Marcella Claxton spoke out to insist she had also been attacked by the Ripper, but her pleas to be included fell on the deaf ears of a police force which kept telling her that her attacker had been black.

The police sought the help of sex workers, while at the same time arresting them in huge numbers. In the months surrounding Jayne's murder, 152 women were arrested and reported for prostitution in Chapeltown and a further 68 were cautioned.

The burgeoning inquiry was now producing such a large amount of paperwork that tentative inquiries were made about utilising the new computer systems which were becoming available at a national level.

On the Monday following the attack on Maureen, the Chief Constable of West Yorkshire, Ronald Gregory, wrote to the Director of the Police Scientific Development Branch asking if they could offer any assistance.

A senior scientist visited the force and wrote a report which concluded that the computerisation of the incident room records was possible. He suggested that a computer at the Atomic Energy Research Establishment at Harwell, Oxfordshire, could be used. The up-front cost would be £25,000 with the cost going forward £156,000 a year. Gregory declined the offer and the incident room continued to operate on a paper-only basis.

A month after Jayne's murder, residents living in every one of the 679 homes in the 21 streets closest to her murder scene had been interviewed and in total 13,000 people had been spoken to as part of the inquiry.

The numbers relating to all five murder inquiries were even more daunting. A total of 343,000 man-hours had been devoted to the inquiries, 175,000 people had been spoken to by police, 12,500 statements had been taken and 101,000 vehicles had been checked.

Despite this mammoth effort, the trail was going cold. By now, both the red and the white phones were silent.

* * *

Jayne Macdonald's family, like others before them, was shattered. Her mother Irene would be on tranquilisers for years to come, and her father Wilf was left a broken man. After identifying his daughter's body at the mortuary, he returned home barely able to speak, only managing to mutter that her beautiful hair had blood on it.

He busied himself by whittling a cross for her grave from the wooden frame of her bunk bed. When it was finished he placed it on her final resting place with the words 'RIP Jayne Michelle Macdonald. Born 16-8-60. Died 26-6-77' painted on it.

But nothing could bring him peace. He had been recovering from bronchitis when Jayne was killed and the shock of her murder knocked him back, and he developed nervous asthma. He was a tough man and tried to fight it, but he never seemed to get any better. What didn't help was that the killer kept killing.

Every time he read about another victim, it pushed him further down the spiral of ill health.

CHAPTER 9

NEW START

It was Sonia's mother Maria who found it for them. She had been helping Peter and Sonia look for a place of their own for a while, and had finally come across what she felt would be the ideal family home for them.

"Sonia's mum Maria first saw that number six was for sale, so she told Sonia and then when I got home from work they told me," said Peter. "So we both went to view it and although it needed a lot doing, we thought it was a bargain."

It was in a lovely street called Garden Lane, in the Bradford suburb of Heaton, considered well-to-do by people who lived in Tanton Crescent or Corny Road in Bingley.

It was the kind of street that Peter's brother Mick would raise his eyebrows at, half in admiration that "'r Pete's going up in t'world", half in disdain that he was leaving his roots behind him.

Number six was the only detached house in a street of bow-fronted semis which had grass verges separating the pavements from the road with attractive trees planted along them.

The street was less than two miles from Manningham Lane, but they felt worlds apart. The owner, a Mr Rahman, a barrister, and his family were selling up to return to Pakistan. The four-bed-roomed house had been on the market for nine months with only two unsuccessful viewings when the Sutcliffes turned up on

Saturday, June 26, to have a look around, a few hours before Jayne MacDonald was beaten and stabbed to death.

Sonia's mother went with them and the women appeared much more taken with the property than Peter, who was worried they might be overstretching themselves with an asking price in excess of £15,000.

"Mr Sutcliffe was very calm, very collected and very polite," said Mr Rahman. "He didn't appear to be too enchanted with the house, certainly not as much as his wife and mother-in-law. He told me he was a long-distance lorry driver and he was away for long periods, so he wanted his wife to be in a quiet, pleasant area."

In the end they agreed on a price of £15,350 with the Rahmans throwing in some bedroom furniture.

They exchanged contracts on August 18 – with Sonia signing them as Mrs Szurma-Sutcliffe and her mother acting as a witness – and the new owners got the keys the following month, with Peter arranging the removal himself.

"When we moved into our house, I borrowed a truck from work to do the removal."

Once he had got over his initial concern about keeping up with the mortgage payments, Peter was delighted with their new home and was too pleased with their move up the social ladder to care about what his brother Mick might have thought.

"It is a posh area. Doctors and surgeons and lawyers and all that lived round there and judges," he said.

He was particularly proud to have the only detached house in the street, which adjoined a strip of land used at the time by a local rugby club.

"You can sit in the attic and watch them play rugby," he said. "Comfortable on a nice sofa, and look out the window watching the rugby."

This was a satisfying period for Sonia. As well as moving into her first home, she had finally landed her first teaching role at

Holmfield First School in Bradford. It was a supply role but, after her years of studying and that breakdown which ended her life in London, she could not have been prouder as she walked into the classroom for her first day as a teacher.

On their days off, there was plenty to keep them busy at their new home, which stretched over three levels. Sonia tended the garden while Peter concentrated on the DIY. As well as being good with engines, he was handy around the house, which was useful.

"It was in a bit of a mess. We had a lot of work to do when we moved in. It had been neglected by the previous owner, who obviously wasn't a handyman.

"You'd think they'd been living in poverty. He should've had a decent wage as a barrister and he let the whole house go to pot. We'd lots to do. Needed decorating and all sorts.

"All the window frames were rotten, the door frames were rotten, we replaced them all, redecorated throughout, bought all new furniture and had the outside completely pebbled dashed.

"It looked completely different inside and out six months after we'd moved in.

"When we first moved in, there was a tall chimney at the back leading up from the kitchen where there once was a fireplace, but I took it down myself, and gave the bricks to our neighbour, Tom Garside."

The neighbours watched with interest on the day they moved in as they carried their belongings in from the borrowed truck, which included a piano.

Barbara Bowman, who lived opposite, wondered if the new man of the house worked in showbiz because of his appearance in a pale green suit and a pair of white wooden clogs along with his moustache, known at that time as a "Pancho Villa" number after the famous Mexican revolutionary.

That notion was shattered when Peter arrived home from work one day in the cabin section of his 32-tonne Ford Transcontinental.

At first, he tried to park it on his driveway but quickly discovered it was too big, so he bumped it up on the grass verge outside his house.

"I never parked my unit in the driveway," he said. "I once tried it, but at eight feet wide the unit was six inches wider than the drive itself, so I parked it half on the road and half on the grass verge between the two trees, leaving the pavement free for folks walking past."

Others in the street worried this might become a regular habit and quickly made their displeasure known to each other.

"This is residential, it's not one of these new estates," Mrs Bowman told her husband.

One of the neighbours finally knocked at number six and politely requested that Mr Sutcliffe might find somewhere else to park his lorry. He readily agreed.

"I didn't take the unit home all that often. If I took the trailer home as well, I'd park the whole rig opposite on the main road."

He continued with his passion for tinkering with engines, but it was no longer his main love as he made efforts to build a happy home life.

"I was happy swapping engines or stripping them down or doing resprays and stuff. But I always had more time for her [Sonia]. If she needed anything I would break off, I wouldn't complain, I'd go in and help her with anything. Got to put your missus first."

The minor disagreement about the parking of his truck was the first and last time there was any reason for disquiet between the new residents and their neighbours. The young couple were considered to be pleasant and quiet and kept themselves to themselves, although they were happy enough to engage in the humdrum neighbourliness which helps such streets get along.

"The Glaziers lived opposite us," remembered Sutcliffe. "They were a nice couple with kids. The kids used to come up and clean my drive at winter time, shovel it clear. I used to give them a £1 note each and a Mars Bar."

Some neighbours had got into a habit of piling garden rubbish on the edge of the rugby pitch, which bordered number six.

Peter didn't mind it, but it eventually got so big that he worried it posed a security risk.

"The only time I ever lit a fire was on the other side of the garden wall where the rugby field is because all the neighbours had been piling their garden rubbish up against the wall. Anybody could climb straight over that into our garden.

"So I lit a fire to get rid of all that garden rubbish and burn it."

He was later accused of burning the clothes he had worn during the attacks on this garden, which he insisted wasn't the case.

"I never burnt any clothes. Would I go and let people see me burning clothes in the garden? The only time I ever lit a fire was to get rid of all that garden rubbish. There was no reason to burn any clothes, I never got anything on them."

After years of living at Sonia's parents, the couple finally had their own place to entertain family and friends.

On Sunday, October 9, 1977, Peter was delighted to welcome his parents, his brother Mick and his girlfriend, his sister Jane and her husband and a friend of his parents who had brought them down from Bingley and who Peter insisted stay to enjoy the small, informal house-warming party.

At first, the atmosphere was awkward, especially when the talk turned to Sonia's various works of art which adorned the shelves. She loved pottery and was enthusiastic enough to later consider doing it as her main career. For now, it was just a hobby, but she was interested in gauging the opinions of her in-laws.

Mick was, for once, at a loss for words. He would have enjoyed a realistic piece of say, a fox, or some other wildlife, but privately thought her modern, abstract work was a "loada bunkum" although he admitted: "I don't know anything about art."

John, wanting to appear sophisticated, offered his opinion that they weren't that far removed from the work of Henry Moore, the renowned Yorkshire sculptor.

After the brief discussion about art, everyone moved to the dining table where Peter's attempt to cook potatoes to supplement his wife's efforts (Sonia had underestimated how much the Sutcliffe men would eat) provided the comedy highlight of the evening. They were undercooked and when Peter tried to stick his fork in one it shot off his plate and onto the floor. The Sutcliffes roared with laughter and kept laughing for the rest of the night, not so much oblivious to Sonia's disapproving looks as just not caring about them.

At the end of the evening, Peter offered to take his parents' home in his red Ford Corsair, having sold his white one a few weeks earlier. After dropping them off safely at their house in Bingley, he headed south, back towards Bradford. But instead of going home, he carried on driving.

It was past midnight, Sonia would be in bed and he had business to attend to in Manchester where the body of his sixth victim had lain undiscovered since he murdered her eight days earlier.

If God was directing Sutcliffe to kill prostitutes, he was also telling him to return to the scene of his latest crime to recover a vital piece of evidence that he had left behind which could blow the entire mission apart.

Peter's God wasn't stupid. It had to be found.

* * *

She was just Jean when she was growing up in Motherwell among the other local Scottish teenagers. But when she hitch-hiked south as a troubled, penniless 16-year-old, Jean Jordan's thick Scottish accent meant she became Scotch Jean when she landed south of the border.

Motherwell, to the south east of Glasgow, was once the centre of the Scottish steel industry and when Jean was a child in the 1960s it was still a boom town, the UK downturn in steel being years in the future. The town's population was rising and there were good job prospects for school-leavers at the Dalzell and Ravenscraig steel plants, the latter employing 12,000 workers at its height helping to give the town the nickname Steelopolis, much as Bingley's close neighbour Bradford used to be known as Worstedopolis thanks to its concentration of mills making worsted wool.

But the attractions of well-paid, secure employment in the steel industry meant little to a teenage girl who was struggling with the challenges of a difficult family life in a town which, despite its Steelopolis riches, was still blighted by slum housing. There had to be a better life out there somewhere.

Without telling her parents, Jean headed out into the world with no real plan of where she was going or what she would do when she got there. She went south, to England. Making her way down the west side of the country she kept going until she came to the first big city where she did what newly-arrived lost souls the world over usually do when they finally arrive, hanging around the transport hubs, busy train and bus stations where the crowds and the bustle offer a glimmer of hope.

Hers came along at Manchester Victoria one day in October 1973 in the shape of Alan Royle, a 21-year-old chef who offered a cigarette to the thin, long-haired pretty girl as he was heading home from work. He bought her a cup of tea and a bite to eat, and they fell into a relationship which, although they never actually married, might as well have been husband and wife.

At first it appeared she had achieved everything she had set out to do when she ran away from home. She had met a man who cared for her and had moved into his flat in the suburb to the south of Manchester which had been developed as a garden city overspill to house inner city slum dwellers.

But the grass is not always greener. Wythenshawe had grown into what was said to be Europe's biggest council estate, their flat wasn't big enough and arguments began to strain their relationship. The arrival of two sons in two years – Alan and James – and the emotional and financial pressure which accompanied those happy events didn't help matters. By the time they moved into a bigger flat in Lingbeck Crescent, in Hulme, they were living separate lives under the same roof.

Jean tried to make a go of things but found that life kept tripping her up. She tried hard to navigate the challenges in her way, but one by one they nudged her down a career path she would never have envisaged for herself.

On Saturday, October 1, 1977, she settled down to watch television as Alan readied himself to go for a pint with his mates.

Jean had become prone to vanishing for days on end without letting Alan know where she was, sometimes hitchhiking back up to her native Motherwell to visit her family. He wasn't bringing in any money these days; he hadn't worked since his job at a bingo hall came to an end, which didn't help the atmosphere.

He sipped a glass of lemonade that Jean had poured him while he got ready as she went to check what was on the box, which is where he thought she would be for the rest of Saturday night.

The Dick Emery show was on BBC1 followed by *Starsky and Hutch* and then *Match of the Day* after the news. On Granada, it was a two-hour long show about a teenager's battle with a brain tumour, but none of it took Jean's fancy. Instead, she turned it off and decided to fit in a couple of hours' work while Alan was out.

The other girls felt Jean wasn't really cut out for the business. They thought she was too timid and shy to work the streets, but money was tight and she was determined enough that she had buddied up with another girl, Anna Holt. They watched each other's backs and in winter took clients to a city centre flat owned by a friend.

The other girls weren't far wrong, though. She was getting sick of the life and, with two soliciting cautions to her name, she had talked about giving it up.

"She was guilty about her kids," said Anna. "She told me that she was going to give it all up, pack it all in, settle down to a decent home life again."

But there was never enough money to go around and tonight she would try and earn a bit before Alan got back.

Jean pulled on her rust-coloured coat – winter was coming after all – and left the flat at 9pm, telling the babysitter she was popping out for a breath of fresh air as she headed down to Moss Lane, one of the main drags through Moss Side.

She had the option of hanging around on Broadfield Road, Raby Street or Westwood street, the network of terraces to the south of Moss Lane where the punters knew the girls would be, or she could pop into the Nile Club, the Reno Club or the Big Ally (the Queen Alexandra pub) in the hope of picking up some custom in the warmth while nursing a half of lager.

With her dark, auburn hair, nice smile and shy, vulnerable look, Jean never struggled to attract the punters. Tonight, while still on the street, she chatted briefly to one driver who had pulled over, but instead she glanced over to the other side of the street and saw a red Ford Corsair come round the corner.

* * *

Two days earlier, Peter Sutcliffe had collected his £75 weekly wages from Clark's, as he did every Thursday. Part of that wage which now nestled in his wallet was a crisp, new £5 note, serial number AW51 121565, which would be part of the deal to tempt a woman into his car. Not that he intended to have sex with her.

It wasn't going to be Leeds or Bradford this time. They had been hotting up for a while now. There were coppers everywhere, and they had even put up a temporary police station in the middle of Chapeltown.

But there were other red light areas.

"I'd seen a religious leaflet, about the prostitutes in Moss Side, Manchester," said Sutcliffe, "so I decided to carry on with my mission there."

He spent the afternoon working on his new Ford Corsair in the driveway. As day turned to night, he decided to take it for a spin, leaving Sonia at home.

He threaded his way out of Bradford, joined the M62 and drove over the Pennines. In no time at all he was in Manchester, heading down Princess Road, the busy four-lane trunk road which connects the centre with the south of the city. He knew where Moss Side was after previous trips there on nights out but he pulled over to check his road map, just to make sure.

He drove on to Moss Lane and parked up near a slim, 5ft 6in-tall young woman in a rust-coloured coat. He asked if she wanted business, and she told him to drive up the road a bit and she would meet him there.

He pulled into a side road and did a three-point turn so he was facing back towards the main road as she walked around the corner. She said it was a fiver and she knew a place to go.

Jean directed him a mile or so south towards the allotments next to Southern Cemetery, the huge burial ground that serves a vast area of Manchester and where the football legend Sir Matt Busby and Factory Records supremo Tony Wilson are buried.

It was a regular spot the girls took their clients to which was ideal, they joked, because it was dead quiet.

The allotments are still there today, but a green metal fence with a locked gate means only allotment holders can now gain entry. A small sign underlines the fact: "Sorry, no key, no entry! Thank you".

In 1977 the security was nowhere near as tight and Sutcliffe drove into the allotments and parked up close to a high hawthorn hedge.

He saw a greenhouse and lied to Jean that it was his uncle's to encourage her to get out of the car and go over to it to conduct their business.

"You're not forgetting about the money, are you?" she asked.

"Of course not," he replied, pulled out the new fiver, serial number AW51 121565, and handed it over.

Jean put it into one of two external pockets on her green, fake leather handbag. What Sutcliffe couldn't see was that inside the pocket was a concealed compartment where she placed the note.

Payment completed, Jean got out and headed towards the greenhouse. They had to climb a small fence to get there, and he let Jean go first. As she lifted herself up, he struck her to the back of the head with a hammer which Mr Rahman had left behind in the garage when he moved back to Pakistan.

He continued hitting her until she stopped moaning, a total of eleven times delivered with such force that four teeth in her upper jaw were almost knocked out. It was 9.40pm. Just 40 minutes after leaving her flat, Jean was dead.

At that point, another car which had driven further into the allotments started up. The driver, presumably having just finished his own business, turned on his headlights and began to drive along the lane toward the main road, in the direction of Sutcliffe. He grabbed Jean and pulled her into a small depression in the ground under the bushes next to a section of disused allotments which had been fenced off earlier that year, ensuring she was out of sight. He glanced around to make sure that nothing had been left lying around that might give the game away and spotted her handbag. He took hold of it and hurled it into the darkness, the excited state he was in causing him to fling it much further than he realised. He crouched behind the hedge as the car passed, barely daring to breathe as he willed it to pull out onto the main road and drive away. The driver hesitated as he checked both ways before pulling out of the allotments. Another close shave. Sutcliffe breathed a sigh of his relief, but it was only temporary. Almost as soon as that car had driven away, another pulled in and went to park in the same spot.

He realised he wasn't safe and, after collecting the hammer and making sure Jean's body was under the hedge and out of sight, he went back to his car, fired the engine and pulled out of the allotments. He drove into Manchester and onto the M62 eastbound, back to Yorkshire.

He double-checked he had the hammer and was happy he hadn't left anything at the scene that could possibly link him to the attack.

But as he drove over the Pennines an awful realisation dawned, which he knew presented the biggest risk yet to his mission.

Serial number AW51 121565.

CHAPTER 10

POSSESSED

Jean's disappearance was not immediately reported to the police, even when Alan returned from his night out to find she wasn't at home. Her lifestyle meant he wasn't concerned, and neither did her absence over the next few days worry him. It wasn't the first time she had wandered off without telling him where she was going or when she would be back.

He still wasn't particularly worried when a week had gone by with no word. He simply assumed she had hitch-hiked to Scotland to see her family and hadn't bothered to phone him when she arrived.

"I didn't think to tell the police because she'd done it so often before," he said.

* * *

"They wasn't frenzied, well, maybe Jordan, but that was after the first attack on her which wasn't frenzied."

Sutcliffe's own interpretation of the frenzied nature or otherwise of his attacks didn't chime with the pathologists and detectives who were forced to inspect the bodies of his poor victims.

But he was accurate in his description of the assault on Jean. She suffered arguably the worst injuries of any of the women he assaulted, but most of them were not inflicted on the night she was killed.

Sutcliffe had slipped easily back into his daily life after murdering her, with no-one around him having any sense that anything was untoward, a common factor with every attack. He fully expected to read headlines in the papers over the coming days about an attack on the other side of the Pennines which was being linked to the murders in Yorkshire, but there was nothing.

Puzzled at first, he realised as the week went on that the answer was obvious. Her body had not been found.

It gave him an opportunity to return to the scene and look for the £5 note. If he could find it, then he would likely be safe from arrest.

He got his chance eight days after the murder following the Sunday night house-warming party, when his undercooked potatoes had proved to be a source of much hilarity.

"People were drinking, but I was taking people home so I wasn't drinking. I used that to my advantage."

When the party ended he gave his parents a lift and after dropping them in Bingley pointed his Corsair in the direction of Manchester.

"I got back there straight away and found it with no problems. I only need to go somewhere two or three times and I can find it every time."

As far as Sutcliffe was concerned, it wasn't just his own mind which had made the decision to cover his tracks, it was also the voices.

"By the following week, I was getting advice again to get the £5 note back. I realised the reason she had not been found was to give me the chance to go back and get the note.

"I'd made a mistake giving her the new £5 note, I thought it could be traced back to me through Clark's where I worked."

After arriving at the allotments, he began searching for the fiver, becoming increasingly agitated when he couldn't find it. He tore at her clothes, frantically searching in every pocket. There was no sign of it, and the thought started to nag that if the voices had directed him to go and get the note, why couldn't they tell him exactly where it was?

"I was puzzled that I did not get advice on where the £5 was when I was looking for it."

Was he in the same frame of mind as when he committed the attack more than a week earlier?

"No."

So how could these two worlds link together if his only motivation was a divine mission driven by a mental illness? On one hand, there was the murderous Peter Sutcliffe, in the grip of a psychotic episode and driven to kill prostitutes by voices in his head. On the other, the calm, sane Peter Sutcliffe, no longer in thrall to his mental illness but still working, in a moment of sanity and clarity, to avoid detection for the actions of his other self.

"Well, even though I wasn't on the mission when I went back, I knew I had to find the £5 to save the mission. I knew it could lead back to me.

"It was the voice that told me to go back to get the fiver. I wasn't on the mission in between, but the voice came back and told me: 'You need to go back and get the £5 note, it will lead to your arrest' and it was right. It could have done because they could trace it back to my place of work."

The note was nowhere to be seen and the more he looked the angrier he became until he lost all sense of control.

He might not have been on the mission but within minutes he was like a possessed, demonic figure of Victorian Gothic mythology as he tore at the body, slashing and tearing at it in an intense fury.

He repeatedly cut her from her left shoulder down to her right knee. One of the wounds was inflicted with such force it cut all the way through to her backbone, causing part of her intestines to spill out. He then took a hacksaw blade and proceeded to attempt to cut her head off.

Yet, he hadn't lost all sense of control or pragmatic thought. This beheading exercise was not done without a calculating reason behind it.

"That was because I didn't want the police to think it was one of mine," he explained. "I didn't do it to put the blame on anyone else, only so it didn't look like it was me that done it.

"So if I was caught for this murder, it would look different from the rest and I'd only have this one murder charge. I didn't use glass to try and cut her head off, I smashed a piece of glass from a window over her. I then tried to use a hacksaw to cut her head off. I couldn't go through with it after a while, I started to be physically sick, I really wasn't feeling right when I was doing that, I really wasn't myself."

The assault on Jean's corpse finally came to an end and Sutcliffe stood over her body, panting and momentarily exhausted but ultimately disappointed in his quest to find the £5 note.

He made his way back to his car and drove back over the Pennines.

"After I went to Manchester and got home I told Sonia I stayed at my mum's for a couple of hours. I didn't but I told her that and used it as an alibi."

Sutcliffe took the weapons with him for the attacks – the knives, screwdrivers and hammers – from his house and garage and almost always returned them after, including on occasion, a kitchen knife.

"I gave them a good clean and put them back, Sonia knew nothing," he said nonchalantly, the thought of Sonia using the murderous implement to later prepare a meal never seeming to bother him.

Following this second assault on Jean, he hadn't hidden her body as well as the first time and the following morning a 23-year-old dairy worker called Bruce Jones discovered her while working at the allotments with a friend.

Nearly 20 years later, Bruce, by then an actor, became a household name when he landed the role as Les Battersby in *Coronation Street*.

Yet despite the fame and fortune which came with appearing for a decade in the world's longest-running soap opera, Bruce suffered depression and suicidal thoughts which he blamed in part on the horrific find in the Manchester allotments.

"She was a mess. I had endless nightmares about it," he said. "He didn't only kill that poor girl and mess up the lives of her family, he messed my life about too."

Once the gruesome discovery had been reported to police, the details were passed to Detective Chief Superintendent Jack Ridgway who drove straight to the scene, arriving 90 minutes before the Home Office pathologist, Dr Reuben Woodcock.

Ridgway was aged 44 and had 23 years behind him on the force, with plenty of murder scenes to his name, but even he couldn't help recoiling in horror when he saw the state that Jean had been left in.

"Jesus – what a bloody mess," he exclaimed as he approached the scene for the first time.

He later recalled: "It was a really bad body. I had never seen anything like it before."

The murder squad's fingerprint expert, Detective Chief Inspector Tony Fletcher, was similarly struck by the brutal nature of the attack.

"As the allotments were quite close to Manchester's huge Southern Cemetery, my first thought was that someone had violated a recent grave and had mutilated the corpse," he said.

The naked body was lying near a wooden hut next to a track. Her clothing was scattered nearby.

In a depression under a hedge a short distance away was an area of significant blood staining where the ground was crawling with maggots.

That area under the hedge was tucked away out of easy view. Yet the spot where the body had been found was out in the open. Ridgway knew that for there to be maggots the body had to have been there for a period of time, but there was no way it could have lain in the spot it was now for any length of time without being noticed. The conclusion was obvious, someone had moved her after she had been killed.

His early thoughts were accurate, with one important exception.

"At that stage, it didn't occur to me that the killer had gone back to move it," he said.

An incident room was established in a facility at Longsight Police station on Stockport Road, four miles from the murder scene, which was kept at a permanent stage of readiness for major crimes.

As detectives and admin staff began collating the initial information to launch a major investigation, Ridgway attended the post-mortem, where Dr Woodcock detailed the extensive injuries which Jean had suffered.

They immediately reminded Ridgway of a special conference he had attended in Wakefield, West Yorkshire, a few months earlier where a local copper by the name of George Oldfield had taken senior detectives from all over northern England through a series of murders committed in Yorkshire over the previous two years.

Ridgway sent a colleague to his office to collect the intelligence report from the conference. He quickly reminded himself of the key points and was left in no doubt; the killer had crossed the Pennines.

As he was digesting the wider implications of what this meant, Dr Woodcock was establishing a strange timeline, which supported Ridgway's early thoughts from his visual inspection of the scene, but with an added twist.

He had found maggots in the head wounds. Yet the wounds to the body contained only fly eggs, no maggots, meaning the two sets of wounds had been inflicted at different times. Not only had someone moved the body, she had been assaulted on a second occasion after she was dead.

The starting point for the timeline was anchored thanks to the first report of the body find in the *Manchester Evening News,* which included a description of her clothing.

Alan Royal was still not particularly concerned that his common-law wife had not returned home until he read in the MEN that the woman found near the allotments had been wearing a rust-coloured coat.

He visited the police and gave them a description of Jean's clothing. He also handed over a photo of her, but the body was so badly decomposed it was difficult for detectives to use the picture for identification purposes.

DCI Fletcher came up with a better idea to confirm her identity and took the set of fingerprints taken from the body to the couple's flat in the hope of lifting a matching print. He finally got a hit off the lemonade bottle Jean had poured Alan a drink from as he got ready for his night out more than a week ago.

The day after the post-mortem, Ridgway drove to Yorkshire to speak with Oldfield.

The two senior officers knew each other slightly but were not close. Their first meeting was cordial but not warm or friendly, with Ridgway feeling his West Yorkshire colleague was stand-offish.

"I told him we had a Ripper murder," said Ridgway. "His reaction is that he doesn't want to know."

Oldfield didn't completely dismiss his colleague's thinking, but Ridgway didn't come away with any sense of him embracing it either. Oldfield suggested they keep any possible link under their hats for now, which Ridgway was happy with, as he was not comfortable dealing with the press and was more than happy to keep them at arm's length.

So he was furious when he was driving back across the Pennines a short time later and heard on the radio that West Yorkshire Police were reporting a woman found dead in Manchester may have been murdered by the same man responsible for the Ripper murders.

"I was so incensed," said Ridgway. "It was something we could have done without. What made me angry was that we had made an agreement, I had gone along with his request that we keep things quiet for a while."

Despite his anger, there was little that Ridgway could do. Oldfield and his men had been working hard to catch their killer for two years now and knew the case inside out. They had interviewed thousands of people and explored numerous leads, whereas he was new to the party.

He was determined, though, to follow his own cautious instincts when it came to dealing with the press in Manchester.

"There are several similarities between our case and theirs, but there are also noticeable dissimilarities," he said at a press conference back on home turf.

He also tried to deflect too many leaps of logic that might link the cases before he was ready. When asked if the dead woman had been a prostitute, he replied: "There is nothing to suggest it."

That hesitancy lasted only 24 hours. The next day, the police were making a direct appeal to the city's working girls to come forward and help with the inquiry.

One detail Ridgway decided early on to not release was the attempt to sever Jean's head. He asked Dr Woodcock to leave it out of his official report, and for years only a small circle of people had knowledge of it.

Eighty officers from Greater Manchester's Tactical Aid Group searched the allotments for clues. They had been instructed to check the area up to a wire fence which marked the boundary between new and disused allotments.

Five days after Jean's body was found, a local man came across a green fake leather handbag on the other side of the fence while working on his allotment, 60 yards from where she had been killed.

Ridgway drove back to the scene as soon as he was told about the find. He checked the bag and in one of the external pockets discovered a concealed, inner compartment which contained a crisp new £5 note, with the serial number AW51 121565.

It was as if a fog suddenly cleared to reveal all as he muttered to himself: "Punter's fiver."

A plausible scenario now lay before him – Jean's last customer had killed her and, later realising he had left behind a vital clue, had returned to her body to recover it days later. Being unable to find it he flew into a rage and ripped off her clothes and tore at her body. Never before had the name "the Ripper" seemed so apt.

As Ridgway was wondering what sort of human was capable of such inhuman ferocity he was also realising that, six murders in, he now had the best clue yet which could finally see the beast in the dock.

Serial number AW51 121565.

CHAPTER 11

QUIZZED

The Great Train Robbery remains as stitched into the nation's fabric as the crimes of Peter Sutcliffe. A gang which included Buster Edwards and Ronnie Biggs stole £2.6m (£45m in today's money) from the Glasgow-London mail train in the early hours of Thursday, August 8, 1963. Various members later fled to Mexico and Canada while Biggs made his home in Brazil after escaping from prison.

The robbery afforded them cult status, but it also marked a watershed moment in the way that cash was transported around the country.

In a bid to prevent a recurrence of such an audacious heist, the Bank of England re-established a strong regional network to ensure banknotes spent less time on the road and rail network during the weekly delivery round to fill workers' pay packets.

It resulted in new regional centres being built which were purposefully designed to appear strong and solid, giving the bank an air of impenetrability. The most striking was Bank House, on King Street, in Leeds.

The five-storey affair, finished with grey Cornish granite and bronze cladding, was a classic of its architectural time. The inverted ziggurat – the formal term for a design which looks like a section of an Egyptian pyramid turned upside down – was inspired by Boston City Hall in the United States and was considered bold and innovative in its day. It would later split opinion, with some considering it iconic while others thought it an eyesore. It was given listed building status in 2015.

Such architectural niceties were on no-one's mind on Tuesday, September 27, 1977, when a bullion van carrying hundreds of thousands of pounds in both new and used notes pulled into the reinforced basement area of Bank House.

On board was parcel number F87947 containing £25,000 worth of recently printed banknotes, one of which had the serial number AW51 121565.

It was part of a batch that was then placed on a bullion van for a run to various banks ready for firms to collect and pay their workers, including the Midland in Shipley.

Jean Jordan had taken possession of the fiver in Manchester on the Saturday, little more than 48 hours after that delivery run.

Jack Ridgway was convinced that the only way it could have made the journey across the Pennines and into her handbag in such a short period of time was if the employee who received it in his wages was the same man who had given it to her and then killed her.

He felt the time frame was too tight for it to have reached her if it had gone into general circulation via a pub or a shop.

George Oldfield was less certain, but this was Ridgway's inquiry, and he was committed to it and sent 30 detectives across the Pennines to work on it. Oldfield, despite his reticence, matched the number with West Yorkshire detectives.

The 60-strong team, based in a disused school house in Baildon, was split into 30 pairs of detectives – one from Manchester, one from West Yorkshire – to begin a laborious game of hunt the thimble.

It was thought most likely that the £5 note was part of £17,500 of notes which had been delivered to the Midland in Shipley.

All the officers had to do now was establish which local firm had collected the batch of notes which included Jean's fiver to complete their weekly payroll.

A total of 34 firms collected cash on Thursday, September 29, and Friday, September 30, from the Midland in Shipley to hand out in wages to 5,943 workers.

The bank kept records of amounts handed out and in which denominations, but unfortunately the serial numbers of the notes themselves were not recorded.

To trace the fiver, the police launched a two-pronged approach. The bulk of the 60-strong team went out into the community, interviewing thousands of workers as they methodically worked their way through the list of every employee from the 34 companies which had received notes from the relevant batch. Each firm had been given a letter to identify it and each employee at that company a number linked to that letter, thereby giving each potential suspect his own unique reference.

If a worker had any notes still in his wallet from that pay packet and the serial numbers were close to Jean's fiver, then that firm might be the one where the killer worked. If the serial numbers were far removed, then the firm could be discounted.

At the same time, a small team was placed in the bank itself to work with the clerks to also try and narrow down the company which received the note based on the way money was distributed.

The clerks stayed back after work each day to help the officers go through the ledgers from the relevant days to try and work out where the note had gone.

Their knowledge of customers and their habits was helpful. For example, a local bookmaker only ever wanted used notes – too much chance of new ones sticking together – so he could be discounted as having received the fiver.

Information from the detectives out on the street was fed back into this team, so if it could be established that a batch of notes far removed from AW51 121565 had been handed to a certain company, then all the men employed by that firm could be discounted.

All the information was entered on a huge wall chart Ridgway had drawn up at the Baildon incident room to track individual notes, effectively a pre-computer age spreadsheet.

A complication, though, was that notes were not all numbered consecutively. Ridgway had started with the assumption that they would be, which was fair, but wrong.

That would have made the difficult task easier, but it didn't account for spoils, notes which had to be destroyed because they weren't of good enough quality for public circulation.

AW51 121565 was 64th in a series of 69-consecutively numbered notes, but after those 69 notes the serial numbers went way off series, making it impossible to be certain which firms received which batch of notes.

Despite all of these hurdles, Ridgway was determined to succeed.

"We are attaching such importance to the banknote that until we have interviewed everybody who could possibly have had that fiver, there is no way I am going back to Manchester – if it takes days, weeks or months," he said.

He was convinced the £5 note inquiry would take his officers right to the killer's door.

* * *

At 7.45pm on November 2, with Garden Lane, Heaton, enveloped in darkness, Detective Constables Edwin Howard and Leslie Smith walked up the drive of number six and knocked on the door.

They were invited in and offered a seat. They were there to speak to F44 – the reference number given to Peter Sutcliffe (employee number 44) from the Bradford engineering and haulage firm T and W H Clark (given the letter F in the list of 34 firms which could have received the £5 note).

It was just over three weeks since Sutcliffe had been gripped by an uncontrollable mania as he ripped Jean Jordan apart.

The contrast now could not have been starker.

"I was calm when the police were questioning me," he said, struggling himself to properly explain how it was possible for one man to exhibit such uncontrollable rage in one area of his life but maintain such a relaxed façade in the rest.

The officers' only task at this stage was to check whether he still had any notes from the pay packet he had been given the week before the killing.

He was unable to produce any but was happy to explain that he had been at home with Sonia on the day in question, and was hosting a small house-warming party for his family on October 9. Sonia confirmed his movements for both dates. Neither made any mention of the fact that after the party he drove his parents back to Bingley. Neither did Sonia offer up the information that, despite the round trip to John and Kathleen's house normally taking around 30 minutes, he had been gone for hours.

Sutcliffe further helped the detectives by saying he hadn't been to Manchester for 12 months since he last visited while making a delivery in his previous job. The detectives jotted down his replies in their notebooks.

This was the first time that Sutcliffe had been spoken to by the police since the murders began two years before. He presented a picture of relaxed innocence, betraying no sign of nerves or the slightest apprehension that they might be on to him.

"It wasn't difficult to keep the mission to myself. I never did [act strangely] even in the days when I was having the voices regularly and going on a mission," he said.

"I could still talk to people, I had to because of my job, I was going delivering stuff and talking to forklift drivers and everybody. I just carried on as normal. I had to, I couldn't let nobody know about the mission. God was in charge, he was conducting everything and I knew everything would be all right. That's why I was able to be so calm when the police were questioning me."

The officers left and were clearly satisfied with the couple's answers, filing just a five-paragraph report when they got back to base. It briefly stated that F44 denied being a punter, had an alibi from his wife for the Jordan murder, and ended with the note: "Not connected".

Sonia was unconcerned that the police had been to their door, knowing that her husband was just one of thousands of men being interviewed in routine inquiries. Sutcliffe was so confident she didn't suspect him that he felt no need to protest his innocence to her.

"She knew why they were questioning hundreds of people, I said they'd questioned other people at Clark's."

The first stage in the £5 inquiry was a total failure with none of the notes in the same 69-note sequence of serial numbers as the Jordan fiver being traced.

Ridgway refused to be swayed, though. He still had confidence in his convictions and he arranged for a second round of interviews with men who worked at firms which had not yet been positively discounted. Firm F – Clark's – remained on the list.

Before this second phase of questioning, a briefing was held by senior officers to inform detectives of a number of crucial pieces of evidence. They were told the murder weapons were thought to be a hammer and an unknown cutting/stabbing instrument, the murderer had previously worn wellington boots or industrial boots about size seven (unhelpful because as Sutcliffe pointed out – "They got it wrong – I'm a size nine") and the killer's vehicle might be fitted with two India Autoway tyres.

The latter wasn't given much credence as it came from the Irene Richardson murder, which was eight months ago and the murderer could easily have changed his car or swapped the tyres.

Sutcliffe had, by then, done both.

"I got some radials and swapped the cross-plys over," he said, "because I had cross-ply on the front, you were allowed to have cross-ply on the front and radials on the back. All I did was took the cross-ply off the front and put radials on."

Detectives were told to revisit the workers to check again their movements on October 1 and 9, to challenge any alibis and, armed with the information from the briefing, to search houses and garages for tools which might fit the bill.

The teams were switched around so the employees were visited by a different pair of detectives from the first interview to avoid the potential of a suspect trying to develop a friendly relationship to dodge difficult questions.

Sutcliffe was seen again at home on November 8 by DC Rayne, of Greater Manchester Police, and DC Smith, of the West Yorkshire force, six days after the first interview. He repeated his movements for the relevant dates, which were again confirmed by Sonia.

This time his mother was also spoken to, and she too confirmed the house-warming party and the lift home he had given them afterwards.

The officers discovered Sutcliffe owned a red Ford Corsair and had previously owned a white one, but they didn't check the tyres. They asked about tools and footwear, but didn't carry out a search of the property and their questioning with regard to his alibis – specifically his movements following the end of the house-warming party – was casual and undemanding, which they were later criticised for.

Another failing was that Rayne and Smith didn't search for a hacksaw, but that was on Ridgway. His decision to withhold it from the press and public was understandable, but his refusal to tell his own officers also came in for criticism later.

Sutcliffe once again answered all the officers' questions calmly and readily. The interview was so inconsequential that when asked about it four years later, after Sutcliffe was arrested, the two detectives couldn't even recall it.

The needle was proving so small and the haystack so large that Ridgway decided he needed the public's help. The serial numbers of the first and last note in the 69-note sequence were released to the press, but not one of the 69 notes was ever traced.

The reports in relation to Sutcliffe's two interviews were filed into the system along with thousands of others. More than three months after Jean's murder, the £5 inquiry was running out of steam and the decision was taken to close it down.

As for Alan, Jean's common-law husband, his life, like all the other relatives left behind when Sutcliffe tore apart their family, was never the same again.

Eighteen months on from her death he was living with the two children in a homeless hostel in Altrincham, he couldn't get work as a chef and instead had taken a job as a labourer in an engineering factory and he had split up with his latest partner.

The children were also struggling. The eldest boy Alan had been almost literally struck dumb by the trauma of his mother's murder. He was nearly five but could still only speak a few words.

* * *

As the £5 note inquiry was coming to an unsatisfactory conclusion, Peter Sutcliffe was back on the prowl.

On December 14, 1977, he was cruising the streets of Chapeltown in Leeds as Marilyn Moore, a 25-year-old mother of two, was leaving a friend's house near the Gaiety pub on Roundhay Road.

As she walked back to her own place in Harehills around 8.30pm, Marilyn decided to try and turn a trick or two to earn some much-needed cash.

She possessed a conviction for soliciting and a similarly troubled background as many of Sutcliffe's victims – she left home at 15, married at 16, divorced shortly after, gave birth to her first child before she was out of her teens and had recently had a second. Neither child lived with her.

As she walked the streets of Chapeltown, Marilyn saw a dark coloured car driving in that slow, cautious manner typical of prospective clients. She positioned herself so the driver would see her as he came back around and as she walked along Leopold Street she saw him parked up ahead. She sauntered slowly past and he asked if she was doing business.

They agreed on £5, she climbed into the car and Sutcliffe pulled away, telling her he was Dave, but preferred David, and that he knew "a right quiet place".

Marilyn, like all other sex workers in Leeds at the time, was apprehensive every time she got into a punter's car. But David had a friendly and reassuring manner and he mentioned a couple of other prostitutes he knew in Chapeltown, both of whose names chimed with girls she also knew.

Suitably reassured, she relaxed and settled back as he drove the short distance to Buslingthorpe Lane, a quiet, dark spot off Scott Hall Road, just a few hundred yards from where Jayne MacDonald and Wilma McCann had lived.

"Let's do it in the back," he said once he parked. She agreed.

She climbed out and went to open the back door but found it locked. He said he would come and unlock it, walked around behind her and began to raise a hammer above his head and slipped.

"I took a swipe at her and it skimmed her, it didn't hit her direct, because it was really muddy and I slipped."

The hammer struck a glancing blow. Marilyn screamed as Sutcliffe struck her again. This time she slumped to the ground, but she was still conscious and continued screaming. The commotion caused a dog to start barking as the hammer blows continued to rain down on her.

Marilyn held her hands up to defend herself and then grabbed his trouser leg and screamed again. The right quiet place was suddenly a maelstrom of noise and chaos.

For the most part in recent years, his established method of attack had become sickeningly efficient. The initial blows to the head with a hammer rendered the victim unconscious, giving him the opportunity to inflict the fatal strikes to the body with a sharpened weapon without disturbance. For once, it hadn't worked and he was now presented with a quandary.

Did he remain at the scene and finish what he had set out to do, running the risk of someone coming to investigate, or did he flee, which carried its own risk of this woman surviving and identifying him to the police?

She was now lying unconscious on the floor, but the dog was still barking. Sutcliffe made his mind up.

"I got back in the car and drove away."

At least he tried to. He fired the engine of his Ford Corsair and hit the accelerator, but the wheels spun on the muddy ground. The car didn't move. With an increasing sense of panic he tried again, the revving of the engine adding to the mounting noise and chaos. The tyres finally bit and he screeched away.

Marilyn came round a few minutes later and staggered out onto the main road with blood pouring from her head wounds. Two shocked teenagers, who were passing, came to her aid and called an ambulance. She was taken to Leeds General Infirmary and rushed into theatre for an emergency operation.

Prof Gee, having been alerted to the attack, made his way to the hospital and was able to inspect her wounds after the successful operation, immediately recognising the tell-tale oval and moon-like shapes left by a hammer.

She was taken to a ward to recuperate as the police put measures in place to keep her safe. She was their most valuable witness to date, a Ripper victim who had survived without any apparent effect on her memory.

From her hospital bed, sporting 56 stitches in her wounds, she was able to give an accurate description of 'David' as 5ft 6in to 5ft 8in tall, aged around 28, stocky build, suntanned or swarthy complexion, a softly spoken voice, brown eyes and a short full beard with a 'Jason King' moustache.

Jason King was a popular television series in the early 1970s, featuring a novelist who became embroiled in James Bond-style adventures involving beautiful women and questionable foreign governments. His moustache was a bold, dark number which extended around the sides of his mouth, just like Peter Sutcliffe's.

The index card system was checked for men called David or Dave. There were 1,037 who had been questioned previously and eliminated. All were spoken to again, but nothing of any significance was discovered.

Tyre tracks were found at the scene of the attack and resin was used to make casts of them. Close examination revealed they appeared identical to those at the Irene Richardson murder in Roundhay Park ten months earlier, although there was disagreement among some of the experts.

The tracking inquiry which had been suspended was restarted now it was considered that the same vehicle had been used in both the Richardson and Moore attacks.

Marilyn was able to give a detailed description of her attacker's car, which brought the list of possibles down from 51 to eight. The short list included five styles of the BMC Farina, a range of cars manufactured in the late 1950s and early '60s, and a Ford Corsair. To narrow the list even further, Marilyn was asked to sit inside a variety of cars and, after studying the interior of each one in turn, she was sure it was a Farina. From then on, the inquiry invested everything into the notion that the Ripper was driving a Farina. Which was wrong.

Despite the police being willing to go with her on the car, they remained reluctant to trust her description of her attacker. She produced a photofit but senior officers were never convinced about her reliability. Other survivors had suffered varying degrees of memory loss, so it was assumed she must have too, and it didn't help when she twice saw men in the street who she was convinced were her attacker and urgently contacted police pleading with them to act. Both men were traced and discounted.

It meant her photofit was never trusted as a particularly strong likeness, which was a shame because it bore a striking resemblance to Peter Sutcliffe.

Her case was formally linked to the series, although not until six months after her attack and her photofit was never published.

There were multiple challenges for the Ripper inquiry, but an ever present one was a lack of resources, particularly staffing, which the force as a whole was labouring under.

In the years after the Second World War there had been a large intake of new officers across all police forces in the country.

By the 1970s this generation was nearing retirement age, meaning West Yorkshire was losing a vast wealth of experience. New officers were being recruited but not at a fast enough rate, and the new recruits were mostly young and inexperienced.

West Yorkshire's authorised establishment – the maximum number of officers a force can employ – was 5,104 at the time but not once during the years that Sutcliffe was at large did the force ever actually have this number. In 1975 there were 4,547 officers and in 1980, despite a recruitment drive, it was still only 5,040.

Crime was rising and it was a turbulent era for industrial action and social unrest, all of which demanded the police's attention.

"The Force was, to coin a Yorkshire phrase, trying to get a pint from a gill pot," said Colin Sampson, the West Yorkshire Deputy Chief Constable.

Every time there was another Ripper murder it placed an extra burden on an already struggling force, and there was no sign of a let up in the attacks. In the seven weeks after Marilyn narrowly escaped with her life, two other women would not be so lucky.

CHAPTER 12

UNCONTROLLABLE

Yvonne Pearson was considered the most professional of all the working girls who fell victim to Peter Sutcliffe. Stylish, streetwise and smart, she regularly visited the hairdresser to keep her Purdy-style haircut looking just so and was considered as "deft as a fashion model" when it came to her make-up.

She had started plying her trade on the streets of Bradford but quickly climbed the working girl ladder and began touring the country to meet clients in Bristol, Birmingham and Glasgow who could pay more than the Manningham regulars. She stepped up another rung when she got into the London scene, using hotels in Mayfair and Marble Arch to meet well-heeled businessmen as well as targeting the conference trade and, she told friends, the "Arab market".

She wasn't blind to the risks. One colleague had fallen victim to a violent robber who stabbed her to death in a hotel room while stealing jewellery and cash. A few months earlier another friend and colleague, Tina Atkinson, was killed in her flat in Bradford by that maniac who was targeting working girls in Yorkshire.

As a result, Yvonne vowed to only go with men on the street when she was back home and began carrying a pair of long-bladed scissors in her bag, although she told other regulars in the Percy in Bradford: "It's just my luck to get knocked on the head."

Yvonne had two soliciting convictions to her name and just after Christmas 1977 had been charged for a third time and was due before Bradford magistrates' court on Thursday, January 26. The courts didn't have an official three strikes and you're out rule but she feared the worst, with jail time a strong possibility.

It was hardly the career path her parents had dreamed of for her while they were bringing her and her three siblings up as good Catholics in a loving home in Leeds.

She had moved out in 1974 after falling for a man from Bradford called Roy Saunders. They had a daughter together, Lorraine, and, in the summer of 1977, a second girl, Collette, but her relationship with Roy was struggling and whatever claims of being a top class call girl she may have made, she was as hard up for money as the rest of the women. Her home was a basic back-to-back terrace house in Woodbury Road, Manningham, and her friends were worried she wasn't eating properly.

Roy ended things between them just before Christmas in 1977 and went to visit relatives in Jamaica early the following month, leaving Yvonne to look after Lorraine, now two, and Collette, five months, on her own.

Her friends and neighbours were never in any doubt about her love for her children and felt that one of the reasons she earned money the way she did was because she was a good mother, not the opposite.

"She only cared about her kids," said one neighbour. "She only went out on the game so she would have enough food and clothes for the children. She didn't do it for anything else."

On the afternoon of Saturday, January 21, Yvonne asked a local 16-year-old girl to babysit while she went into Bradford shopping. After returning home she counted her cash, noting she had enough for at least a couple of drinks, and asked the babysitter if she wouldn't mind staying on so she could have a Saturday night out.

Yvonne was actually on a curfew ahead of her impending court case. She was supposed to be at home between the hours of 7pm and 7am, but she wanted to have some fun and it wasn't as if there were electronic tags to monitor her movements.

She went to the Flying Dutchman for a pineapple juice and game of pool with a friend before moving on to the Percy, staying for only one before stepping out on to Lumb Lane. It was cold now, and dark.

As she walked past Southfield Square loud soul music from the Young Lion Café, popular with the small Caribbean population in the area, provided the soundtrack to her final journey as she headed along Lumb Lane, up onto Church Street and round towards the junction with St Mary's Road – a spot known locally as 'Kinky Corner' thanks to the number of working girls based there. She saw a friend over the other side of the road, shouted a greeting and waved at him.

She wandered back towards Lumb Lane and vanished off the face of the earth.

It was a mystery which baffled police, family, friends and the media for weeks, although there was one person who knew where she was.

"I wasn't actually looking for a prostitute that night," said Sutcliffe. "I wasn't on the mission, I was simply on my way home from work at the time and the road I was going to take was busy, so I decided to drive up Lumb Lane."

As he threaded his way through the throng on the lively street, a car suddenly reversed out of a side street, causing him to come to a halt.

He heard a tap on his window and glanced across to see an attractive young woman with a Purdy hairstyle opening the passenger door with a smile.

"Are you looking for business?" she asked.

"I didn't have any weapons with me, I only had a lump hammer which I used at work. It had a short handle. The only reason I had that in the car was because the head was loose on it. I was taking it home to fix it, knock some nails into the head and bend them over to hold it tight.

"I didn't like leaving stuff in my truck because there was a lot of thieving going on, people taking stuff out of people's wagons like maps and tools, so I was taking stuff home with me.

"Pearson tapped on the window and opened the door, it was a complete surprise to me because I wasn't looking for a prostitute at all. She said: 'Are you having business?'

"I said: 'Where did you spring from?' She said: 'It must be fate.' Well, that sealed her fate."

After picking up Yvonne, Sutcliffe drove down on to White Abbey Road and turned into Arthington Street, a dead-end behind Silvio's Bakery and Globe Mills, where his dad used to work, as she directed him to a patch of derelict land where there was only one reason to go to after dark.

They had a brief discussion about how much this was going to cost before she got out and went to get into the back of the car, undoing her jeans as she was trying to open the locked door. He came round to her side of the car, walked up behind her, gripping the lump hammer in his hand.

"When we got to where we were going, I hit her on the head with the hammer," he said.

As he had done with a number of other victims, he dragged her further into the darkness, close to a discarded sofa. Yvonne was still alive and was moaning loudly. Sutcliffe frantically looked around for something to quieten her as he noticed a car parked nearby with a man and woman inside.

"I used horse hair from an old sofa to keep her quiet. I stuffed the horse hair down her throat. When the car left, I started jumping up and down on her to kill her, as I didn't have a knife with me, that was the only one I done where I wasn't initially on the mission.

"I just thought God had made this happen, that he doesn't make mistakes. I thought I was doing them a favour by killing them, saving them from themselves, you see."

Yvonne's jeans had been partly pulled down as he dragged her over to the sofa, and he now took them all the way off as his rage grew. He kicked out at Yvonne, repeatedly striking at her head, shattering her skull with repeated blows before leaping up and down on her torso.

"I was senseless with rage," he said. "Afterwards I talked to her and apologised for what I had done, but she was dead. I was distraught. Maybe if I'd fought a little more, in my own mind, I maybe wouldn't have killed her. I worried over what control I had over myself. Did I have any?"

He dragged her body underneath the sofa, making sure it was out of sight, before heading back to his car. He later claimed that before driving away he was suddenly overcome with the enormity of what just happened. This was the first and only attack which had occurred without a build-up of depression and voices, and he said he now found himself weeping uncontrollably.

"I was in tears. It was the first time I had apologised to anyone I had killed."

It wasn't long before he regained his composure and felt able to drive home. He went to bed and the following morning, as if nothing out of the ordinary had occurred, he drove to Bingley to wish his mum Kathleen a happy birthday. His parents were moving house that day, they were downsizing as the children had long since flown the nest and their eldest son helped them move the last of their things to the new flat in Rutland House.

* * *

The babysitter looking after Yvonne's children was concerned when she didn't return and contacted some friends. They reassured her that worries over her possible jail sentence had likely got to her and she had probably just gone to ground.

By Monday, it was clear something was seriously wrong. No-one thought she would just vanish and leave her children behind. She had also left without taking any possessions, particularly, it was noted, the family allowance book.

The police were informed and began making inquiries to trace her, but they didn't make a public appeal until the Friday of that week, the day after she had been due in court.

It was small and understated, a simple request for information about a missing person with no hint of the wider fear about the fate she may have suffered, and at whose hands.

The appeal was massively ramped up the next day with banner headlines announcing: "Ripper fears over missing mum".

Det Chief Inspector Roger Wiseman, of Bradford CID, stressed they were keeping an open mind, but he couldn't help but admit that her disappearance was odd. The way she had left the children and hadn't taken any clothes, money or personal items, not even a toothbrush or that family allowance book, didn't bode well.

Police conducted door-to-door inquiries and interviewed her family and friends, but no-one had any idea where she was. They tried to speak to her former partner Roy, but he was still in Jamaica.

He returned and the children went to stay with him. Their mum's 22nd birthday, 12 days after she vanished, came and went without celebration.

As the weeks rolled by her case drifted out of the media and from most people's minds and without a body, a confirmed sighting or any other solid lead to follow, there was little the police could do.

* * *

A couple of days before Yvonne's 22nd birthday, as her body lay undiscovered beneath a discarded sofa half a mile from her home in Bradford, Helen Rytka and her twin sister Rita were being careful on the streets of Huddersfield.

They had a system which they thought would keep them safe in this new venture of theirs, selling sex under the railway arches of the Leeds-Manchester line as it passed through Huddersfield town centre. They worked opposite sides of the road, aiming to pick up clients at the same time and meeting back at the public toilets at the bottom of Great Northern Street 20 minutes later. Neither would go with the next client until they knew the other was back safe and sound. It was hardly perfect, but it made them feel better.

The twins ended up under the arches following a wretched start to their young lives, crippled by broken dreams. The ambition Helen clung most keenly to – the international pop star – had not yet been realised, but she was still only 18 and had enough youthful optimism left to think that anything was possible.

Such optimism was fast vanishing on the cold, dark streets of Huddersfield in the harsh winter of 1978 when eight inches of snow fell some nights and a 90-strong team of council workers wrestled with frozen fuel lines on their snowploughs as they tried to keep the town's roads passable.

The twins were born on March 3, 1959, to a Jamaican father and an Italian mother, Bernadina, whose own difficult upbringing would be mirrored by that of her children's.

She grew up in Venice, where she spent seven years in a foster home after her father died. She moved to England in 1953 seeking a better life and. after a brief spell in London, travelled north to Leeds where she met Eric Rytka.

Their relationship was marked by the challenge of both being recent immigrants in Leeds in the late 1950s. Their small, cramped accommodation was damp and money was always tight.

When the girls were just four months old, it all became too much for Bernadina, and they were taken into care, going to live at St Theresa's, a children's home run by the Sisters of the Holy Family of Bordeaux, in Knaresborough, 15 miles north of Leeds.

A couple of years later, Bernadina fell pregnant a second time, again with twins, Tony and Angela.

When the older girls were five, Eric and Bernadina finally felt able to look after all of their children under the same roof and Helen and Rita moved back home, which was now a cramped flat in Leopold Street, Chapeltown.

After a few years of relative happiness, the couple divorced. Bernadina remarried, but the presence of a step-dad in the house failed to bring a calming influence. When Helen and Rita were ten, the children were sent back to St Theresa's.

Unsurprisingly, they pined for family life and watched in envy as other youngsters left the home to be fostered or adopted. They were classed as "hard to place", though. Mixed race twins weren't top of many potential foster parents' shopping list.

They never gave up hope and in May 1974, after reading a series of articles on fostering in the *Yorkshire Post*, they took the innovative step of sending a poem to the paper accompanied by a moving letter in which they pleaded for loving foster parents to take them in.

It found them in the headlines four years before Helen grabbed them again for all the wrong reasons.

The poem, written by Rita, began: "Loneliness is to live in a world; Where people do not care", and went on: "Unloved is to miss the love that all parents should give… yet they cast you aside."

In the letter she wrote: "If my twin sister and I got fostered out together, it would be like winning £1,000 on the football pools. But money is not involved. LOVE is…

They didn't have to wait long. The letter struck a chord with a civil servant and his wife and within days of its publication the girls, on the verge of their 16th birthdays, were offered a fresh start in a large detached house in a well-to-do area of Dewsbury. The next two years would be contenders for the happiest of their lives.

The house had a huge garden and they even had their own bedrooms – a luxury unheard of in Leopold Street.

The girls enjoyed the kind of opportunities which had never been available to them before, at one stage taking part in a German exchange programme in 1975.

Helen and Rita were close, but they were very different characters. Rita, a talented artist who also loved to write, was quiet and withdrawn. Helen was much louder and chattier. She was outgoing and vivacious, with a love of singing and dancing. She could only afford to go out at weekends, but when Friday came around she was a regular at the Pentagon Nightclub in nearby Mirfield, often dragging a reluctant Rita along with her.

At 18, they appeared to have achieved a degree of stability with Rita studying at Batley School of Art, Helen earning £20-a-week at a sweet factory in Heckmondwike, with a vague plan of one day training as a children's nurse, and the two of them finding a flat to share in Manningham, Bradford.

Yet the seemingly solid start to adult life was built on foundations of sand, hardly a surprise given their turbulent early years. Rita quit her college course and, shortly after, Helen left her factory job. For the first time in their short lives the girls became separated when Rita moved out of the Bradford flat and, for a brief period, they lost touch. Towards the end of 1977 Helen finally traced Rita to Elmwood Avenue, on the edge of Huddersfield town centre. She was living in a once proud Victorian villa which had been chopped up into tiny bedsits. The rent for Flat 3 was £5 a week, toilet and bathroom facilities were shared with other residents and the only heating to keep them warm was a small, gas fire.

The girls shared a double bed, pots of tea and meals of stew and dumplings as the never-ending winter raged outside. Helen also decided to share the new approach Rita had opted for in an effort to earn some money, down in the arches on Great Northern Street.

Their age and looks meant they were earning decent money, while the system they had developed to stay safe meant the life they had chosen was proving as satisfying as that life can be.

UNCONTROLLABLE

On Tuesday, January 31, 1978, they got up at 1.30pm and made a cup of tea before cooking up another stew, with potatoes, sweet potatoes, yam and black-eyed beans joining the meat in the pot. They had a snack at 5.30pm and a short time later got dressed ready for an evening on the streets.

Two chauffeurs who had dropped off a couple of businessmen at an evening dinner picked them up around 9pm and drove to Huddersfield Town's football stadium, where they parked in different areas of a deserted car park.

Helen and her client were done first and he dropped her back at the toilet block just before 9.25pm.

A few minutes later, the twins' fragile arrangement to stay safe was shattered when a red Ford Corsair pulled up alongside Helen and she climbed in.

Peter Sutcliffe wasn't as familiar with the red light district in Huddersfield as those in Leeds and Bradford, but a few days earlier he had been making a delivery to a local firm and saw a number of women on Great Northern Street.

It didn't take much to bring him back.

"The urge inside me to kill girls was now practically uncontrollable."

Helen directed him to a nearby timber yard, where he parked in a darkened spot he thought was out of sight of the road. Helen began undoing her trousers but hesitated, telling him: "It will be better in the back."

He agreed and she got out of the car. As she went to open the rear door on her side, he reached under the seat to his usual hiding spot and wrapped his fingers around the shaft of a hammer.

He got to the rear passenger door as Helen was halfway into the car, but he slipped as he swung the hammer. It clipped the top edge of the door frame, lessening its force, so when it struck her head it was soft enough for her to mistakenly believe he had hit her with his hand.

She was still understandably concerned and quickly tried to talk her way out of what she knew was a rapidly worsening situation as Sutcliffe realised with horror that he wasn't out of sight of the road at all.

"I could hear two taxi drivers talking with their engines running. After hitting her, she was making a noise. I said: 'If you keep quiet, you'll be all right, just keep quiet.'"

He shoved Helen in front of his own car, out of sight from the taxi drivers, dropping his hammer in the melee as he leapt on to her and covered her mouth with his hand, desperately trying to stop her from calling out.

Sutcliffe later told police he had sex with Helen – the only one of the victims where that was the case. He insisted that the motivation for the intercourse was not sexual, but to keep her from making a noise and alerting the taxi drivers.

Later, desperate to rebut any suggestion he was a sex attacker, he offered another version of what happened.

"I never had sex with her, I never had sex with any of them, I told the police I had sex with her, but I didn't."

If so, why lie to the police in the initial interview?

"I had to because I had to cover up for the mission, I couldn't tell them why I was doing it. So I had to make excuses and, of course, I'm the person involved, I know the truth better than anybody. The police forced me into telling them lies by trying to demand explanations, and I told them what I thought they'd believe."

Whether the sex did or did not take place, Sutcliffe was soon engaged in his by now familiar and sickening routine. He found the hammer where he had dropped it and struck her hard to the head before taking a kitchen knife from one of his pockets and stabbing her to death, repeatedly thrusting the blade 13 times into two wounds. Just like with Jayne MacDonald, this would take on particular significance at his trial.

He dragged her to a small gap between a wall and a pile of timber and covered her with a sheet of corrugated asbestos.

As Sutcliffe was driving Helen to the timber yard, Rita was being dropped off at the toilet block by her client. They had missed each other by minutes. Rita hung around for a while and when her sister failed to show she returned to the bedsit, a feeling of dread quickly building inside their cold, cramped home.

She didn't report her missing straight away because she was worried about how the police would react, but by Thursday, her concern for her sister trumped any worries about a soliciting charge and she went to Huddersfield's Castlegate police station.

A search was launched of the Great North Street area and the following day a police dog and its handler discovered Helen's body in the timber yard.

Darkness – and a rain shower – descended, and mobile lights were erected to illuminate the scene and a sheet of polythene erected above to protect it as Prof Gee arrived to conduct his initial examination.

There was little doubt in anybody's mind who was responsible and Oldfield was already there waiting for the pathologist.

One of the first tasks Prof Gee performed was to carefully reach around the back of her head where he felt a wound. He reported this back to the waiting crowd of senior officers.

Any doubts that may have been floating around the timber yard as to whose work this was vanished at that moment.

Days off and annual leave were cancelled, and an incident room was set up in a cramped corner of Castlegate police station with officers working a 12-hour shift – 9.30am to 9.30pm – as they set about trying to trace everybody who had been in the red light district area on the evening of the murder. Another indication of the lack of resources which often handicapped the inquiry was that the incident room had only three phones.

Oldfield gave a brief update to journalists at the scene on Saturday morning. The reports which came from this briefing would refer to Helen as a "half-caste Jamaican prostitute".

He went on to make repeated statements over the coming days to the media which suggested the police were just one small step from an arrest.

"We are making good progress," he insisted.

As well as his high optimism levels, Oldfield was maintaining his high work rate of 14-hour days, on-call 24/7. A greenhouse he began building in his back garden around the time Anna Rogulskyj had been attacked in the summer of '75 remained unfinished, nearly three years, eight murders and five more non-fatal attacks on.

Keeping himself front and centre of the inquiry, he went on *The Jimmy Young Show* on Radio Two in the hope of recruiting help from the millions of listeners to the 'housewives' favourite'.

"He must have aroused suspicions," he told the audience in between the record requests and recipes, making it as bluntly clear as he could that the killer could be their "relative, workmate or associate".

After the programme, he said: "I am hoping that the broadcast will have done a lot of good. After all, the Ripper is someone's neighbour, and he is also someone's husband or son. It may be that someone who has been listening might have their memories jogged about some suspicious person or event."

Rita was photographed in identical clothes to those Helen was wearing on the night she was killed to help make an appeal poster with Helen's head superimposed onto her body. They were printed in English, Urdu and Punjabi. The Punjabi version was headed 'Sympathetic murder', a phrase used in the Punjab to describe a killing where the victim is considered wholly innocent. The police hoped it would be more likely to elicit a response from that particular community if the victim – who was still being described elsewhere as a half-caste Jamaican prostitute – was "innocent".

A £10,000 reward was posted by a local newspaper and businessmen, to the delight of West Yorkshire's Chief Constable, Ronald Gregory.

"It may well be that this could be the break we have been looking for," he said.

More than 90 letters were sent in by members of the public and 200 phone calls were received offering snippets of information or potential names for the killer, but Oldfield's repeated appeals began to sound desperate. This murder inquiry was rapidly heading the same way as all the others.

More than 5,000 people had now been interviewed in the hunt for the Ripper since he murdered Wilma in Leeds more than two years ago, but police were no nearer catching him now than they were on the foggy morning when she was found.

The latest unforgiving winter was finally receding as train drivers were threatening to strike, the National Front was fighting on the streets with police and anti-fascist protesters, pupils were being sent home for lunch because teachers refused to supervise school meals in a pay dispute and Helen was being buried.

Her funeral took place on March 9 at St Anthony's Roman Catholic Church in Clayton, Bradford, six days after what would have been her 19th birthday. A Special Requiem Mass was attended by around 30 people.

Three days earlier, Kirklees coroner Mr Philip Gill appealed to the public for help in catching her killer as he adjourned Helen's inquest to allow the funeral to take place.

He also warned that if the Ripper was not caught soon, then there was the "gravest possible likelihood" that he would kill again.

Unbeknown to Mr Gill, he already had.

CHAPTER 13

FALSE TRAIL

Around noon on Easter Sunday, March 26, a young man was taking a shortcut across the patch of litter-strewn wasteland at the bottom of Arthington Street.

He glanced across to the charred, khaki coloured sofa that had been there a while now and did a second take. He walked over and saw what he at first thought was the arm of a mannequin poking out from under the old piece of furniture.

As he leant in, a sickly sweet, putrid stench grabbed the inside of his nostrils and refused to let go. He turned and ran to a nearby phone box to call 999.

Detective Superintendent Trevor Lapish was one of the first officers at the scene. As soon as he walked up to the sofa and spotted the arm, clear as day, he was struck by the thought that there was no way that the body could have laid there like that for very long without being seen.

It might have been a desolate piece of wasteland, but enough people used it as a shortcut and kids as a playground for someone to have spotted the arm soon after it became visible under the sofa.

The officers at the scene knew Yvonne was still missing and it was clear to Prof Gee when he arrived that the body was decomposed to such an extent that it strengthened her as a favourite for whichever poor soul it was.

Yet she vanished more than two months ago, and Lapish kept coming back to the way the arm was in clear view, leading him to wonder if the killer had returned to the scene and disturbed the body. Or it may have been something more mundane.

"It may be an animal that pulled out a hand or an arm," he said.

The mystery deepened on closer inspection of the body when a copy of the *Daily Mirror* dated February 21, 1978, was found beneath her right hand.

Appropriately, given the recent weather, the front page splash was about the continuing big freeze which was gripping most parts of the country. Today was cold but dry, the almost daily snow and rain had let up for one day at least, but recent months had seen some of the heaviest snow falls in 30 years.

Despite the decomposed nature of the body, the fingerprints were intact and it was confirmed to be Yvonne who had gone missing on January 21 – a full month before the newspaper was published.

Forensic tests established that she had been killed around the date she had gone missing, meaning there was no way the newspaper could have been on the ground when she was murdered and her body simply placed on top of it. It didn't make any sense for a random person who was not the killer to find the body and instead of reporting it to police, place a newspaper underneath it and leave the scene without alerting anyone.

All of which led to only one conclusion – the killer had returned to the body at least once when the paper ended up under her body – and perhaps a second time, to place her arm on clear display so she would be found.

So did Sutcliffe revisit the body?

"No, that wasn't me. I never went back to any of the bodies apart from Jean Jordan, which was because of the £5 note. The others, I didn't have any reason to go back."

But why would someone else place the paper there?

"I suppose they didn't want to put themselves in the frame, so they didn't say anything when they found the body."

That doesn't feel plausible. Some people might not feel a natural inclination to help the police, but why place a newspaper under the body?

The mystery of the newspaper under Yvonne's body – how it got there, when and why – remained unexplained, but it paled into insignificance compared to another intriguing event a few weeks after the publication date of the *Mirror* newspaper, but before Yvonne was found.

On March 8, a letter addressed to "Chief Constable (sic) George Oldfield, Central Police Station, Leeds, West Yorkshire" was placed in a post box on Hylton Road, Sunderland, in the North East, around 100 miles north of where the Ripper had been operating.

The author, who had inadvertently given Oldfield a promotion, had written a short letter in a distinctive, thin writing style laying claim to be the murderer.

"Dear Sir," it politely began, "I am sorry I cannot give my name for obvious reasons. I am the Ripper, I've been dubbed a maniac by the press but not by you, you call me clever and I am. You and your mates haven't a clue that photo in the paper gave me fits and that bit about killing myself, no chance. I've got things to do. My purpose is to rid the street of the sluts. My one regret is that young lassie McDonald, did not know cause changed routine that nite. Up to number 8 now you say 7 but remember Preston 75, get about you know. You were right I travel a bit. You probably look for me in Sunderland, don't bother, I am not daft, just posted letter there on one of my trips. Not a bad place compared with Chapeltown and Manningham and other places. Warn whores to keep off streets cause I feel it coming on again. Sorry about young lassie."

It ended politely: "Yours respectfully, Jack the Ripper.

"Might write again later I not sure last one really deserved it. Whores getting younger each time. Old slut next time I hope, Huddersfield never again, too small, close call last one."

A few days later, on March 13, a second letter written by the same hand was also posted in Sunderland but this time addressed to "Chief Editor, Daily Mirror Publishing Office, Manchester (STD code 061), Lancs."

It read: "Dear Sir, I have already written to Chief Constable, George Oldfield a "man I respect" concerning the recent Ripper murders. I told him and I am telling you to warn them whores I'll strike again and soon when heat cools off. About the Mcdonald lassie I didnt know that she was decent and I am sorry I changed my routine that night. Up to number 8 now you say 7 but remember Preston 75. Easy picking them up don't even have to try, you think they learn but they don't. Most are young lassies, next time try older one I hope. Police have'nt a clue yet and I don't leave any I am very clever and don't think of looking for any fingerprints cause there arent any and don't look for me up here in Sunderland cause I not stupid just passed through the place. Not a bad place compared with Chapeltown and Manningham can't walk the streets for them whore. Dont't forget warn them I feel it coming on again if I get chance. Sorry about lassie I did nt know. Yours respectfully Jack the Ripper. Might write again after another ones' gone maybe Liverpool or even Manchester again. Too hot here in Yorkshire. Bye. I have given advance warning so its yours and their fault."

The letters triggered a degree of excitement among some detectives, who felt there were enough indicators to suggest the author was the killer, although there was not one critical piece of information which proved it. None of the elimination material from any case was included, for example.

The numerous grammatical errors and mistakes such as getting Oldfield's rank wrong suggested the author was not highly educated (although that could have been a diversionary tactic) but his desire to be seen as "clever" and "not stupid" suggested an insecurity which felt authentic.

No fingerprints had been left on the letters or envelopes.

One anomaly in the letters appeared to be the tally of murders. Up to that point, there had been seven acknowledged Ripper murders. The murder of Joan Harrison in Preston in 1975 had been hovering around the edges of the inquiry for a while, but the author was insistent that she was part of the series. If he was right, then the total should be nine, the seven the public knew about, plus Joan and Yvonne, whose body had yet to be found when the letter was written.

Yet he stated: "Up to number 8 now you say 7 but remember Preston 75."

It felt strange not to claim credit for Yvonne's killing, which the police were not yet aware of. If a killer was motivated to contact the police in this way, surely he would want to gloat as much as possible.

Unless Prof Gee's doubts about the identity of her killer were right, that is.

There were a number of factors at this scene which did not chime with the others. None of the other victims had been hidden so comprehensively, and the tell-tale oval and crescent-shaped wounds to the back of the head were absent, as were the stabbing wounds to the torso. The injuries inflicted to her head were far more brutal and extensive than with previous attacks. She had been struck repeatedly with a heavy object, leaving 17 wounds. Her skull was so badly shattered it had to be rebuilt around a ball of modelling clay to try and assess the exact injury pattern.

It was difficult to determine what weapon had been used and in an attempt to unlock the mystery, three-quarters of a ton of rocks and discarded concrete was taken from the patch of waste-land where her body had been found and transported to the Home Office forensic lab at Wetherby for testing.

After the post-mortem, Prof Gee cautiously expressed his view that Yvonne was not a Ripper victim and Lapish repeated that position to the press.

But the similarities were unavoidable, leading to speculation a copycat was on the loose.

Another intriguing find at the post-mortem was the discovery of the ball of horsehair which had been shoved into Yvonne's mouth. Lapish kept that under wraps, treating it as his elimination information.

A team of detectives began digging into Yvonne's life to try and find any clue, however small, which might point towards the man who had done this to her.

Every house in the surrounding Lumb Lane area was visited by a 50-strong team of Task Force officers hoping to find someone who might have seen or heard something of interest on the night Yvonne vanished. It was a big ask given the amount of time that had lapsed and little of any value was gleaned. Local businesses were visited, although the time of year hampered early inquiries. It was the Easter weekend and most were closed until Tuesday.

As the Task Force was working the streets, a team of detectives took on a more targeted approach, based around a pocket-sized cream and gold-coloured address book which had been found among Yvonne's possessions.

It contained a list of 36 names who were reckoned to be regular clients. Lapish put out an appeal for any man who thought he might be on the list to come forward, stressing that he wasn't interested in the nature of their relationship with Yvonne, he just wanted their help in solving her murder.

Unsurprisingly, not all of them rushed forward to be interviewed so Lapish had to change tack.

"We can wait no longer to spare the feelings of these people," he said as he announced plans for a more front-foot approach in tracking them down. All 36 were finally traced and interviewed at their homes, and all co-operated. None could help with the murder inquiry. The detectives were as sensitive and tactful as possible when they knocked on their doors to explain why they wanted to speak to the men. It wasn't recorded how many of the 36 later had some explaining to do to long-term wives and girlfriends.

Maggots discovered on Yvonne's body were found to be larvae from the trichoceridae fly, commonly known as the winter gnat or crane fly. One of Prof Gee's colleagues from Leeds University's Department of Pure and Applied Zoology took on this particular line of inquiry with gusto, even consulting with an expert at the British museum to understand the likely distribution of such a fly in the area where Yvonne was found. The flies feed on rotting organic matter and are found in potato and turnip crops but also in cow dung, so a small team of officers set off to begin inquiries with farmers and farmworkers in the rural areas outside of Bradford. Nothing came of it.

Six days after Yvonne's body was found, a rookie WPC called Lena Markovic retraced her steps in a reconstruction wearing identical clothes. She was chosen because there was a striking resemblance to Yvonne, save for the hair. A Purdy-style wig was acquired to disguise her own black hair, and she set off to wander around the rain-soaked red light area for two hours in the hope that someone who hadn't previously come forward might have their memory jogged. Two uniformed officers and ten detectives followed her to talk to people who were on the street or to flag down passing motorists. A police Land Rover drove slowly by their side, broadcasting regular appeals for help.

One witness did come forward to say he had seen Yvonne on the evening she vanished near 'Kinky Corner' shouting and waving to an acquaintance across the road, but none of the lines of inquiry got any closer to discovering what had happened to her.

Around this time in Leeds, the police were becoming increasingly exasperated that prostitutes were not helping themselves. They couldn't believe the working girls were still working given what had happened to so many of their colleagues, so they stepped up efforts to save them from themselves and from the Ripper – by arresting them.

Around 70 were picked up between January and March 1978 in the hope that repeated fines and jail time would drive them off the streets, reducing the Ripper's ability to claim further victims. Unsurprisingly, the tactic didn't end prostitution in Leeds, and Lapish was finding that the stigma attached to the profession was hampering his own inquiry in Bradford.

"The fact that Yvonne was a prostitute means that a lot of people are saying 'So what?' when they hear that she was murdered," he said. "A lot of people are simply not bothered about Yvonne's murder. On this inquiry, we have had nothing like the response from the public that you would get with most murders."

He was facing an uphill battle in persuading the public to take a more compassionate view of sex workers.

"A bad man's a bad man, but a bad woman's a bloody bad woman, and you can't say 'owt else about them," said one local housewife in a television news report about the murders.

Although Yvonne's murder was still not officially included in the series at this stage, even some senior officers were unable to completely discount it.

Around a week after her body was found, the Chief Constable, Ronald Gregory, visited the murder room and gave a press interview in which he spoke about his "deep concern over the prostitute murders", effectively lumping Yvonne in with the rest of the attacks, despite Prof Gee's position.

In an effort to help crack the case, Gregory also made the slightly unrealistic offer to meet the killer, as if the three years the murderer had spent successfully evading capture could be put to one side.

"This man must feel in his own mind that he is likely to go on killing and needs help. I am willing to see him personally at any time and discuss the situation," declared Gregory.

Perhaps it was the pressure that pushed him into making such an unrealistic offer. Gregory had an air of relaxed confidence common to those in senior ranks, but privately he was racked with doubt over the failure of his detectives to catch the Yorkshire Ripper.

"I even lay wide awake at night wondering whether I was the right man for the job, or whether I should resign and let someone else take over," he said later.

But it wasn't in the nature of this career officer, the fourth generation in his family to become a cop, to give up so easily. By his own account he was tough, ambitious and "perhaps over-confident" so it was no surprise that he might try and solve the Ripper case by making a public offer for him and the perpetrator to meet.

The number of seasoned detectives who rolled their eyes at their Chief's suggestion of how to solve the case can only be imagined. As for the Ripper, he never did get in touch.

Copies of the anonymous letters which had been posted to Oldfield and the *Mirror* were sent to Northumbria Police so they could be checked against handwriting samples they possessed for people in the Sunderland area, but no match was found. Similar inquiries were made in West Yorkshire but, again, nothing of significance was discovered. There were no clear clues within the letters which pointed to the identity of the author and, of course, they were far from the only anonymous letters the Ripper squad was receiving at the time.

The initial ripple of excitement felt over them by some in the Ripper squad faded and they were placed in the "cranks file". For now.

One comment which the Chief had made in his press interview which did ring true was of the unique challenge the case posed.

Gregory declared that the Ripper investigation was now one "of the most difficult this country has ever known."

CHAPTER 14

THE VOICE

By his own admission, Peter Sutcliffe was not on the mission when he first spotted Yvonne Pearson on a street in Bradford. Unlike all the previous attacks, the voices in his head had not spent the last hours or days telling him to kill a prostitute, yet a short time after he first set eyes on her, he murdered her anyway.

With Jean Jordan, he returned to her body more than a week after killing her to pursue the very pragmatic aim of evading arrest. He drove to Manchester in a focused, forensically-aware frame of mind to retrieve a piece of vital evidence which he knew could convict him if the police found it first.

These two examples raise fundamental questions about Sutcliffe's thought process surrounding the attacks.

The central issue which arose after he was arrested – was he mad or bad? – will be considered in detail later when, for the first time ever, Sutcliffe himself gives his opinion about the many theories which try to explain why he became a serial killer.

But for now, it is worth considering just what was going on in his head during, before and after the attacks.

What exactly was 'the voice'? What did it sound like and what did it say? Did it only talk about the mission to kill prostitutes?

"The voice can also come and talk to me about everyday routine things," he explained. "I might be trying to think of doing something and then all of a sudden the voice will say what about this, or have you thought about? I know it's me thinking these thoughts, but it is a voice that gives me the answer, it tells me what I need to know.

"The voice gives me advice. It interferes with you all the time, it's telling you things that you got to do, instructions. And you can't shut it out, can't block your ears. It knew it wasn't appropriate to give me these messages regularly when I was driving the truck. But even though I believed what I believed at the time I still was in kind of awe of it, sort of dread, because I was half expecting what it was gonna be saying. You can't shut it up."

Did he ever talk back to it?

"Oh yeah, if there were people around I'd just think what I wanted to say, if I was alone like in my truck for instance, I used to talk out aloud."

What was the voice like in the run-up to an attack?

"It was usually similar in that it could be two or three days before an attack. It was a steady build up and then I did the attack. But it can sometimes be over a couple of hours. It can be that quick.

"I might have been hearing the voices for a few days, but once it felt like I was primed I couldn't stop myself. When it started escalating, at the start I could stop myself, but after a while I couldn't stop myself.

"I couldn't fight it. Once I had killed that was it, it was a release from the pressure it was over.

"I knew what I was doing, it was controlled, there were only a couple of times when it wasn't. When I wasn't fully primed for the mission, I got really angry at what I had to do.

"It is a clear voice, I know it's in my head, but it is a clear voice. It's a male authoritative voice. It seemed to come from things, trees, walls.

"It's not like anyone I've ever known. It doesn't remind me of my dad or anyone else I can pinpoint. The voice gives my advice.

"The only time it was different was Yvonne Pearson. With the other ones I had to be primed, but with her, it was the words she used… she asked me 'do you want business?'… that's the term they used. I never wanted business with them.

"I said: 'Where did you spring from?' She said: 'It must be fate'. Well, that sealed her fate. It was because she said that, that it turned me to be on the mission."

Discussing his attacks over many years in the visiting areas at both Broadmoor and Frankland Prison, Sutcliffe returned to the subject of fate a number of times.

It appeared a favourite subject, perhaps because, like his mental illness, it absolved him of responsibility for his terrible deeds. It wasn't his fault, it was down to fate, he appeared to be saying as he leant back in his chair, happy to discuss the attacks in a relaxed manner which ignored the actual bloody reality of the injuries he inflicted.

Suddenly leaning forward, he felt the need to stress that on the night Yvonne was killed, he wasn't on the mission.

"I never went out intending to kill one."

He went on to explain how that attack came about, his eyes coming alive as he got into his stride, accompanied by the tiniest flicker of a smile.

The change in him is almost imperceptible when he starts discussing the attacks. His body doesn't shift much, for the most part remaining in the statuesque pose common to all his visits. The difference is in his face, framed by that greying beard, especially those dark, peering eyes which appear almost excited now.

With his and his visitor's face just inches away, he continues talking in his quiet, soft voice, which lacks any emotion or compassion for the woman in his sights.

"Unfortunately for her, I thought this was my direct signal and it triggered off the mission. I was then thinking of how I could kill her, I realised I only had the lump hammer in the car."

A silence descends as the enormity of what befell her sinks in, although it fails to move Sutcliffe himself as he quickly reverts to discussing the voice, an ever present in any conversation with him.

He mentions the voice regularly and to his mind it was always the invisible, guiding hand, directing him to commit murder.

Did he ever have any sense of free will to disobey what the voice told him to do?

"At the beginning I could fight against it, I could try and stop myself from doing what I was going to be doing. But as time went on it was harder and harder to fight the urge and I couldn't stop myself.

"That mission was only a small part of my life. It only lasted a short time each time I went out on it. And it was only now and then, you know, rarely. In the meantime, I was living my life, doing my job and everything."

So he did retain a degree of free will to disobey the voice, although it faded over time. Did he ever exercise this free will?

"Yeah I did, I went once and I was on my way to Leeds and I were changing up and down the gears, arguing with God. I went faster and slower, and I managed to turn round and go back, and he said: 'I know that I can see you're not ready', because I used to have to be primed up to it. I went back home and I was so relieved when I got back home when I'd not gone through with it. I didn't know it was schizophrenia, I didn't know what it was, I just thought it was a miracle.

"I didn't know best, but I believed I did. That was the dangerous thing about me, believing what was happening to me was a miracle. Divinely inspired."

An aspect of his behaviour which is difficult to comprehend is the ease with which he slipped from mundane domestic duties into a murderous frame of mind and back again, without anyone else observing any change in his behaviour. Just hours after murdering Yvonne Pearson, for example, he was helping his mum celebrate her 59th birthday and move house.

Leaning back in his chair, as if to emphasise how simple this was for him, he said: "It was easy [to separate the attacks from everyday life]. The crimes were only a small part of my life. I always knew what I'd done, but I had total belief in what God was telling me, how could he be wrong? After all, he created everything."

And no-one, not his workmates, friends or family, ever noticed anything untoward?

"No. Even in the days when I was having the voices regularly when I was outside and going on a mission. I could still talk to people, I had to because of my job. I was going delivering stuff and talking to forklift drivers and everybody. I just carried on as normal. I couldn't let nobody know about the mission."

How long did this rapid transformation from brutal killer back to ordinary bloke take?

"Not long because it didn't affect me as though I'd done anything wrong, I thought I were doing something right. That I was supposed to be doing something good and righteous."

The mission required, of course, that he only murder prostitutes. Yet at least thirteen of his admitted 22 attacks were women who were not prostitutes. How does he explain that contradiction?

"I was absolutely convinced [that they were all prostitutes]. I thought it couldn't be wrong because God doesn't make mistakes."

But some of the women were so clearly not looking for business on the streets, it's difficult to accept that he had no inkling at all that they might not be sex workers.

"That's beside the point, it's what I believed at the time. Otherwise, I wouldn't have attacked them."

Did his mind ever turn to the police and their apparent inability to get anywhere close to catching him?

"I never really thought much about the time it took them to catch me. I believed I was caught up in a miracle, so when things happened to thwart the police I simply believed it was divine intervention and thought no more of it.

"They had no reason to suspect me. People forget, other people were being questioned more than I was at the time, it's just looking back now at where I was questioned so many times people now think it was a big thing. It wasn't, it was happening to lots of other people."

* * *

Peter Sutcliffe might not have been giving any thought to the police catching him, but it dominated Ronald Gregory's mind.

In April 1978 the Chief Constable called a special conference at force HQ where it was decided that a 12-strong elite group of detectives dedicated solely to catching the Yorkshire Ripper would be formed.

It was headed by Det Chief Supt John Domaille, the SIO from the Tina Atkinson case, and was to be based at Millgarth in Leeds just down the corridor from the Ripper incident room.

Domaille was a likeable, popular and diplomatic officer who preferred to persuade a suspect to come quietly rather than drag him in 'cuffs.

His ability to rub along with most people meant he was the perfect choice to take a long, hard look at everything that had been done so far on the Ripper murders.

He spoke to the SIOs from all the previous attacks, using all those diplomacy skills to reassure his fellow officers he wasn't looking for faults, just trying to find a better way of doing things.

The one relationship he had difficulty with was potentially the most important – George Oldfield. Any suggestions for a strategic shift or rethink in the overall inquiry had to go through Oldfield, and the two didn't always see eye to eye. Oldfield didn't like the way Domaille dealt with the press. He thought he was too open with them and gave up too much information early on. Domaille disagreed. He felt that, as long as the relationship was a professional one, the media was a valuable weapon.

Domaille didn't let this conflict with Oldfield bother him as he had endless discussions with other detectives to try to think up new or different approaches.

He was forward-thinking and was keen to utilise the most modern computer systems available at the time to streamline the manual card index system.

All Major Incident Rooms across the country at the time were based on this paper-and-pen approach. Information about people or vehicles was filed on cards using an established structure of reference numbers and letters that should, in theory, be easily searchable throughout the investigation.

The system worked well for smaller inquiries and West Yorkshire's was considered a sophisticated version of it.

But a uniquely large and complex inquiry such as the Ripper case was placing an unbearable strain on it.

Every time an officer was tasked with an action, a piece of paper with a number of coloured copies was filled out. Before the officer went to complete the task, they would check the indexes to see if there were any previous references relevant to this action. If anything was found, it would be photocopied and stapled to the new form. If nothing already existed in the system, a new nominal index card would be filled out and filed.

West Yorkshire's filing system was structured by letters and numbers. For example, the reference 'B' is for anyone actually seen by an officer in relation to the inquiry. So if an eyewitness who saw something suspicious on the night of a murder was the 135th person to be seen since the attack, they would be B135.

One action could lead to multiple new actions as the inquiry mushroomed, all needing a new form with its coloured copies.

No force anywhere in the country had ever used the system on such a wide-ranging inquiry with multiple victims at different locations.

By now the system amounted to many thousands of cards and action forms. Guaranteeing that every piece of information had been filed correctly and nothing was misplaced was impossible.

The use of computers was still in its infancy. Not a single officer anywhere in the UK had any experience of a major investigation being run using computers rather than paperwork, but senior officers in West Yorkshire were not blind to the advantages of a computerised approach.

The previous year, Gregory had considered and then rejected the offer to use a mainframe computer at the Atomic Energy Authority Establishment to computerise the Ripper investigation's existing records.

The force had also consulted with the best IT brains in the private sector. The task was considered so large and complex that only IBM were prepared to take it on. But their proposal made clear that it would take years to computerise the existing records and the sum quoted – £500,000 – was deemed unrealistic.

It was suggested that the fledgling Police National Computer (PNC) system could be used to assist the officers noting down registration numbers in red light areas.

The PNC was already up and running, so this was green-lighted and ten screens were installed in the Ripper incident room. Officers could now obtain printouts of cars seen in red light areas, a development considered cutting edge at the time.

But there were shortcomings.

Only the car registration numbers could be printed out, not the name and address of the owner. These could only be acquired by feeding registration numbers back to the PNC mainframe via a computer terminal, and then waiting for a hard copy of those details to be posted back. Eventually the system was altered so the name and address could be printed out in the incident room, but the printout gave the time and date the information had been inputted, not when the actual sighting was made in the red light area.

That information could, of course, be essential in challenging alibi evidence.

If a potential suspect claimed he had been at home on a particular night and therefore couldn't have been in a red light district, the interviewing officer had no idea if he was telling the truth because the information he possessed only had the time and date when it was entered into the system, not when the suspect's car had been sighted.

It meant detectives were going to potentially critical interviews with one arm tied behind their backs, but it wasn't completely without value and did lead to detectives calling once more at Garden Lane in Heaton, Bradford.

By then, the quiet, unremarkable man they wanted to talk to after his car had been seen in Chapeltown and Manningham had committed yet another brutal murder.

* * *

There was a tragic irony to Vera Millward's body being found in the grounds of a hospital. She had been ill for years and suffered almost constant pain due to a stomach condition. Three times she went under the surgeon's knife for it, but it still gave her regular cause for complaint. The pain got so bad some nights that she would walk for 30 minutes from her council flat in Hulme, Manchester, to the Royal Infirmary seeking medication to dull the agony.

That's where her common-law husband Cy Burkett thought she had gone when she popped out one spring evening in 1978 taking her other frailties with her. She only had one lung and would often drag one of her feet as she walked. People thought she looked far older than her 40 years.

Life had been hard when she was born in Madrid in 1937 as the Spanish Civil War raged around her, and it didn't get much better for her and her family following General Franco's victory in 1939. By the time she reached her late teens in the 1950s, she followed the established route of many of her fellow countrymen and women and moved to the UK for work, acquiring a job as a domestic help in Manchester.

She met a man called Yusef Mohammed Sultan and they had five children together but the family splintered after he died, and

Vera once more found herself struggling, turning to prostitution to help make ends meet. She received a number of convictions for soliciting over the years, the last of which was in November 1973.

By May 1978 she was living with Cy and their two children in Grenham Avenue. He was aware of her past life as a working girl but thought she had given it up, which wasn't strictly the case.

Each Tuesday, a man would pull up outside the flat in his 1963 maroon Mercedes and flash his lights so she would know he was there. Vera would head out and climb into the posh motor, and for a few hours he would whisk her away from her hard life in one of the toughest parts of Manchester. They would chat and laugh together and have sex before he delivered her back to reality, often paying her in gifts and compliments rather than hard cash.

On Tuesday, May 16, 1978, the established routine fell through. The man in the Merc failed to turn up and by 10pm Vera needed some fresh air. She told Cy she was going out to buy cigarettes. The stomach pain was also playing up again and he assumed that, as well as her Benson and Hedges, she was going to the hospital for painkillers.

She bought two packets of her favourite filter-tipped cigarettes and, with her regular Tuesday night appointment having fallen down, she said yes when a man with a dark beard and striking dark eyes pulled up alongside her in a red Ford Corsair and asked if she was doing business.

Prostitutes in Manchester tended to take their clients to one of two spots. The allotments next to the Southern Cemetery – where Jean Jordan had been murdered – or the grounds of Manchester Royal Infirmary, which was much closer to Moss Lane.

Vera directed Peter Sutcliffe to the hospital once they had settled on a price of £5. He pulled into the car park behind the private patients' home and as he killed the engine he suggested it would be better in the back. She agreed, but he waited until she opened the passenger door and climbed out before reaching under his seat to collect a hammer. He went around the car, walked up behind Vera as she was about to reach down and open the back passenger door, and struck her across the back of the head. She was still conscious and began to scream: "Help... help... he-".

The third yell for assistance was cut short as Sutcliffe brought the hammer down again. A man not far away had heard her cries, but thought it was a patient in pain in the hospital and didn't react.

Sutcliffe dragged Vera's unconscious body a few yards across gravel into a more secluded location next to a chain link fence. He stabbed her with a knife, repeatedly thrusting the blade into the same wound, as he had done with Jayne MacDonald and Helen Rytka, before jumping back into his car and driving away.

A few hours later, just after 8am, six landscape gardeners turning up for work at the hospital saw what they thought was a large doll of some description or a tailor's dummy before realising it was a body.

Det Supt Jack Ridgway, who had led the Jean Jordan case, arrived at the scene shortly after and 20 officers began a fingertip search of the immediate crime scene as police dog teams conducted a wider check of the area.

When Dr Reuben Woodcock performed the post-mortem, he discovered that one of the stab wounds to her chest had passed between her ribs and penetrated her one remaining lung.

Less than 48 hours after she was killed, newspaper headlines announced details of the "Ripper's new victim".

Over the following days, detectives flooded the red light area in the hope of talking to as many of Manchester's estimated 400 prostitutes as possible to both glean useful information and to warn them about their own safety.

Any information they gained was fed into the system, which was now creaking. At the peak, up to 27 officers in the main Ripper incident room were controlling as many as 1,000 detectives who were making inquiries elsewhere.

A nine-month backlog developed on reports from these officers being filed, and the various appeals for help on the different murders were bringing in an unmanageable 1,200 phone calls a day from the public.

As the police struggled with their own challenges, Vera's family faced a more immediate, emotional crisis.

Cy and the children were devastated. He spoke to the press to pay tribute to her and revealed an anecdote which showed how Vera had enjoyed precious little luck in her life. In 1973, she won £40,713 on the football pools, a huge amount and worth more than ten times that in today's money. She was delighted and saw it as the answer to all of her troubles, but a dispute over the coupon arose and she ultimately never got the money.

The agony of her death eventually became unbearable for Cy and he moved back to his native Jamaica with the children.

The search of the murder scene had discovered tyre tracks, which forensic officers were able to take casts from. Detailed impressions were obtained from all four tyres which allowed the North-West Forensic Science Laboratory to produce a list of 11 vehicles which could have left the tracks.

These matched the vehicles which could have left tracks at the Irene Richardson murder scene in February, 1977, and the Maureen Long scene a few months later, both in Leeds. The Farina remained the favourite for those attacks, although the Corsair was also on the list.

Two detectives on the Manchester squad went deeper into this line of inquiry and following extensive research were able to prove the car used in the Millward attack could not have been a Farina.

Ridgway went to see George Oldfield armed with these findings, but he was not well received. The tyre tracks were one of the few pieces of hard physical evidence the police had and a huge amount of resources had been invested into it, leading to the firm belief they were looking for a Farina driver.

To accept Ridgway's new information would mean that nearly 18 months of detective work had all been in vain, and Oldfield was hardly the kind of character who would readily admit to such an error.

"He would not have it at any price," said the Manchester detective after his meeting with Oldfield.

Ridgway had as much faith in his own detectives as Oldfield did in his, and he informed his West Yorkshire colleague that his investigation into the Jordan and Millward murders would not be following the Farina line.

His officers did even more work on this point and concluded that Marilyn Moore could only have been attacked by a man driving either a Ford Cortina Mark I or a Ford Corsair.

It was an excellent piece of detective work but, by now, Ridgway had lost all faith in the tracking inquiry and rejected it as a basis for further investigation. Over the Pennines, Oldfield remained convinced the killer was a Farina driver, a belief he held until Sutcliffe's arrest. A golden opportunity to catch the killer had been squandered.

By now £1.5million had been spent on the Ripper inquiry, a vast amount in the 1970s. More than 48,000 people had been interviewed, 11,600 statements had been taken, 130,000 vehicles had been checked, and the police had in their possession a couple of hard bits of physical evidence pointing directly towards the killer. Despite all of that, they still didn't have a clue who he was.

CHAPTER 15

FAMILY GRIEF

Peter Sutcliffe was a taker of mothers. As a direct consequence of his murderous activities 25 children would never again send a Mother's Day card, yet he never seemed to appreciate the full extent of the crushing, debilitating pain he caused others, even when his own mother passed away.

Kathleen Sutcliffe had never appeared particularly healthy ever since the incident at the Bankfield Hotel when she arrived for what she thought was a date with her lover only to be confronted by husband John, who had arranged it as a trap to expose her infidelity.

The psychological hangover from that episode joined forces with her ailing physical health, which wasn't helped by the daily grind of juggling three jobs with every domestic chore on the home front. She developed angina in the mid-1970s and began to feel increasingly unwell, although in her typically stoic manner, she kept the full extent of her illness from the rest of the family.

"We hardly knew how serious it was," said Sutcliffe. "We knew she had angina, but she never complained. She was in pain all the time... she never said anything."

By then, she and husband John were settled in their new place in Rutland House. The flat was closer to Bingley town centre making it easier for her to go to the shops, and it was smaller and easier to manage than the house in Corny Road.

But John's extra-curricular activities of drinking and woman-ising were showing little sign of abating, which hardly helped her condition.

As autumn was turning to winter in 1978, Peter suddenly realised how serious things were when he received a panicked call from her one day.

"She'd been cleaning at a woman's house in Gilstead and she rang me up," he said. "I had just got home and I were eating my tea, and she rang and said: 'Pete, can you come and get me?' I said: 'Where are you?' She said: 'I'm on Priestthorpe Lane in a telephone box, I can't walk.' I said: 'What's wrong?' She said: 'I've got terrible pain in my chest.' So I dropped what I was doing, I dashed out, jumped in the car, shot down to Bingley, up to Gilstead to Priestthorpe Lane, and she was there in a phone box looking as white as a sheet.

"I got her into the car and took her down, it was only about 200 yards from her flat where she lived and it's downhill, but she couldn't do it. I took her there and helped her up the stairs. I said: 'Will you be all right?' She said: 'Yeah, no need to come in, I'll be all right, your dad will be home soon.' So I went home. She never made a fuss and she must have been in terrible pain if she couldn't walk."

Her condition worsened, and she gave up her cleaning jobs and got to the stage where she hardly went out. She was already on medication and insisted people didn't make a fuss, so no further medical advice was sought on her worsening heart condition.

"She never complained and she was in pain all the time, a lot of pain," said Peter. "She could have had some kind of treatment. She never had any heart valve treatment or anything for it. They hadn't got the modern treatments, but they might have been able to do something if she'd opened her mouth.

"She never said anything and next thing she knew it was a massive heart attack."

Peter's sister Maureen found her on a Wednesday afternoon in early November. She had popped in to see her mum around 4pm after picking up the children from school and found her collapsed on the bed. She was seriously ill, but still alive.

Maureen called 999 and then set about alerting the rest of the family to let them know that Kathleen had been taken to Airedale General. Her dad was at work, but she managed to get a message to him and understood that he would head straight to the hospital.

As it turned out, Peter was the one who got there first, but he still didn't make it in time.

"Maureen rang my house and said she's gone to hospital. I left my dinner, jumped straight up, jumped in the car and shot off to Airedale. I got there as fast as I could.

"Maureen told me my dad had already gone to the hospital, so I expected him to be there with Mum before I arrived. He wasn't there and she had died alone before I got there."

Peter wandered outside the front of the hospital, devastated and in shock. He slumped onto a bench to wait for his father to arrive, puzzled as to why he was taking so long.

When John finally got there, 90 minutes after he had been due, it triggered a furious row between father and son, because father wasn't on his own. Instead of racing to the hospital to be by his wife's side, he had gone to the home of one of his women friends to ask for a lift.

"He went to his fancy woman, waiting for her to get a bath and get ready to take him in her car, instead of hopping on the bus," said Sutcliffe. "He'd have been there before she died and he could have talked to her a bit.

"He turned up laughing and joking with his fancy woman, so I had a right go at him and told him if he hadn't waited so long for this woman to get ready and bring him in her car, he'd have been there before Mum died.

"I had a big row with him outside the hospital. I said: 'Where were you? You could have been here hours ago, she's died since then.'

"Then I just had a damned good cry.

Bingley Cemetery where Peter Sutcliffe worked as a grave digger and first heard the voice that later instructed him to kill prostitutes

Serial killer Peter Sutcliffe in 1976, sitting in the cab of his lorry at the Bradford engineering firm where he was a driver

Olive Smelt, a survivor of an early attack by Peter Sutcliffe, who would go on to murder 13 women

Forensic officers search for clues at the timber yard where the body of Helen Rytka was discovered in January 1978

Detective Chief Superintendent Trevor Lapish leads a team of detectives in Savile Park, Halifax, where the body of Josephine Whittaker was found in April 1979. Wearing the sheepskin coat is Assistant Chief Constable George Oldfield, head of the search for the Yorkshire Ripper

The funeral of Yorkshire Ripper victim Barbara Leach was held at Kettering Parish Church in September 1979. Barbara's parents, David and Beryl Leach, watch alongside her brother as the coffin is carried into the crematorium

Police play the Ripper tape from Wearside Jack to Bingo players in Bradford in September 1979

Detectives at work in the Yorkshire Ripper incident room in Leeds

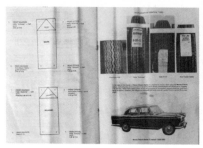

The Ripper hunt created a mountain of paperwork, which ultimately did not help the police

Jacqueline Hill, the final victim of the Yorkshire Ripper, Peter Sutcliffe

Police searching for clues after the body of Jacqueline Hill was discovered just a few hundred yards from her home in November 1980

Richard McCann, the son of the Yorkshire Ripper's first recognised victim, Wilma McCann

Peter Sutcliffe's best friend Trevor Birdsall, who finally reported his suspicions to the police. He is pictured with his girlfriend Gloria Conroy

Psychiatrist Dr Hugo Milne at the Old Bailey for the opening day of the trial of Peter Sutcliffe in May 1981

Peter Sutcliffe's wife, Sonia, leaving the Old Bailey during his trial in 1981

Detective Chief Superintendent Jim Hobson, head of West Yorkshire CID

Assistant Chief Constable George Oldfield

John Sutcliffe, father of Peter

Carl Sutcliffe, brother of Peter

1 WILMA McCANN, 28 LEEDS, OCTOBER 1975	2 EMILY JACKSON, 42 LEEDS, JANUARY 1976	3 IRENE RICHARDSON, 28 LEEDS, FEBRUARY 1977	4 PATRICIA ATKINSON, 32 BRADFORD, APRIL 1977
5 JAYNE McDONALD, 16 LEEDS, JUNE 1977	6 JEAN JORDAN, 21 MANCHESTER, OCTOBER 1977	7 YVONNE PEARSON, 22 BRADFORD, JANUARY 1978	8 HELEN RYTKA, 18 HUDDERSFIELD, JANUARY 1978
9 VERA MILLWARD, 41 MANCHESTER, MAY 1978	10 JOSEPHINE WHITAKER, 19 HALIFAX, APRIL 1979	11 BARBARA LEACH, 20 BRADFORD, SEPTEMBER 1979	12 JACQUELINE HILL, 20 LEEDS, NOVEMBER 1980

Twelve of the Ripper's 13 victims. He also murdered Margo Walls in 1980

An angry mob gathers outside Dewsbury Magistrates Court for Peter Sutcliffe's first court appearance

May 1981 – a handcuffed Peter Sutcliffe at court

"I had deep regrets, I believed I could have done a lot more for my mum. I really regretted when she died. I really kicked myself. But I didn't know. She wouldn't tell us how bad she was.

"I couldn't sleep properly for quite some time after she passed away as she was on my mind so much.

"I just wish my mam would have confided in us more about her heart condition, but it was just like her not to want to alarm anyone. She was far too considerate for her own good, bless her.

"Sonia said to me: 'You're taking it very hard.' I said: 'That was because it all happened so quickly, I had no time to say goodbye'.

"You've got to do everything you can for your mum. When they've gone, you always say, oh I could have done that and I could have done that. After she died I thought, Oh no, I wish I'd done that and that, put her first. Give her all the love you can because she's your mum."

Tragic though Kathleen's death was for the Sutcliffe family, it did have one positive effect for which the women of Yorkshire were the main beneficiaries.

"Things dropped off a lot then, I was too distraught, I couldn't do anything," he said, explaining why there were no attacks for another five months. "I don't know if that was affecting my mind, you see. I might have been grieving for a long time, nothing happened after she died. I asked God to give me a break, give me time to grieve."

But how could he continue taking other women's lives when he now had first-hand knowledge of the devastation a bereavement brings to a family?

The question caused him no discomfort at all and in a flat, emotionless voice he simply replied: "Well I didn't think of them as mothers, or daughters or sisters or anything like that, they were just to be removed."

Sutcliffe never did acknowledge the irony of the grief he felt at losing his mother while also creating exactly the same feelings in others.

He later clung to the one positive he could think of that arose out of his mum's death – that it came before his arrest, meaning she went to her grave never knowing her firstborn was the Yorkshire Ripper.

"She would have stuck by me," he said, "but it would have been extra pressure on her with the press and all that. She never knew, so that's as well really."

In keeping with the skewed, self-centred way in which he viewed his crimes and everything that flowed from them, Sutcliffe couldn't accept that it would have been his actions that would have caused her pain, if she had lived. He laid the blame for the distress she would have felt elsewhere, on the press, an inability to accept responsibility for his own actions which ran through his whole life.

* * *

While he was at large, the Yorkshire Ripper gained a kind of mythical reputation, seemingly possessing the ability to float into city centres undetected, claim another victim and then vanish without trace. Like a ghost in the night.

The police knew that ghosts didn't exist, so they decided to up their game in relation to the covert surveillance operation in red light areas. The killer's pattern of seeking victims was by now well-established. So it followed that if a list of registration numbers of kerb crawlers could be compiled each night, then when the next murder occurred, the police should already have his car details.

The Automatic Number Plate Recognition (ANPR) system – a network of 11,000 cameras across the UK which can instantly identify registration numbers – only existed in the realm of *Tomorrow's World* in the 1970s, so the police had to do it the old-fashioned way.

A squad of 100 officers was tasked with manning 26 observations points in Chapeltown, Manningham, and around the Great Northern Street area of Huddersfield each night to write down the numbers of cars driving through the red light areas to pick up women for sex.

At some locations, cars were driving too quickly to note their number, so they began using tape recorders.

It was manpower-heavy and morale-sapping work, and sometimes other demands elsewhere meant not every minute of every night of the week could be covered.

Detectives working lengthy shifts could become tired, or lazy, meaning not every number plate was recorded accurately, or recorded at all.

Nevertheless, officers across the north of England were committed to this line of inquiry and it was expanded to include 13 locations in Moss Side, in Manchester, four in Sheffield and three in Hull.

It was known as the Cross Area Sightings inquiry with drivers being seen in more than one red light area being placed on a list called the 'Punters' Index', a record of men who regularly sought the services of prostitutes in towns and cities across the M62 belt of northern England.

A plan was drawn up for everyone on the Punters' Index to be interviewed, leading to detectives once more knocking on the door at number six, Garden Lane in Heaton, Bradford. It was August 13, 1978, three months after Vera had been murdered in Manchester.

* * *

Peter Sutcliffe's red Ford Corsair had been sighted by police in red light areas seven times over two and a half weeks – six in Bradford, one in Leeds.

He had also been sighted a further nine times in a recently acquired Sunbeam Rapier (he owned the Rapier and the Corsair at the same time for a number of months).

But the limitations of the computer system meant that Detective Constable Peter Smith was not aware of the Rapier sightings when he knocked on the Sutcliffes' door. He thought it was just the seven in the Corsair, and he had no idea at what time of day or night they had been made.

He was invited in and offered a seat by what he quickly decided were a pleasant, ordinary couple. The man of the house was dressed in overalls as he was decorating the kitchen, but he was happy to interrupt his work to chat to the officer.

Detectives had been given the strict instruction to make no mention of the covert observations in red light areas. They had to question vehicle movements, but could not reveal how they knew that a car had been in a particular spot at a certain time. They were also tasked with inspecting cars to see if they could have left the tyre tracks at the three murder scenes and were told to confirm alibis by checking paperwork such as diaries, holiday bookings forms or records of hospital visits.

With all of that in mind, DC Smith asked Sutcliffe about his movements for Tuesday, May 16, when Vera was killed.

"He would have come home from work and stayed with me all evening," Sonia told him confidently.

The couple explained that they had only recently bought their house and were spending all their spare time doing it up, which DC Smith could see for himself was true with the decorating of the kitchen in full swing.

They added that they hardly went out and when they did, it was always together, with Sutcliffe confirming he was almost always home on an evening.

He appeared calm during the interview, not giving off the slightest hint of nerves.

He was so confident of evading capture, he began to chat un-prompted about the large number of men being spoken to in relation to the Ripper to underline how routine this current interview was.

"One time at home when they were questioning me again and Sonia was there, I said: 'I bet you've questioned the same people numerous times, have you?' Yes, they said. I said: 'Oh well, I'll just have to tolerate it then.'"

At one stage Sonia popped out of the room and DC Smith used the opportunity to ask the delicate question of whether Sutcliffe ever used prostitutes, which he denied.

Officers were under strict instructions from on high to tread carefully when it came to this line of inquiry.

"The detectives were there to alibi the driver for the Ripper murders, not for driving in red light districts," explained Dick Holland, Oldfield's right-hand man. "We did not want to stir up divorces or domestic problems. We didn't want police officers who had witnessed such activities in prostitute areas being subpoenaed in divorce hearings."

Sutcliffe was also asked about the use of his car and explained that any sightings of it in Bradford could be explained by his journey to work.

He repeated that he rarely went out in the evening. It was a lie, but it highlighted the weakness of the system which meant DC Smith was unable to challenge him on it.

The earliest sighting of his car in a red light area had been at 8pm, the latest at 12.50am, making a mockery of Sutcliffe's claim that he rarely went out in an evening.

But all DC Smith had in his possession was the time that the information about the sightings had been entered into the computer.

In relation to his car being seen in Chapeltown, Sutcliffe simply denied ever being in the area. DC Smith was again hampered by not being able to reveal how he knew that Sutcliffe's car *had* been in Leeds' red light area.

No particular importance was attached to the fact that Sutcliffe was being interviewed for a second time in relation to two separate lines of inquiry – the £5 note and the Cross Area sighting. DC Smith simply assumed that it was not unusual for men in this area of West Yorkshire to be questioned on both.

He didn't bother to check the tyres on Sutcliffe's car because his understanding was that he had owned a Corsair at the time of the relevant murders, which he didn't think could have left the tracks, even though it was still on the list of possibles. Neither did he make any search of the house or garage for a hammer that fitted the bill because he thought this had been done at the previous interview.

Both Sutcliffe and his wife were happy to make written statements confirming everything they had told the officer, and once done he bade them good day.

Despite having just interviewed the Yorkshire Ripper, DC Smith walked away from the house harbouring no suspicion whatsoever.

One of the reasons for his lack of concern was that they seemed such an ordinary couple and Mrs Sutcliffe was clearly supportive of everything her husband said. It was an unintended, but effective consequence of her affection for him.

"There can be no doubt that the support of his wife, her obvious intelligence and open demeanour, long delayed the capture of Peter Sutcliffe," said the Chief Constable, Ronald Gregory, later.

It's true that they were a loving couple who to the outside world appeared to be just like any other ordinary couple. But there was another side to the relationship which the outside world never got to see, although Peter used to worry that the neighbours would hear some of it.

Sonia was obsessed with cleanliness. The house was immaculate and plastic sheets covered the chairs to ensure they didn't get worn or dirty, and the surfaces were clean enough to eat off. But she never seemed content and would spend hours with a dustpan and brush in her hand inspecting the carpets for the tiniest speck of dirt, and as soon as she found one it was consigned to the dustbin.

Her husband was a constant target and it began even before he entered the house. The rules were that he was never allowed in with his shoes on as that presented too much danger of bringing dirt into the house.

There was an invisible but established barrier at the entrance to the house, beyond which dirty clothes and boots weren't allowed. On a regular working day, once he had changed out of his dirty clothes and was cleaned up, he liked nothing more than to settle in front of the television with the paper, perhaps with a snack from the fridge.

But his wife's highly-strung nature meant that even this simplest of pleasures was not without its difficulties. She would often effectively ban him from making himself a snack from the fridge, and it wasn't unknown for her to march up to the television set, grab the plug and pull it from the wall.

Temperamental and over-excited, Sonia would fly into a rage at her husband as he sat quietly reading his newspaper. Sometimes it got physical. She would swipe a hand at him and kick out, causing him to restrain her, although he insisted he never retaliated by striking her back.

"It happens quite often," he said, as he insisted that he never retaliated. "I have never hit her. When she loses control over absolutely nothing, or when she hits me or starts kicking me, I hold her wrists."

These interactions left Sutcliffe embarrassed that the neighbours might hear.

Sonia, cold and at times appearing unstable, didn't seem to care, but it got her husband down.

"I was feeling very depressed because she always nags me," he said. "I was just fed up with her constant nagging."

Another aspect of their marital life which brought its own pressure was that Sonia suffered three miscarriages, each in the early stages, although all three pregnancies were apparently unplanned.

"We didn't plan to have a family, but these things sometimes occur," he said. "We didn't try for kids, it was just accidental, but she just fell pregnant three times and had three of them – I wasn't aware that four out of ten pregnancies end in a miscarriage. I'd have been really good to the kids if I'd had them but, it worked out for the best because it would have been a bit harassing for them in the circumstances if we'd have had kids. Perhaps it's as well."

DC Smith filed his report, which his supervising officer was happy with. But when Dick Holland reviewed the paperwork he noted that Sutcliffe had owned two Ford Corsairs which were on the list of suspect cars, even though the Farina range was still the favourite.

Sensing there was more to explore here, Holland instructed for a follow-up interview to be carried out.

It was authorised by the incident room 16 days after the previous interview with DC Smith, but the pressure on the investigation meant it wasn't conducted until three months later, on November 23, a fortnight after Sutcliffe's mother Kathleen had died.

DC Smith was tasked with going back to speak to Sutcliffe (the demands on manpower had resulted in the earlier instruction of officers never interviewing the same person twice going out of the window), this time accompanied by a colleague, DC Bradshaw.

It should have been a hugely significant interview. The man they were about to see worked for a company which could have paid out the Jordan £5 note in wages, his car could have left the tyre tracks at three murder scenes, it had been seen regularly in red light districts, and he had not been positively alibied for any of the attacks which now numbered 15, nine murders and six attempted murders.

But they approached it as a matter of routine, and DC Bradshaw didn't even get out of the car for it.

He waited outside while DC Smith went to speak to Sutcliffe and his wife to go over the same ground as before.

The Corsair couldn't be examined this time as Sutcliffe had by now sold it. The new owner was traced, but he had changed the tyres.

DC Smith returned to the incident room and filed his report, which, although it didn't raise any pointed suspicion, did make it clear that Sutcliffe was now in the crosshairs of all the major lines of inquiry.

Every alarm bell in the Major Incident Room down at Millgarth should have been ringing.

But what happened when DC Smith filed his report into the system?

It went missing. For nearly a year.

CHAPTER 16

OVERWHELMED

By early 1979, the Cross Area Sightings inquiry which noted down punters' car numbers in red light areas had produced another tsunami of information to overload the inquiry.

Around 20,000 vehicles had been sighted in two red light areas, far too many to be interviewed quickly, so drivers were prioritised in terms of geography. Those who lived in West Yorkshire or Greater Manchester were at the top of the list, those who lived far away were unlikely to ever be spoken to.

Even with this change, this line of inquiry was placing too much strain on resources, so it was fine-tuned. From now, only drivers sighted in *three* red light areas would be interviewed. The Cross Area Sightings inquiry became the Triple Area Sightings.

A fresh list of drivers was printed out each week and the second list, printed on Friday, February 23, 1979, included a Black Sunbeam Rapier, registration number NKU 888H, registered owner Peter Sutcliffe.

But there was no chance of him being seen promptly.

Detectives were forever being redeployed to other more urgent tasks, such as a fresh attack or a seemingly crucial tip-off from the public.

By the time he was interviewed in relation to this matter, another woman would be dead and the life of yet another would be changed forever.

On March 2, 1979, Sutcliffe crept up behind 22-year-old student Ann Rooney as she walked near a college in Horsforth, Leeds. Ann wasn't a sex worker, and nothing about her behaviour suggested she was. That vital criteria which Sutcliffe always insisted was central to his attacks had collapsed. From now on, not a single other attack would be on a prostitute.

He hit Ann over the head three times with a hammer. She survived and was able to give police useful information. She said her attacker was in his 20s, around 5ft 10in tall, broad build with dark curly hair and a drooping moustache. Even better, she was positive she had seen him sitting in a dark coloured Sunbeam Rapier shortly before the attack.

But it ended up being for nothing when her attack was rejected as a Ripper case for the narrow reason that the width of the hammer used to inflict her wounds was different to previous attacks.

Senior officers were so worried about including attacks due to the mass of information it would produce from the public, some potentially misleading, that they used the slimmest of reasons to rule them out, in this case a matter of millimetres.

Three weeks after Ann was attacked, another letter landed on Oldfield's desk from the North East.

Addressed to Assistant Chief Constable Oldfield, it read: "Sorry I havn't written, about a year to be exact, but I hav'nt been up North for quite a while. I was'nt kidding last time I wrote saying the whore would be older this time and maybe I'd strike in Manchester for a change, you should have took heed. That bit about her being in hospital, funny the lady mentioned something about being in the same hospital before I stopped her whoring ways. The lady won't worry about hospitals now will she. I bet you be wondering how come I hav'nt been to work for ages, well I would have been if it hadn't been for your cursered coppers I had the lady just where I wanted her and was about to strike when one of your cursing police cars stopped right outside the lane, he must have been a dumb copper cause he didnt say anything, he didn't know how close he was to catching me. Tell you the truth I thought I was collared, the lady said dont worry about the coppers, little did she know that bloody copper saved her neck. That was last month, so I don't know when I will get back on the job but I know it wont be Chapeltown too bloody hot there maybe Bradfords Manningham. Might write again if up North.

Jack the Ripper

PS Did you get the letter I sent to *Daily Mirror* in Manchester."

No great importance was attached to the first two letters, but 12 months on, the third letter changed things.

They contained various bits of information which, when taken together, took on a greater significance and Oldfield and Holland were now confident the author was the killer, rather than just another hoaxer.

In the first letter, he had talked about targeting an "old slut next time", possibly in "Liverpool… or even Manchester again."

The next attack took place in Manchester. The victim was Vera Millward, who, at 40, was older than all but two of the previous victims.

The third letter noted that Vera had been treated in the same hospital where she had been murdered. Oldfield thought, wrongly, that this information had never been released to the press meaning that only someone who knew Vera well, or the killer if she had told him, would know it.

The first two letters also mentioned Joan Harrison's murder in Preston, and the police were also under the mistaken belief that her attack had never been reported in the press.

Strongest of all, though, was a forensic clue which the envelope for the third letter had thrown up.

Analysis of saliva revealed that whoever had licked the envelope was of the relatively rare 'B' secretor blood group, just like the killer of Joan Harrison. Her murder had never been conclusively included in the Ripper series, but this was considered too much of a coincidence. Oldfield was now convinced that the letter writer, the Harrison killer and the murderer operating in Yorkshire were one and the same. He would stubbornly stick to this view to the bitter end.

* * *

The winter of 1979 was a bad one. The previous one had been harsh enough, when Yvonne Pearson and Helen Rytka braved the snow and sub-zero temperatures to continue working the streets and paid with their lives, but 12 months on and that one felt like child's play as the cold north winds paralysed a nation already reeling from widespread industrial action.

Towns and villages were cut off as drifts towered over the roofs of the snow ploughs sent to clear a route through them. With temperatures dropping to -24C overnight in places and failing to rise above -5C through the day, it would be the coldest winter for nearly 50 years. Never mind hell, it felt like the United Kingdom had frozen over and Halifax, in West Yorkshire, bore the brunt as much as anywhere with its lofty position up on the high slopes of the Pennines.

Life was tough enough even without the weather. Inflation was threatening to spiral out of control as the Labour Government struggled to maintain its wages policy, which limited public sector awards to 5%. Strikes were rife, there were food and fuel shortages and rubbish piled as high as the snow drifts when the dustbin men joined in.

The Winter of Discontent more than earned its title.

In Halifax, teenager Josephine Whittaker was too young to take too much interest in the problems of the outside world as the Labour Government collapsed and campaigning began for a general election which would see the country's first woman Prime Minister, Margaret Thatcher, sweep to power.

In Bingley, Peter Sutcliffe wasn't too diverted by national events either. Like most of Britain's workers, he battled on through the winter as best he could. He was constantly looking at ways to improve his working day, an approach which found him at the workbench one day, patiently filing the worn end of a Phillips screwdriver until it came to a sharp point.

"It was a giant Phillips screwdriver, having been badly worn and converted into a bradawl," he explained later.

It could, indeed, be used as a bradawl, the piercing tool used to indent wood or other material to make it easier to insert a screw. It was also a lethal weapon.

The weather showed no sign of letting up. Even into May there was snow in some areas, delighting the children and depressing the adults who wondered if it was ever going to end.

On the evening of Wednesday, April 4, there was enough of a pause for the snow to turn to sleet and rain, but Josephine – Jo to family and friends – had other things on her mind, namely her new watch. She had been saving up for the silver timepiece and that morning had finally collected it from her work colleague who ran a mail order catalogue.

It had cost £60, a hefty amount, but she really wanted it and had saved up money from her wage as a clerk at the Halifax Building Society to pay for it.

She couldn't wait to get home to show it off, including to her beloved grandparents, Tom and Mary Priestley, who lived a short walk from Jo over the Moor.

Savile Park was no longer a moor in the normal sense of the word, instead it was a large urban parkland peppered by sports fields and where people walk their dogs and go for a morning run, much like Soldiers Field in Roundhay Park in Leeds, but people still called it the Moor.

Jo normally went to see her grandparents on a Sunday afternoon but she and her mum had had a row over the cost of the electricity to run her fish tank and, after stewing in her bedroom for a while, she decided to get some fresh air. She would go and see her grandparents and at the same time show them her watch.

As she left her house, Peter Sutcliffe was in his black Sunbeam Rapier heading her way.

"I'd been driving around aimlessly, the mood was in me and no woman was safe while I was in this state of mind. Without realising or without having a particular destination, I arrived in Halifax late at night," he said.

Grandad Tom was delighted to see Jo when she turned up unexpectedly at 8.50pm. Mary was at a church function, but Tom popped the kettle on, Jo showed off her new watch and they settled down to watch television.

Mary returned after 11 and after a brief chat, Jo said she should be heading home. Given the hour, the couple suggested she stay the night but Jo declined. She wore contact lenses and the boxes she kept them in overnight were at home.

They tried to insist, but she won the debate and headed out into the night, waving goodbye at 11.40pm.

"I drove along through the centre, passed the Bulls Head, round the roundabout, past the Halifax Building Society," said Sutcliffe. "I came to a wide road with a sweeping curve to it. I took a right turn and eventually came to a big grass open area."

He climbed out of his car when he saw a lone female walking purposefully next to the Moor. He caught up with her and struck up a conversation.

Then, in a strange and cruel irony given what had been the highlight of Jo's day, Sutcliffe asked her the time.

Perhaps still not used to having a watch on her wrist, Jo glanced up at the clock tower of the nearby Holy Trinity and St Jude's Church instead of her new timepiece.

Jo didn't scare easily according to her friends – one of her hobbies after all was a love of horror stories – but even she must have been concerned as the stranger refused to leave her side when she cut across the Moor.

"I realised she was not a prostitute, but at that time I wasn't bothered, I just wanted to kill a woman," he said later. "She told me that she normally took a shortcut across the field. I said you don't know who you can trust these days. It sounds a bit evil now, there I was walking along with my hammer and a big Phillips screwdriver in my pocket ready to do the inevitable."

Sutcliffe later insisted the large screwdriver had not been adapted with murderous intentions in mind.

"I had one big one that was sharpened up, not for that purpose though, it was for putting holes in the bodywork and putting rivets in the sills and on cars and that. It wasn't sharpened up for that."

It hadn't been fashioned into a sickeningly efficient weapon of murder?

"No, not at all. It's the only one I ever sharpened, and it wasn't for that purpose."

His denials ring hollow given that it was now tucked in his pocket along with a hammer, which he took hold of as he dropped behind Jo, pretending to concentrate on the church clock.

"I took my hammer out of my pocket and hit her on the back of the head twice," he said. "She fell down and she made a loud groaning sound."

As Sutcliffe glanced around him, he saw somebody walking along the main road not far away. Terrified he was about to be caught, he dragged Jo further onto the Moor away from the street lights. He paused to make sure he hadn't been seen or heard, only to see two other people walking across the Moor. He hesitated until they had passed, relieved that yet another near-miss had gone his way.

When he was sure the coast was clear, he tore at Jo's clothes and stabbed her 21 times to her abdomen and back, but also to her breasts and vagina before fleeing into the night.

OVERWHELMED

Around 6.30am Jean Markham walked down to the bus stop on Savile Park Road on her way to work at the Rowntree Mackintosh sweet factory where she was a machinist (the factory, still in operation, is where Quality Street chocolates are made).

As she tried to warm herself in the bitter morning cold of this never-ending winter, she looked across and saw a bundle of rags. She looked closer and realised there was a lone shoe lying a few yards away.

Walking over to take an even closer look, she recoiled in horror. She turned and ran home to call 999.

Local officers quickly attended, but the nature of the injuries meant the Ripper incident room was immediately informed.

A short time later, with Jo still lying in situ and covered by a sheet, her 13-year-old brother David was passing the park on his early morning paper round, still unaware, like the rest of the family, that she had not returned home the previous night. Everyone else had gone to bed while she was still at her grandparents and they assumed she had arrived home safely after they were asleep.

David stopped to watch the unfolding police drama like other passers-by, but as he did so his eyes fell on the shoe which Jean had also seen, 10 yards from the tarpaulin-covered body.

He immediately recognised it as Jo's and raced home, yelling at his mum, Avril, as he burst into the kitchen. With a sickening panic rising inside her, Avril sprinted upstairs to check on Jo's bedroom, only to find that her bed hadn't been slept in.

Praying for the best, but fearing the worst, she picked up the phone and called the police.

Officers called round as others gathered at the scene a few hundred yards away, including George Oldfield and Dick Holland. Jack Ridgway from Manchester drove over as soon as he heard.

Prof Gee's six-and-a-half-hour post-mortem later that day confirmed everyone's worst fears, and the local paper announced on its front page: "IT WAS THE RIPPER".

Oldfield didn't pull any punches in his first press conference.

"There is a homicidal maniac at large in Halifax," he said. "This man will continue to kill until he is caught. We cannot stress how careful every woman must be. Unless we catch him, and the public must help us, he will go on and on."

The response from the public had been sluggish at times in relation to some of the previous attacks. Oldfield was convinced that the best way to address that was to emphasise the difference in lifestyles between the victims, stressing the "innocents" vs the "good time girls" divide.

"This was a perfectly respectable girl in a respectable area, and that touches emotions," he said.

Oldfield's faith, however unpalatable viewed from today, was not misplaced and calls flooded in as yet another huge murder inquiry swung into gear. Easter leave was cancelled, dog teams headed to the area to sniff out any clues, house-to-house inquiries were launched and a fingertip search was conducted of the corner of the Moor where Jo was killed.

Oldfield, intent on driving home the advantage, kept pushing the notion that this murder was somehow different to some of the other attacks.

"In the past, the public response to help catch the murderer has not been very good," he said. "So far the response we have had from the people of Halifax has been most encouraging. We hope this continues."

In the first few days the incident room was receiving 360 calls an hour from the public offering up all manner of tips, suggestions and theories.

"We are receiving information from people all over the country," said Oldfield, delighted with the response. "It's coming in so fast that we are having our work cut out coping with it. But I want people to come forward all the same and give us their help. Only with their help will we catch this man."

His appeals also included a direct yet subtle approach to the killer's ego. He had, as far as Oldfield was concerned, sent those letters in which he made it clear that he wanted to be seen as an equal to Oldfield, who now acceded to that request.

"We are looking for a clever, intelligent person," he said, further building a direct relationship between him and the letter writer.

The police desperately needed the public's help, but there was a downside to the huge flow of information. It overwhelmed the incident room and almost all the inquiries from previous cases, including potential suspects who still required their alibis checking, ground to a halt. There just wasn't the manpower to cope.

After ten days, the police had spoken to more than 5,000 people and taken around 1,000 statements.

They were no nearer finding the killer yet Oldfield refused to let his optimism, always expressed in his under-stated Yorkshire fashion, slip.

"This inquiry is not dead. It is still bubbling. We are nearer now than ever before," he said.

There was a reason for this optimism which had so far been kept from the public, but it was decided to reveal more at a press conference 12 days after Jo's body was found.

Journalists had a hint that something big was about to break when the daily press briefing was switched from the usual 10.30am to 3.30pm, timed so that whatever Oldfield was about to reveal would receive maximum exposure on the tea-time television news.

Yet when it came, it was only a halfway house.

He told reporters that the killer could be an engineering worker with connections to West Yorkshire and the North East. He wanted firms to check their records to see if any employers had been in the North East on three specific dates.

They were the dates when the letters had been posted, but Oldfield didn't reveal that, although he didn't need to. Newspapers discovered it for themselves and the existence of the "Jack the Ripper" notes was soon being reported, a development Oldfield described as being of "vital importance to the inquiry".

Detectives interviewing potential suspects were now instructed to ask for a sample of handwriting. If it didn't match the letters, they could be eliminated. If it looked similar, the sample would be sent for expert analysis to the Home Office Forensic Science Laboratory.

By early May, the murder of Jo Whittaker and the hunt for the Yorkshire Ripper had been elbowed out of the headlines by the election of Margaret Thatcher with a swing to the Conservatives larger than any election since 1945, the year before Sutcliffe was born.

Oldfield was less gripped by the political developments than most and all his attention remained on the job in hand.

He was sure the letter writer was the killer, and a little over six weeks after Thatcher's landmark election victory that conviction became anchored in his mind even more securely with the arrival of a small package, postmarked Sunderland.

Inside was a cassette tape which had recently been bought in Woolworths in the city's Fawcett Street.

It would lead to the Ripper case stampeding back into the headlines, even leading to the new Prime Minister expressing her annoyance at the police's inability to catch the killer.

It would also drive the investigation down a new route with no way back, with disastrous and tragic consequences.

CHAPTER 17

VOICE OF JACK

Dozens of photographers, television correspondents and their camera crews crammed into the lecture theatre at the West Yorkshire Police Academy at Bishopgarth, Wakefield, in readiness for the most electric press conference of their careers.

Sitting in front of them was the Ripper team with George Oldfield at the centre, seated behind a low table on which was placed a chunky tape cassette player.

Alongside him were Dick Holland, Jack Ridgway, from Manchester, Wilf Brooks, from Lancashire, and Brian Johnson, Assistant Chief Constable of Northumbria Police.

The other four looked younger and fresher-faced than Oldfield, who had the last four years etched on his face. He appeared tired and not particularly well as he reached forward to start the recording.

The room fell silent in anticipation, but there was a brief delay when Oldfield couldn't find the 'on' button.

Holland reached across and pressed it for him.

The silence was suddenly shattered by a flat, North-Eastern monotone voice. The voice of the man that Oldfield was convinced was the Yorkshire Ripper filled the auditorium, the first time the public had heard what would become one of the most iconic voices in British criminological history. Yet there was a haunting disconnect between the terrible deeds he laid claim to and his low-key delivery.

"I'm Jack, I see you are still having no luck catching me."

Oldfield had long ago turned this into a personal fight, him versus the Ripper, good versus evil. His obsession to catch the killer gave his appeals an emotional, personal feel which nobody around him felt able to challenge. A police force is a strictly rank-based organisation and the upper tiers of West Yorkshire were staffed by men who had either fought in the Second World War or who had done National Service in the years following it. They respected the rank and obeyed orders, and no-one was going to question the boss.

Now his personal approach was coming back to haunt him in spades. The 'Ripper' was taunting him and the world was watching.

As for the real Yorkshire Ripper, he couldn't believe his luck, although he quickly reminded himself it wasn't luck at all, it was the voice carrying God's will.

"I thought that it was diverting the police when that [hoaxer] came on to the scene. I thought well they can't win 'cos God's on my side directing everything," he said.

The tape had arrived at Millgarth police station eight days before the press conference, on June 18, in an envelope addressed to 'ASST CHIEF CONSTABLE OLDFIELD, LEEDS CID, LEEDS CENTRAL POLICE HQ, LEEDS, WEST YORKSHIRE'. It was handwritten and printed in capitals rather than the joined up, upper and lower case writing of the other envelopes and the letters. As an added layer of reassurance that it got to the right desk, the author had written 'From Jack the Ripper' on the reverse of the envelope.

Inside was that cassette bought from Woolworths, but no letter. The cassette had no writing on it and the manufacturers' label had been scraped off. Forensic checks of the tape and envelope found no fingerprints.

Oldfield, Holland and Jim Hobson listened to it again and again in the days after it arrived. There were a few doubts to begin with, but one by one they fell away until the men were confident it was genuine.

"I must have played it 20 times to analyse all the information the tape contained," said Holland. "I thought the Ripper was taunting us for not having caught him. The voice was so distinctive we felt sure that we were going to get him."

Two days later, a hastily arranged – and very secret – conference of all the senior officers from the various forces involved was held in Halifax. Senior detectives from Northumbria, Lancashire and Greater Manchester were in attendance as the tape was played half a dozen times.

West Yorkshire then did a briefing to take the officers through all the evidence which they were sure meant the man who sent the letters was the same man who had made the tape and was also the same man who had killed 11 women (including Joan Harrison) across the north of England in the last four years. Handwriting analysis confirmed that all four envelopes were written by the same person. The detectives, with hundreds of years' experience between them, began discussing the evidence and whether the tape should be made public.

Lancashire quickly repeated their concerns about whether Harrison should even be included in the series, but their objections were weakening.

The entire room listened attentively as Oldfield spoke to express his view that a portion of the tape should be released to the public at some stage, but not all of it.

Others questioned that approach, but the most persuasive view was that in the tape the killer had threatened to strike again. Imagine if he carried out that threat, and it later became known that the police were aware of it but had kept quiet?

"All hell will break loose," said one officer.

Detective Superintendent Peter Docherty, head of Sunderland CID, chipped in to confirm the accent was from Wearside.

The meeting finally agreed that an edited version of the tape be released and a press conference was arranged for 2pm on Tuesday, June 26, six days away.

It was decided that the bulk of the three minute, thirty-seven second tape should be played rather than a smaller edited extract and, after Holland had helped his boss start the tape, the journalists in the packed lecture theatre leaned forward as the man with the flat, slow, almost considered, Wearside voice, taunted Oldfield.

"I'm Jack. I see you are still having no luck catching me. I have the greatest respect for you, George, but Lord, you are no nearer catching me now than four years ago when I started. I reckon your boys are letting you down, George. They can't be much good, can they? The only time they came near catching me was a few months back in Chapeltown when I was disturbed. Even then it was a uniformed copper not a detective. I warned you in March that I'd strike again. Sorry it wasn't Bradford. I did promise you that but I couldn't get there. I'm not quite sure when I'll strike again but it will be definitely some time this year. Maybe September or October. Even sooner if I get the chance. I'm not sure where. Maybe Manchester. I like it there. There's plenty of them knocking about. They never learn, do they, George? I bet you've warned them but they never listen. At the rate I'm going I should be in the book of records. I think it's eleven up to now, isn't it? Well, I'll keep on going for quite a while yet. I can't see myself being nicked just yet. Even if you do get near, I'll probably top myself first. Well, it's been nice chatting to you, George. Yours, Jack the Ripper. No good looking for fingerprints. You should know by now it's clean as a whistle. See you soon. Bye! Hope you like the catchy tune at the end. Ha! Ha!"

In case anyone was still in any doubt that this was now personal and that Oldfield was being taunted, the tape ended with an excerpt from the 1978 song by Andrew Gold, *Thank You For Being A Friend*. Reaching number 42 in the UK charts and later being used as the theme tune for the American sitcom *The Golden Girls*, the song included the lyric: "Your heart is true, you're a pal and a confidant."

The man who this was aimed at stared as intently as anyone in the room at the cassette player as it played the message. Holding his glasses between both sets of fingers, he leant slightly forward, appearing mesmerised by the words. It was almost as if he felt that if he concentrated hard enough, then some fresh and vital clue would magically emerge from the inner workings of the machine itself.

He listened impassively, his expression never changing apart from once when 'Jack' said: "I reckon your boys are letting you down, George." The jab appeared to find its target, triggering an almost imperceptible lifting of his right eyebrow.

Oldfield gets mentioned by name four times in the recording, always the informal 'George' underlining the personal nature of the battle and making the recording sound as if it was a private message between friends.

Although the words, when read on the page, feel cocky and taunting, the way they sound on the original recording don't give the same impression. The delivery is slow and ponderous. At times, it sounds like they are being read off a script with all the confidence of one of the less able pupils reluctantly reading his English essay to the rest of the class. There is no smooth flow to it, there are lots of pauses and it appears he might be about to falter at some words, triggering a debate among the experts over whether he had a stutter that he was hiding.

But the editing of the tape had a strange effect. To make it easier to digest for the press and the public, the large number of pauses – there were at least 18 noticeable ones with the longest being 13 seconds – were edited out.

That gave the message a much punchier feel, the delivery was now quicker, more confident. The editing process made the taunting of Oldfield feel more effective.

The effect on the room of journalists was immediate and marked. They had just heard the voice of a killer and the drama of that ensured the exposure to the tape, and the Ripper story in general, now made headlines around the world.

Oldfield took questions from reporters and it was inevitable that some would focus on the personal nature of the battle.

"The man has taunted you – he has set a challenge to you – what is your reaction to that?" asked one journalist.

"I am prepared to take it on," replied Oldfield, who looked tired and ill-equipped to take on any challenge.

Northumbria's assistant chief constable Brian Johnson also spoke to emphasise the belief that the man on the tape was from his area and that his force and West Yorkshire were committed partners in the hunt for the Ripper.

The reaction from the public when they heard the tape on the radio news or saw the television coverage was electric.

Dedicated telephone lines were set up for people to listen to it, which instantly became jammed due to the huge level of interest.

There were 238 officers working full-time on the inquiry, with 100 dedicated solely to answering calls about the tape, but they were quickly swamped.

Eleven West Yorkshire detectives were despatched to Sunderland to help colleagues in Northumbria follow-up leads about potential names for the voice on the tape.

Within 24 hours of the press conference, there had been 1,000 calls to the inquiry – this in an era when many people still didn't have their own phone at home.

A lot were requests to hear the tape, others were suggesting names of people they thought was the man on the tape. Most were genuine, but it was also the perfect opportunity to gain revenge on a hated ex-boyfriend or abusive husband. The officers had no way of knowing whether a caller was genuine or malicious, but they all had to be checked out.

People wanting to just hear the tape and not speak to an officer could do so by phoning Leeds 469111 to connect to the Post Office's dial-a-disc service (first introduced in 1966 and ironically launched in Leeds, it usually allowed people to listen to songs from the charts), but so many were doing so that by the weekend after the press conference it was constantly ringing engaged and the police asked the Post Office to provide more capacity to ensure everyone could get through.

Within the first four days, 3,000 calls had been received in West Yorkshire and another 600 in Sunderland.

Just like the rest of Yorkshire, Sutcliffe was fully aware of the news broadcasts following the press conference.

"I was quite aware that the hoaxer was misleading the police, but I wasn't in a position to let them know that, of course, as my duty at the time was to a much higher entity – God.

"I said to myself, 'Thanks to God'. I believed God had used him to distract the police and get the attention off me. It was God's will.

"I had a duty to protect the mission at all costs.

"I felt fully protected and at the time believed God had influenced the hoaxer."

Examples of the handwriting were released at the press conference, with copies of the envelopes available to photograph and film.

The letters themselves were not revealed, but three days later the police did release limited extracts which helped add to the flurry of interest which had, by now, gripped the nation.

One of Britain's foremost experts on phonetics – the branch of linguistics that studies human speech and accents – had been brought onto the inquiry before the press conference to help the police nail down exactly where the voice came from.

Stanley Ellis was a senior lecturer at Leeds University and regularly appeared on television and radio programmes as "The Dialect Man" discussing the fascinating subject of why such a small country as Great Britain has such a rich variety of accents.

He concluded the voice on the tape came from Castletown, one of the coal-mining villages along the north bank of the River Wear to the west of Sunderland.

Castletown gets called a village without ever having looked like one. It is an unremarkable estate on the edge of Sunderland, but for a while in 1979 it became the centre of everything as the nation helped the police try and track down the Ripper.

Ellis's colleague at Leeds University's Department of Phonetics, Jack Windsor Lewis, assisted him and although he was less certain of the specific location for Wearside Jack (as he quickly became known) they agreed on the general area. They were both convinced that the accent was genuine and had not been put on for the benefit of the tape.

Lewis also examined the letters. They had previously been inspected by a handwriting expert but not a linguistic expert, who focussed on the actual words and phrases used rather than the way they were written.

After careful studying, he declared himself certain that the letter writer and the person on the tape were the same person.

But what the academics could not be certain about was that that person was also the killer. Oldfield might be sure, but their analysis carried an important caveat – this person was either the killer *or* a 'super-hoaxer' (so called because there were plenty of other hoaxers who had bedevilled the inquiry over the years, but none who had shifted its direction in such a fundamental fashion as Wearside Jack).

Oldfield, though, was deaf to any suggestions that he was dealing with a super-hoaxer rather than the killer himself, and West Yorkshire pressed on with a huge publicity campaign.

They took the recording everywhere. Officers visited nightclubs and asked the DJ to pause the music for a few minutes so the revellers could stop dancing and listen to the tape, although there were fewer dancers than there used to be. The Ripper's campaign of murders had seen attendances at late night venues significantly reduced.

The tape was played in pubs and clubs, bingo halls and sports events.

Police even interrupted regular strip shows at the region's earthier pubs to play the tape to the dancers and their audience.

It was played again and again on the television and radio news programmes and publicity posters were printed, written in the spirit of Oldfield's unshakeable belief that Wearside Jack was the Yorkshire Ripper.

"The Ripper would like you to ignore this!" was the bold headline on the posters, which listed the most important clues that could help people identify the murderer.

It urged people to ring Leeds 464111 and "listen to the killer's voice". Not the voice of the man who claimed to be the killer, but "the killer's voice".

Northumbria were more hesitant. Their publicity material stated that the author of the letters and the man in the tape "*claimed* to be connected with the murders".

It was a subtle difference likely lost on most people, but it did underline the difference in opinion between the two forces which would only grow over time.

CHAPTER 18

BLUNDERS

It was the lack of detail that bothered Detective Inspector David Zackrisson. The killer was intent on taunting the police, so why not ram the point home with more detail? Just a few specifics would have nailed their incompetence and underlined how he was always a few steps ahead. Details such as how he had dodged their surveillance operations in the red light areas or how they had taken so long to find Yvonne's body, perhaps. But there was just vagueness such as: "The only time they came near catching me was a few months back in Chapeltown when I was disturbed…"

Which night? Where in Chapeltown? Was it an actual attack he was referring to – if so which one?

The lack of detail was so marked that when he first got to read the letters he was underwhelmed.

"It was a bit of an anti-climax," he said: "I expected them to say, do you see what I did with such and such a body… [details] only the murderer would know… but there was nothing there."

Another concern was the similarity between some phrases in the letters and those used in a famous letter sent during the original Jack the Ripper murders.

Known as the Dear Boss letter and received by the Central News Agency on September 27, 1888, it was dismissed as a fake at first, but police had a rethink when two women were murdered in one day with one having part of her ear cut off, as predicted in the letter.

When read together, that letter and the Wearside Jack letters raised eyebrows.

From one of the old letters: "I keep on hearing the police have caught me, but they won't fix me just yet," and the new correspondence: *"I see you are still having no luck catching me... you are no nearer catching me now than four years ago when I started."*

Old: "I have laughed when they look so clever and talk about being on the right track."

New: *"I reckon your boys are letting you down, George... They can't be much good, can they?"*

Old: "I am down on whores... I love my work and want to start again... I shan't quit ripping them till I do get buckled."

New: *"There's plenty of them knocking about... I'll keep on going for quite a while yet... My purpose to rid the streets of them sluts."*

And, most strikingly – old: "The joke about the leather apron gives me real fits."

New: *"That photo on the paper gave me fits"*

"I was worried about these letters," said Zackrisson, known as Zack to colleagues. "They didn't appear genuine, and I felt the old-fashioned phraseology could have been copied from elsewhere."

Another concern was Yvonne Pearson's murder. She was killed before one of the letters was sent but was not found until after it arrived yet the writer didn't include her in his tally of murders, a perfect opportunity to draw attention to police failings yet one he hadn't taken.

It didn't make any sense for a killer to write to police to gloat, but pass up on the chance of maximum gloating.

But wind forward 15 months and throw in the tape recording, coupled with the mounting desperation to catch the killer, and the doubts over the Pearson anomaly were put to one side as the investigation went full speed ahead in the North East.

The huge publicity campaign meant that information was being received from as far afield as Africa, Hong Kong, New Zealand, Canada and all across Europe.

But it was in Castletown that the police were concentrating their inquiries.

The tape was played in hundreds of pubs and clubs. Officers visited pits with tape recorders to play it to miners before they went underground for their shift and they played it to thousands of factory workers.

A team of 15 officers trained in handwriting analysis checked 100,000 official forms such as applications for council houses. More than 7,000 letters from men on probation were also analysed.

Officers were even stationed in the regional sorting office to try and intercept a fourth letter as early as possible so they could work out where it had been posted.

More than 15 million letters were checked by this team over the next 18 months, but a fourth letter was never sent.

Oldfield accepted the similarities with the original Jack the Ripper letters (although he felt it might have been an inspiration for the author rather than a reason to doubt the authenticity of the new letters) and libraries were checked to see who had withdrawn books on the Whitechapel murders in recent months.

There were 1,500 homes in Castletown and every one where a male lived was visited to check his handwriting and voice.

Throughout all of this work, the Northumbria detectives had Zack's cautious words ringing in their ears.

"Zack would say: 'Keep an open mind'," said one officer. "He would say he was not convinced the man who had sent the tape and the letters was responsible for the murders. If he was responsible, he said that would be a bonus, but he always stressed: 'For God's sake, keep an open mind'."

He wasn't the only one with concerns.

The linguistic experts, Stanley Ellis and Jack Windsor Lewis, had become convinced the police were chasing a super-hoaxer, not the killer.

They were sure that such a distinctive voice from such a small, concentrated location would have been identified within days.

If that person didn't have a cast iron alibi for the murders (as, of course, the murderer couldn't have) then he would have been arrested. After a while, they were sure the voice on the tape must have been spoken to by the police and, as they had not been arrested, must have an alibi. The voice was, therefore, a hoaxer and not the killer.

Desperate to alert the police to their mistake, and with an earlier 1,400-page report analysing the letters being sat on by West Yorkshire, Lewis went public.

In late 1979 his concerns were published in the *Yorkshire Post* under the headline: "Voice expert dismisses vital clue as just a red herring – Ripper tape made by super-hoaxer, says police adviser."

The police effectively ignored it.

Zackrisson also considered going public, but that would have been professional suicide, so instead he wrote a nine-page report entitled 'Commentary on the 'Ripper' Letters and tape' which he passed to his superiors at Northumbria Police.

It listed in forensic detail why Wearside Jack was a hoaxer and not the killer, but again was ignored.

It became official policy – a suspect could be discounted if they were not Blood Group B or have a North Eastern accent, a stance that was in the forefront of the minds of the two officers who went to speak to Peter Sutcliffe for the fifth time on July 29.

* * *

The Major Incident Room was by now so overwhelmed with paperwork it was at breaking point. There was a huge delay in new information being filed and a crippling inefficiency in old information being retrieved or cross-referenced.

So when Detective Constables Andrew Laptew and Graham Greenwood went to speak to Sutcliffe, they had no idea he had ever been spoken to before.

They had been tasked with interviewing him because his black Sunbeam Rapier had been spotted in three red light areas.

The action had actually been waiting to be picked up since February 23 of that year, five months previously, but such was the extent of the backlog that interviews like this were taking months to be conducted.

More than three years earlier, Laptew had been a keen young copper on the Task Force helping to search for clues after Sutcliffe's first victims were murdered in Leeds.

An enthusiastic young officer with a fascination for the process of detective work, Laptew, a former trainee Merchant Navy Officer, made sure he followed the normal routine when tasked with this interview – he checked the index card system to see if the person he and his colleague were about to see had been spoken to before. This was to be Sutcliffe's fifth interview, but they could find no mention of him. Such were the failings of the system that neither was there a card, in place of where his should be, stating that another officer had taken the cards out.

Despite this, Laptew and Greenwood were both struck by a sense of unease as they began the interview with the softly-spoken man who allowed himself to be talked over by his wife.

"They seemed an odd couple," said Laptew. "He was very quiet, she was quite vociferous. Usually when we went to an interview, as an icebreaker we'd tell the wife: 'Now's the chance to get rid of your husband'. You'd get a laugh, some reaction or other, and one bloke once threw me out of the house. There was always some reaction. But from those two, nothing. Not a bloody thing.

"It was like drawing teeth. It was, 'What do you do for a living?' 'I'm a driver.' 'Who do you work for?' 'Clark's at Shipley'. He was being as defensive as he could be without arousing suspicion. "

Sutcliffe later explained how he found it easy to evade the questioning because it was so routine.

"He never asked anything of importance really, he was just there to eliminate me from the crimes."

He added with a smile: "I was happy to help him."

In relation to the joke Laptew made to Sonia about getting rid of her husband and its failure to raise a smile, Sutcliffe, as if talking about the crimes of another man he was appalled by, said: "Laptew said we never laughed, well, why would we? Trying to be a wise guy. It was a serious matter."

As the man in front of him was responding willingly but blandly to his questions, Laptew was thinking about the Marilyn Moore photofit, which bore a striking resemblance.

Sonia went to make a pot of tea in the kitchen and the officers used the opportunity to ask Sutcliffe if he ever paid for sex. He denied it. He explained that his car had been seen in Bradford's red light area often because it was on his way to work. He said he had taken his wife to a nightclub in Leeds once which could have explained the sighting in Chapeltown, and he flatly denied ever being in Manchester.

He couldn't give specific alibis for the dates of the murders, but insisted that whenever he went out on a night it was always with his wife.

He handed over a letter to give them a sample of his handwriting and said he was happy for them to search his garage and also to provide a blood sample if necessary. The officers checked the garage but couldn't find any incriminating tools or any other evidence.

The two officers thanked Sutcliffe and his wife for their time and left the house. Their suspicions were so great that as they headed back to the station they debated whether they should have arrested Sutcliffe there and then on suspicion of murder.

But they knew that that would have resulted in a major bollocking from the higher-ups, who had given strict instructions to the rank and file to not arrest for the murders without first seeking authority to do so.

Laptew began making further checks, speaking to Sutcliffe's employers and checking any previous convictions. That produced a positive result, but as with so much of the inquiry, the poor record-keeping tripped him up.

"I sent off for Sutcliffe's previous convictions and got a slip of paper about three inches long, two inches wide from the National Criminal Records Office just saying: 'Going equipped for theft'.

"What it didn't say was Sutcliffe had been arrested in a garden with a hammer.

"Going equipped covers a multitude of sins. If that had come back 'Going equipped for theft with a hammer' I'd have been faster than shit through a goose knocking on his door and pulling him in. In fact, I wanted to pull him in, but we had instructions 'Do not under any circumstances pull any person in'."

Instead, he detailed his suspicions in a 600-word report which suggested that Sutcliffe be subjected to further questioning.

He delivered the report to the incident room and tried to press home the case for further action to Holland, but got short shrift in return.

"I pointed it all out, but Dick Holland said: 'Is he a Geordie?' I said: 'No, but he is a dead ringer for the photofit,' to which he replied, 'If anyone else mentions a photofit to me, they will be in uniform till the end of their service.' This was interspersed with numerous expletives.

"There were about 50 people in the incident room at that time and I felt so small I could have crawled under the crack in the door."

His report was filed with all the others and was never acted on. Holland would later say he couldn't remember any of this.

Despite his serious misgivings about Sutcliffe, there was nothing more Laptew could do. The inquiry was committed to the man on the tape being the killer and Sutcliffe had the wrong accent.

"Senior officers weren't gods," he said, "but they did advise God on policy. In other words, you didn't question them."

They weren't gods and they weren't indestructible. Oldfield had been driving himself too hard for years, sustained by whisky and an obsessive urge to catch a killer who was now publicly taunting him for failing to do so.

He had had a cough for months and was left breathless whenever he walked up the stairs. In July, he went to see a heart specialist, and a few days later his wife Margaret found him sitting on the edge of their bed early one morning, gripped by a terrible pain in his arm and an overwhelming sense of fear. He urged Margaret to ring the heart specialist and pour him a whisky, later convincing himself that the shock to the system triggered by the tot is what kept his weakened heart going and saved his life.

He was taken to hospital and spent the next six months recovering from three heart attacks.

When officers from Northumbria who were working on the Sunderland end of the inquiry got to hear the bad news, they had a whip round and bought him a bottle of whisky.

CHAPTER 19

DERANGED

The Mannville Arms in the 1970s summed up all the best qualities of Bradford. It welcomed all comers to create an eclectic mix of clientele who might not be expected to get along but for the most part did, including punks, rockers, bookish students and a loyal band of locals.

It was the kind of place that inspired great love and affection among regulars and which would, years after it was closed and converted into a convenience store, inspire sentimental blogs about a slice of time gone forever.

But that was in the future. In the late 1970s it was thriving and a popular destination for a host of different groups, including Barbara Leach – Babs to friends – and her flatmates.

The Mannville was situated at the corner of Great Horton Road and Southbrook Terrace in the heart of the city's student area. Babs lived a matter of yards away on Grove Terrace.

In September 1979 she was looking forward to the third and final year of her social sciences degree. She was a popular young woman who made friends easily. She loved animals – she had monthly subscriptions to the RSPCA and the Canine Defence League – and on weekends she would catch the bus to the nearby village of Tong to go horse riding.

On Saturday, September 1, 1979, as she was looking forward to a night out at the Mannville, she realised she had forgotten to send her dad a birthday card. She phoned home to apologise and during the conversation with her mother asked her to book an appointment at their local hairdresser in Kettering for the following week when she was due back home for a few days. When she arrived, she planned to give her dad his belated birthday card as well as his present, a mug with the inscription: 'Life is too short not to live it up a little'.

That evening, Babs and her flatmates had an enjoyable time in the Mannville. Babs was wearing a long-sleeved, beige cheesecloth shirt and a pair of jeans with the jocular patch reading 'Prime Rump' on one of the back pockets. It was a busy night, busy enough for no-one to give a second glance to the man with distinctive black hair and beard, who ordered a half and drank it slowly and quietly as his dark eyes took in the surrounding scene.

At one stage, those eyes alighted on the backside of a young, dark-haired woman and the "Prime Rump" patch.

"I seen her in a pub, walking around," Sutcliffe said later. "I was inside the pub, I'd bought myself half a pint. I noticed she had a badge on the back of her jeans which said – Prime Rump. What type of respectable person wears a badge on their jeans like that?"

He was well away from Bradford's red light area but in his sick, twisted mind, "Prime Rump" could only mean one thing.

"They say she was a college student, she maybe was, but that doesn't mean she wasn't trying to make extra money on the side, for books or whatever.

"I only had a half a pint, then left the pub and went outside to my car. I drove up a road taking a left, I remember I drove the wrong way down this one-way street. I parked up."

When Babs and her friends left the pub, they debated whether to head to one of Bradford's famous curry houses that were open until 2am. But it had started to rain and they'd had enough for tonight, so they went home instead. As they got to the junction with Grove Terrace, a few yards from safety, everyone did a left, apart from Babs who said she was going for a stroll.

It wasn't unusual, she often went for a little walk on her own at night to clear her head.

As she headed up the road, ignoring the soft drizzle now falling, she had the misfortune to pass Sutcliffe, who was still parked up in his brown Rover 3500 which he had become the proud owner of just a couple of months before.

"She was walking slowly, looking around, that's why I thought she was a prostitute," he said. "My urge to kill remained strong and was totally out of my control. I got out of the car."

He hadn't recognised Barbara from the pub and hadn't followed her. It was just a tragic coincidence that when she decided to go for a short stroll, she passed his car.

Barbara wasn't a sex worker and nothing in her behaviour suggested she was, but Sutcliffe would later insist that by now, his deranged mind had convinced itself that any woman alone at night was a prostitute, or so he would claim after his arrest.

"People think she wasn't a prostitute because she was a student, but a lot of them don't have much money, so she could've been on her way to find a punter to pay for books or whatever. Why else would she go in that direction away from where she lived, especially if it was raining?"

He checked all around and, despite it being a busy area of the city, he considered there was a low risk of being seen as he watched her walk up the street.

"There was hardly anyone around, plus I knew I was being protected, so I wasn't too bothered about that."

Clutching a hammer in one hand and the same sharpened screwdriver he had used to kill Josephine Whitaker, he attacked Babs following the by now sickeningly similar pattern.

The following morning her flatmates thought it odd she hadn't returned home as it wasn't like her to stay out all night without telling them.

By the late afternoon they were so worried they called the police. Officers began making inquiries and that evening called the Leach family home in Kettering as Barbara's parents David and Beryl were watching *The Onedin Line*.

The rest of the episode went unwatched as Mr and Mrs Leach began trying to comprehend what they were being told on the phone.

Her body was found at 3.55pm on Monday by a constable who was part of the group checking the filthy, overgrown yard behind 13 Ash Grove.

It was only later that Sutcliffe realised the woman he had killed was the same one he had seen in the Mannville.

Recalling that attack nearly 40 years later while in Frankland top security prison, Sutcliffe leant back in his chair in the visiting area and took a long, deep intake of breath before he launched into his memories, as a chilling smile spread across his face.

"They later said I'd dumped her like rubbish because I left her where they stored bins. It was also said she had a badge on her jeans saying 'Prime Rump'. It was the same girl I'd seen in the pub."

It was the same girl, and her fate at his hands was retold with the same sinister smile which would pass across his lips whenever he tried to justify his actions or when he felt that fate had played a part.

Sutcliffe never missed an opportunity to evade full, moral responsibility for what he had done and if he could blame something else such as fate, he would grab it with both hands. Always accompanied by that brief, telling smile.

A 100-strong team of officers was assembled and an intensive search launched of the crime scene and surrounding streets.

Detective Chief Superintendent Peter Gilrain, head of West Yorkshire's western area CID, echoed the language used following Jo Whittaker and Jayne MacDonald's murders when he told the press: "This girl was perfectly respectable, and I think that any female is in jeopardy until the attacker is caught."

Chief Constable Ronald Gregory revealed that the cost of the Ripper investigation had now passed the £2m mark, but he insisted his force was as determined as ever to achieve a successful outcome.

"The morale of the men is high because they are confident that eventually they will get this man," he insisted.

Demands had begun to be made to call in Scotland Yard to assist, but the very idea stung the proud West Yorkshire officers. As they pointed out more than once: "They haven't caught their own Ripper yet."

For his part, Gregory said: "I am affronted by talk of Scotland Yard being called in. I have never considered asking for help from Scotland Yard, and neither they nor the Home Office have suggested we need their help."

Officers spoke to 200 people, which gave rise to 34 potential new witnesses, but further questioning took them no closer to an arrest. The murder weapon was never found either because the killer had taken it with him and later discarded it.

"I threw it at Woolley Edge, the first service station down the M1," said Sutcliffe.

Barbara's murder brought all the horror flooding back for Wilf MacDonald, whose 16-year-old daughter Jayne had been murdered by the Ripper two years earlier, although the truth is that it was never far from his mind on any given day.

"The man is a monster," he said when he spoke to the press following Barbara's murder. "How many more innocent girls must suffer before he is caught?"

Wilf's never-ending battle against ill health had weakened him, but he still had some fight left in him.

"I may be a sick man, but I'd just like a few minutes with him. I remember to this day the night my daughter died. She looked like a film star when she went out. She kissed me and said 'I won't be late tonight, Dad'. The next time I saw her was after that evil monster had done his worst."

It was the following month that Barbara's heartbroken mother Beryl finally felt able to make her own appeal for help, directing it at anyone who might be close to the killer and harbour suspicions.

"It would be horrible to have to live with the possibility that you may have been able to prevent these needless killings and yet did nothing."

As she was making this appeal, Wilf MacDonald was finally giving up his fight.

He had never fully recovered his health and now, just over two years after his daughter was murdered, he died at the family home in Leeds aged 60 and was buried next to Jayne. His wife, Irene, was under no illusion as to the cause of death.

"He died of a broken heart," she said.

As tragedy after tragedy mounted, the police remained committed to searching for a man with a North East accent.

They made inquiries at hotels, B&Bs and guest houses in Bradford to check if any guests had been staying around the time of the murder with the right accent.

The 'I'm Jack' tape was still available to listen to for the public on the Post Office's dial-a-disc service, but since Barbara's death the numbers calling each day had doubled. The Post Office had to change the number and increase the number of lines so people weren't constantly getting the engaged tone.

Around 30,000 people a day were calling, with the total number who had called since the tape was first released reckoned to be more than one million.

The tape was famous all round the world, but especially in northern England where the words "I see you are still having no luck catching me" were branded into the public's consciousness.

The case permeated every aspect of life. Sunderland fans even sang sick songs at matches hailing the killer as one of their own, such as "One Jack the Ripper, there's only one Jack the Ripper" and "10,000 coppers and only one Yorkshire Ripper".

It was something that the real killer took great amusement – and comfort – from.

"The crowd were all shouting at the police 'Ripper 11 – Police nil', stuff like that, trying to get at the police and wind them up."

With the police and public convinced he was from the North East, it made Sutcliffe's continued freedom ever more secure and it was, he was certain, all thanks to the Lord.

"God was in charge," he said. "He misled the police several times and I just knew it was a miracle happening every time."

A huge PR campaign surrounding the tape and letters was launched on October 2. A Leeds-based advertising agency volunteered to run the campaign and was able to obtain the equivalent of £1million worth of free advertising space on 5,500 roadside billboards and in 300 newspapers ads across the country, as well as radio and television commercials.

Running alongside this increased publicity was a rising anger from the public, who were fast losing patience with the police and their inability to catch the killer.

Women, especially, were furious with the police's clumsy, old-fashioned attempts to keep them safe.

"Don't go out at night," was the message directed at women, whereas they took the view that the unofficial curfew should be directed at men not women.

The Bradford-based Women's Right to Self Defence group campaigned for women to be allowed to carry weapons to protect themselves and a week after Barbara died a protest march was held through the city with women carrying placards reading: "Men off the streets not women" and "Reclaim the night."

With fear and anger growing, an inspector in the incident room at Millgarth came across the paperwork from the fourth interview which had been conducted with Peter Sutcliffe, eleven months earlier.

This was the one *before* the Laptew interview, and had taken place because Holland was not happy with the outcome of the third interview.

Sutcliffe couldn't be positively alibied for any of the attacks other than by his mother and wife, and he had been flagged in connection with the £5 inquiry and Triple Area Sightings.

When the paperwork was found, it was decided to question Sutcliffe again and two more detectives were dispatched to speak to him. They were aware of the first four times he had been interviewed, but had no knowledge of the Laptew interview or the suspicions he and his colleague harboured about Sutcliffe.

When they called at the house the door was answered by Sonia who was by now exasperated at the repeated visits.

"Oh, not again," she said to them.

The officers, DC Tony Vickerman and a DC Eland, were, just like Laptew and Greenwood at the previous interview, uneasy. They considered Sutcliffe a slightly strange character, and the fact that he didn't have a positive alibi for any of the murders bothered them.

DC Vickerman had such a strong gut feeling that he even wrote in his report that Peter Sutcliffe could be the Yorkshire Ripper. It came to nothing. He had previously been eliminated and, of course, didn't have a Sunderland accent.

The paperwork from this interview was marked to be filed.

CHAPTER 20

ARRESTED

The start of a new decade was, to say the least, tumultuous. The 1980s began with 65 countries boycotting the Olympic Games in Moscow in protest at the Soviet invasion of Afghanistan the previous year, John Lennon was shot dead in New York and 40 people succumbed to a new disease called Acquired Immune Deficiency Syndrome (AIDS). A national steel strike rumbled on in Britain as unemployment soared past two million for the first time since 1935. It would keep going, contributing to a raft of social and economic problems that would come together in an orgy of violence and destruction. A host of inner city areas were about to go up in flames.

In Yorkshire, Peter and Sonia were also unsettled.

He loved his job as a long-distance lorry driver, it was what he had always wanted to do. But as he climbed into the cab of 'Wee Willie' each morning, he was starting to contemplate a radical change in his life. Should he walk away from it all to enable Sonia to follow her lifelong dream of running a pottery business?

"We had it all planned out to sell the house and buy this obsolete pub and change it into an arts and crafts place, a really nice pub we used to go in opposite a cinema on Legrams Lane, going up to Clayton where Sonia used to live," he said. "We were going to run that. I wasn't going to re-tax my car and insure it, I was going to trade it in for a big van that we could work with the pottery and the art stuff.

"It was a fairly modern building; they closed it down and it was for sale, so we were gonna buy it. We might have been doing great now if it hadn't have been for what not..."

'What not' was his offhand way of describing his ongoing campaign of murder. But a new hurdle now lay ahead in relation to his need for transport to both develop the business idea and trawl the night-time streets for victims – a drink drive arrest.

On June 25, 1980, officers who were conducting a covert observation in Manningham saw a brown Rover 3500 speed past them. They followed, but it was going so fast they were unable to pull it over and only caught up with it when the driver arrived home in Garden Lane.

He was breathalysed and found to be over the limit, the consequence of one drink too many when he had bumped into an old friend earlier in the evening.

"I met an old school friend, Mick Peart, and we went for a few drinks," he said. "He worked for the AA driving a yellow van, and he saw me getting out of the truck. I stopped off at Halfords to pick something up for the car, and he stopped and said: 'I thought it was you Pete, how are you doing?' I hadn't seen him since school days, so we went for a few pints. I got picked up and done for driving over the limit. I'd never been done for speeding or drink-driving before."

The two officers didn't just nick him for drink-driving. As was second nature for police in West Yorkshire who stopped anyone in a car after dark, they also grilled him about where he had been and what he had been up to.

They weren't happy with his answers and contacted the Ripper incident room to run his name, but were told he was in the clear. Wrong accent.

The outcome at court following his arrest on the drink-driving charge would be inevitable, as would the consequences at work. They couldn't keep on a driver who had lost his licence, however much he was one of their star employees, so he decided to pre-empt it. He would hand in his notice at Clark's so they could follow Sonia's dream of owning their own pottery and art place.

They would finance it by selling their house, which was now worth more than twice what they had paid for it. They put it on the market at £37,500 with their fingers crossed for £40,000.

"I knew I'd get a ban, so I wasn't planning on driving. I was giving my notice so we could sell the house and buy that big pub. Sonia would make pottery and sculptures and I would have done art work, which I'd always wanted to do if I had the time."

They were settled on their future career move, but more up in the air was their dream of having children. They confided in friends and family that Sonia was having tests at hospital to see if she could have children after those three miscarriages. If it was bad news, they planned to adopt two Vietnamese boat children, orphans who were among the two million people who fled the country in the years following the end of the Vietnam War in 1975 and who needed a home.

"I would have been a good dad… I'd have been really good to the kids if I'd had them."

In terms of that other issue in his life, the one for which the police kept coming to interview him, he could be forgiven for thinking he was now invincible. In quick succession over a period of three weeks he was interviewed three more times, yet still he remained at large.

The long-called-for development of bringing in Scotland Yard had also happened, after a fashion, but that didn't result in a breakthrough either.

It came about in the autumn of 1979 when the pressure had become impossible to resist.

As the Home Secretary Willie Whitelaw was preparing to visit the incident room to be updated on the progress of the investigation, West Yorkshire's Chief Constable, Ronald Gregory, travelled the other way for a meeting with Sir David McNee, the Metropolitan Police Commissioner.

Following this, it was agreed that one of the Met's most senior and experienced officers, Commander Jim Nevill, would travel to Yorkshire to conduct a review.

It was a halfway house. Gregory had agreed to a fresh pair of eyes checking things over to ensure his own war-weary detectives hadn't missed anything obvious, but he hadn't ceded any operational ground.

While this review was taking place in Yorkshire, the £5 note investigation was being reactivated in Manchester. Ridgway had never lost faith in this line of inquiry and the Bank of England offered to replicate the exact printing run from the 1977 batch of notes, which included the Jordan fiver. Using fakes, they produced exactly the same number of notes with identical serial numbers in the correct order. Ridgway's team were then able to reconstruct how the money had been issued by the Midland Bank in Shipley.

It was a long, slow process but by reconstructing each banking day over a period of months they were able to confidently say that the note had gone to one of, not 34 firms as originally thought, but 11. And not 5,943 potential recipients, but 240.

T & WH Clark was on the list, contributing 49 workers to the list of 240, which was increased to 241 when Oldfield insisted that a man he had long felt was a red-hot suspect, but who was in fact totally innocent, be added. Peter Sutcliffe was employee number 44 at Clark's, number 76 on the total list.

It was a huge step forward. Checking movements and alibis of nearly 6,000 men was a massive task, but less than 250 was something else altogether. They could each be closely scrutinised to the extent that any gap in their stories would hopefully become apparent.

Once again, a number of Ridgway's officers headed over the M62 to link up with colleagues from West Yorkshire to work through the list. Before the interviews began, the card index was checked to see if any had featured in the inquiry before and should, therefore, be the focus of these fresh interviews, but one of the finest pieces of detective work in the entire investigation was about to run into its greatest weakness.

The incident room wasn't just creaking under the weight of paperwork in a metaphorical sense. It also presented literal challenges. Structural engineers had to be brought in to strengthen the floors at the incident room over concerns that the vast amount of files meant they were in danger of collapse.

The failings were extensive and systemic, but many could have been avoided or at least reduced if the force management had allocated the necessary resources. At the height of the biggest murder investigation the country had ever known, only one typist was based in the incident room. Not a single telephonist was employed to take calls from the public, with the workload instead being borne by police officers, including the inspector who was in charge of the incident room. Police cadets performed important filing and admin tasks for which they were not trained.

These failings meant that out of the list of 241 men, the system showed that only seven had had previous dealings with the investigation, whereas the true number was 25. The other 18 were lost in the system.

By the time that officers were preparing to interview the latest list of possible suspects, there were almost a quarter of a million names in the index system with cards. It was inevitable that cards would go missing, but unforgivable.

Ridgway insisted that the 241 must not be eliminated on the basis of hand-writing or accent, they had to have a verifiable alibi to be cleared, and that meant verified by someone other than their wife or mother.

Six days later, on Sunday, January 13, 1980, Sutcliffe was interviewed at his home in relation to this fresh £5 note inquiry – the seventh time he had been spoken to in relation to the Ripper attacks.

Detective Sergeant Boot and Detective Constable Bell called at his house at 1.25pm, but were still hamstrung by the failing index card system. They were aware of Sutcliffe's interview in relation to the initial banknote checks, but none of the other interviews. Sonia opened the door to them wearing a nightie and dressing gown and let them in, calling her husband down from upstairs. Sutcliffe was asked about his movements around the time that Barbara Leach was murdered the previous September. He was unable to give a firm alibi, but did mention that he had previously provided a handwriting sample, which was a surprise to the officers who weren't aware of that information.

They checked his boots and tools in the garage and questioned him about his work. One of the officers wrote in his notebook that Sutcliffe was a "strange runner", but neither came away with the same strength of suspicion as Andrew Laptew had done.

Back at the incident room, they checked the system and this time found three separate cards detailing his various interviews. They referred to more extensive paperwork relating to him, but most of that couldn't be located.

It was also noted that a Ford Corsair, which Sutcliffe had previously owned, may have been involved in the Millward attack. It clearly wasn't satisfactory and an inspector ordered yet another interview.

Seventeen days later, Detective Sergeant McAlister and Detective Constable McCrone went to speak to Sutcliffe, the first interview which had taken place away from his home.

The officers caught up with him at Kirkstall Forge Engineering works in Leeds, one of Clark's main contractors, where Sutcliffe would call in each day and load up with whatever items would need delivering.

"I went there every morning unless I was away on overnights. I picked up axles and gearboxes and took them all over the country, that's where Clark's were mainly contracted. All our trucks went there."

As well as checking movements on certain dates, they wanted to question him about his boots. They had a photograph with them showing the tread left at various murder scenes that they wanted to compare with boots that potential suspects owned, but appeared to miss an open goal with Sutcliffe.

"I had the same wellingtons on that they had on the photograph. They showed me a picture of the tread and I had them on and climbed into the cab. They could see them, but they didn't say anything."

One reason for the officers' lack of interest in Sutcliffe may well have been that everyone still thought they were looking for a suspect with a Wearside accent.

The interview lasted just 30 minutes, during which time they also searched the cab of his lorry. When their report – which mistakenly said his car and home had also been searched – was delivered back to the incident room, an inspector decided the interview hadn't been anywhere near as fulsome as it should have been and ordered another one. That took place on February 7 – the third in the space of 25 days – at Clark's yard, when Sutcliffe repeated his answers from all his previous interviews.

Nothing new or hugely suspicious leapt out, although the nagging doubts remained because he couldn't be positively alibied for any of the attacks.

The report from this interview – the final one before his arrest – stated that if there was another murder, then he should be interviewed all over again.

It was accepted by the incident room inspector and, feeling there was nowhere else to go with this particular entry on the list of 241 men, he recommended he be filed. Ridgway agreed.

Sutcliffe had got away with it again, but he sensed things were closing in. Nine interviews. How long before they finally stumbled across a piece of evidence that led to his arrest?

He had to stay one step ahead. To his mind, that meant changing tack. He needed a new method of murder.

CHAPTER 21

LUCKY ESCAPE

The Yorkshire Ripper. Peter Sutcliffe hated the name by which he was now known around the world, for a number of reasons.

For a start, he reckoned it was inaccurate.

"I hate that title because it didn't apply. It was just a fantasy nickname. I haven't ripped anybody, it's a misnomer that name."

He also objected to the way it linked him to his 19th century namesake. Jack the Ripper had also killed women by selecting them at random on the street and inflicting horrific injuries, just as Sutcliffe had done. But the modern-day Ripper didn't like the comparisons.

"Making people think I was linked to the similar things that 1888 Jack did. I never done that sort of thing, I haven't ripped anybody.

"They gave me that nickname so that they could make a big fuss of it every time. Keep it in the public eye because of the original person in 1888. They're still on about that aren't they and it happened in 1888. It's ridiculous, only because of the nickname.

"He did live up to his nickname, but I didn't. I don't deserve that name."

He accused the media of inventing it just to get their readers and viewers interested, as if his crimes would not have attracted widespread attention without it.

"The press gave me that nickname and that is what triggers it all. People's imaginations go wild and nothing like that happened, it's just stupid.

"It's a sick obsession they've got with me, it only arises because of that false nickname they gave me 'The Yorkshire Ripper'.

"It's just to grab a headline, that's all.

"They try and play with people's imaginations to make them imagine things worse than they are."

Later, he would accuse the press of perpetuating it as part of a wider conspiracy to foil his dreams of being released.

"It's only there to catch the public's attention. That's the press for you. They stick labels on people just to make life difficult and it's bad enough as it is. They don't leave you to get on with you doing your time."

He hated the name so much that it was one of the many things swirling around his mind through 1980. But how to get people to stop using it?

By August of that year, it was almost 12 months since his last attack, the murder of Barbara Leach in Bradford the previous September. This was the longest fallow period since the first attack of the series in 1975, but it also heralded the start of the bloodiest period, with the next four attacks occurring at the rate of just over one every three weeks.

Civil servant Marguerite Walls was a quiet and unassuming woman who lived a simple life. She worked hard at her job at the Department of Education and Science office in Richardshaw Lane, Pudsey, on the western edge of Leeds, not far from Bradford, where she was well-liked and respected by colleagues and bosses alike. Marguerite, known as Margo, was a private woman who didn't like to share, preferring to get on with her work rather than engaging in office gossip. It wasn't unusual for her to stay back late, as she felt she was more productive in the quiet solitude of an empty office.

Most days she walked to work from her detached stone-built house. She liked walking. She was a keen hill walker and was looking forward to a holiday in the Lake District.

She was 47 years old, single and lived alone and on Wednesday, August 18, 1980, she worked later than usual to make sure everything was up-to-date ahead of her ten-day break, which was starting the following day.

She finished around 10pm, packed up her things, collected her blue mackintosh coat and headed out of the office for the last time.

Despite it being the height of summer, it was windy outside, but that didn't bother Margo the fell walker. She put her head down and braced herself for the mile walk home.

Women were still cautious despite it being nearly a year since the last attack, but in an area like Farsley, pleasant and respectable and a world away from the red light areas, they could be forgiven for thinking the risk was even less. So Margo walked home alone, but made sure she stuck to the well-lit main road.

Peter Sutcliffe was behind the wheel of his Rover and was "on my way Leeds with a view to killing a prostitute", when he spotted her walking on New Street.

He pulled over, killed the engine and grabbed a hammer and a length of rope – but not a knife or sharpened screwdriver. He followed Margo for a short distance, catching up with her as she walked past the stone pillared entrance to a large home set in its own grounds called Claremont House.

He hit Margo over the back of the head with the hammer and as soon as she slumped to the ground dragged her down the driveway, over a rockery and into a wooded area of the garden. He looped a length of rope around her neck and began strangling her. But Margo was still conscious and fought back.

She hit out at him with clenched fists as she desperately fought for her life. Sutcliffe was alarmed at how difficult this new method of murder was proving to be, and his strong hands gripped the rope tighter. Years of bodybuilding and driving an HGV had given him an upper body strength which was no match for a middle-aged, desk-bound woman.

He stripped her naked apart from her fawn coloured tights. A post-mortem would later find three small scratches to her vagina, leading police to conclude that he interfered with her in some way, possibly with his fingers.

He made tentative efforts to hide the body using Margo's tartan-lined mackintosh coat and some grass clippings and straw before fleeing the scene.

After five years and 18 attacks, why had he fundamentally changed the method of attack, substituting a ligature for a stabbing implement?

The reasons were varied and complex.

He said that one was down to his dislike of that nickname. As unlikely as it sounds, he thought that by killing someone without inflicting massive injuries with a sharp weapon, it might result in the media and the public not using it as much.

"I hated that name from the start, The Yorkshire Ripper. I thought, if I done it that way, killing her that way with a rope, they'd stop using it."

He also offered up a more practical reason – a lack of time to prepare when he saw her on the street.

"With her, I wasn't prepared. I didn't have a knife or anything sharp. I hit her on the head, knocking her out as I'd done with them all, that way they didn't suffer, they felt nothing afterwards, I done that with them all, every one of them."

Yet another reason was his hope that a different method of attack would put police off the scent. If he changed his approach, detectives might think another killer was at large, muddying the waters for the entire Ripper investigation.

There was also a fourth, sickening reason for strangling instead of stabbing. After all this time, he was finding his traditional method of attack increasingly hard to stomach.

"I thought it would be easier, quicker to kill that way, strangulation, but it wasn't, it was horrible, slow. [Stabbing] can be very quick and effective... but it was traumatic having to stab them, I thought it might be better to just strangle them, but it wasn't. [It took] about three minutes or so [to strangle her] she was unconscious at the time, so she didn't suffer, they were all knocked unconscious, that's why whenever the survivors have spoken about the attacks, they say they knew nothing until they woke up in hospital."

His suggestion that Margo was unconscious and therefore didn't suffer is contradicted by the defensive injuries to her hands. The way he persuaded himself that his victims somehow didn't suffer is another example of his refusal to take responsibility for his actions, as well as an attempt to hide the true horror of them from himself. When it was pointed out to him that they suffered terribly and his survivors also carried a terrible physical and mental toll for the rest of their lives, all he could offer was: "They weren't meant to have survived."

* * *

Margo was found the next morning by gardeners arriving to work at the property.

Her murder gave rise to immediate speculation that after all this time the Ripper had struck again, but one of the reasons for using a different style of attack appeared to have succeeded. Within 48 hours, Detective Chief Superintendent Jim Hobson publicly ruled out any connection to the Yorkshire Ripper.

* * *

Just over a month later, on September 24, 1980, a 34-year-old Singaporean doctor called Upadhya Bandara, was walking through Headingley, in Leeds, after a night with friends. She was in the city on a World Health Organisation scholarship, studying for a health services postgraduate at Leeds University.

She walked past the Arndale shopping centre and did a right past the Skyrack pub on her way to her digs at St Michael's villas.

It was 11pm, but this was Headingley, not Chapeltown, the area of the city popular with students which was considered safe in the same way that Farsley, where Margo was killed, was.

When Upadhya heard footsteps behind her, she stepped to one side to let whoever was behind her pass. She caught a glimpse of a beard, then felt a rope around her neck and could remember no more.

She didn't realise it as she slumped to the ground, but the cause of her sudden loss of consciousness was not the rope around her neck, but a single hammer blow to the back of her head.

As with Margo's attack, police kept the details of the rope from the public as their private fears began to grow that a second serial killer could now be on the loose.

Upadhya recovered and was able to help police stage a reconstruction before she returned to Singapore.

Just as with so many other attacks, Sutcliffe had a close escape during the assault on Upadhya.

As he was trying to strangle the life out of her, a car drove past and then a short time later a police car also passed by.

By this time Sutcliffe had fled, but it wasn't the closest shave. That was yet to come.

* * *

Fireworks exploded above Huddersfield, illuminating the dark November sky. Bonfire Night, 1980. Peter and Sonia had been due to go to a party, but he cancelled at the last minute, phoning home to say he was on a long run for work. It was a lie. He clocked off at Clark's at his usual 5pm and drove to Huddersfield.

At 39 Willwood Avenue, Theresa Sykes and her boyfriend Jimmy Furey, a mill worker, didn't have much time this year for the fireworks as they had a little one to think about.

Theresa was just 16 and had left school a few months ago, but had already moved in with Jimmy and all of their focus was now on five-month-old Anthony.

At 7.30pm they turned on *Coronation Street,* but before it had finished they realised they were out of cigarettes. Theresa pulled on her coat and popped out to go and buy some from the Purewal convenience store next to the Bay Horse pub down on the roundabout.

To get there, she had to walk down a path that ran alongside the playing fields opposite their house. The fields were in darkness, but Theresa was 16 and invincible, too young to harbour the same worries about the Ripper that the adults did.

After buying the cigarettes she came back along the dimly lit path, watched by Peter Sutcliffe, who needed only the mildest trigger to convince himself that a woman alone at night was a prostitute.

"In this state of mind, I think all girls are pros," he said later.

And what made him so sure with Theresa?

"She was wearing a split skirt."

There were only a couple of street lights along the path, and there were shadows everywhere.

"It was just before I got to the lamppost and once I got under the light that I looked around and he was behind me," said Theresa.

The shock of a man appearing out of the dark gave her a fright and as she stared into those dark eyes, framed by thick black hair and beard, she froze.

"I looked at him and he looked at me, it was a couple of seconds and he walked off down the path. I thought he had gone."

Relieved, and just yards from home, she pressed on, but within seconds the relief vanished as a sixth sense told her the man was still close by.

"I still got the feeling there was something behind me. I carried on walking and got past the second light and noticed the shadow on the floor."

She froze for a second time.

"I couldn't run. I didn't do half the things you think you can do. I couldn't do it.

"So I grabbed hold of the gate and that's when he hit me."

Sutcliffe had brought a hammer down on the back of her head, but it didn't result in the usual, immediate unconsciousness. Instead, it launched an almighty commotion.

Theresa's scream sliced through the night, her next-door neighbour came out and rushed over to see what was happening. Jimmy was looking out of the bedroom window. He sprinted down the path, shouting at the top of his voice as the figure took off into the darkness.

"He shouted something out from the window," remembered Sutcliffe. "He saw me attack her through the bedroom window. He shouted something out, but it was dark.

"I thought 'I'll scarper' and I went down this snicket, and he went down the snicket and went across the road. It was lucky he didn't catch up with me."

Jimmy kept searching the nearby streets, looking in gardens and checking the shadows, determined to find the man, but he was probably lucky that he didn't come across him.

Sutcliffe, hiding in those shadows, was still driven by a deep, unshakeable belief that he was on a mission that was yet to be completed. The one thing he couldn't let happen, he told himself as he clutched the hammer, was to be apprehended either by the police or an interfering member of the public.

If Jimmy had found him, would this finally be the time that his weird run of luck ran out?

"Not really, because if he'd caught up with me, I'd have attacked him, he wouldn't have stood a chance as I had a hammer. I couldn't let him identify me. I was tooled up."

As Jimmy was searching the streets, Theresa was being taken inside by her neighbour, still unaware of the full extent of her injuries.

"I didn't feel any pain, but I was soaked in blood from head to toe," she said. "I had no idea how badly I had been hurt."

A dog handler was brought in to repeat the search that Jimmy had already done of the area, but by then the attacker had vanished.

By the morning, a squad of 60 police officers had been assembled and eight-strong teams dressed in protective forensic clothing crawled along all the nearby roads to conduct a fingertip search for clues. Nothing was found.

Public appeals for information were made and a description of the attacker was issued – 5ft 8in or 5ft 9in tall and wearing an overcoat. But no mention of a beard.

Any possible connection with all those other attacks was dismissed as detectives insisted they were looking for a local man, not the Ripper.

Within two weeks of the attack, the number of officers working on the case had been halved as the investigation drifted away.

Theresa underwent emergency surgery and at first appeared to recover well, but she suffered a relapse and had to be taken back into hospital.

By the New Year, she was struggling to cope and moved back in to live with her parents. Her physical wounds slowly healed, but the psychological scars were harder to shake off and she and Jimmy, who had planned to marry, split up.

She still didn't feel safe, especially at night, and when she went to bed she would pull the wardrobe across her door. There was always a knife under the pillow.

Dick Holland, who lived just a mile and a half away from Theresa and whose own daughter lived around the corner from her, was left to rue just how close they had come to catching the Ripper.

"It is frustrating every time you get near a criminal and just miss them," he said. "All the luck ran on his side right up until when he was finally caught, that was the first time the cards fell our way."

But that was still two months away, and the mission wasn't over yet.

CHAPTER 22

BACKLASH

The number one bus has always been a welcome sight for students in Leeds. All day and into the night it rumbles up and down the spine of student life connecting the city centre with the campuses, the under-graduate heartlands of Hyde Park and Headingley and all the way up to Bodington, the huge halls of residence on the northern edge of the city, just beyond the outer ring road of doubles, which closed in 2013.

At 9.13pm on Monday, November 17, 1980, Jacqueline Hill, a 20-year-old modern languages student, climbed aboard the number one at a stop in Cookridge Street in the city centre.

She had just come out of a seminar about becoming a proba-tion officer, the career she had set her mind on once she graduated next summer.

Jacqueline was a caring young woman who had been a Sunday School teacher, volunteered at a camp for disadvantaged children and completed her Duke of Edinburgh Award. Her long-term boyfriend Ian Tanfield, 22, who also came from her home town of Middlesbrough, was at the start of a career with the RAF, and they were planning to announce their engagement on her 21st birthday the following May.

As her bus neared the university where the gleaming white tower of the Parkinson building stood out against the black winter skies, Peter Sutcliffe was two miles up the road in Headingley, walking back to his car behind the Kentucky Fried Chicken.

He had earlier called Sonia to say he was on a long run to Gloucester. Just as with the lead-up to the attack on Theresa Sykes, it was a lie and in reality he had clocked off at 7.03pm and driven to Leeds, where he was now climbing back into his Rover to begin eating the meal he had just bought.

The bus approached Headingley, passing the Skyrack pub on the left and the Original Oak on the right.

Jacqueline got ready to alight as Sutcliffe was finishing his meal.

He wiped his fingers, started his engine and drove back out into the centre of Headingley. The number one bus pulled up and Jacqueline got off along with five other passengers, making sure she had her fluffy wool scarf, Fair-isle mittens and cream raffia handbag with her as she went.

It was 9.23pm. The time when he first saw her.

She crossed over the main road and walked towards the Arndale Centre, ready to turn left into Alma Road which would take her up to Lupton where she shared a flat with four other women students.

Sutcliffe drove into the street and parked up ahead of her, waiting until she walked past before he quietly got out with a hammer and screwdriver in his pocket. She was just 80 yards from her front door when he attacked her. He struck her from behind and she slumped to the ground making a groaning noise, her cream raffia handbag dropping from her grasp.

He dragged her into the scrubland under the ramp which takes vehicles up to the Arndale's car park and hit her again until she fell silent, but her eyes remained open as her body went into shock, the adrenaline racing as she desperately clung to life.

He pulled off most of her clothes and stabbed her in the chest until he thought she was dead, but when he glanced up, he was horrified to see her eyelids open.

"Due to the way my mind was at the time... paranoia... I thought she was looking at me in an accusing way," he said. "So I stabbed her in the eye, but she was already dead. Yet just before

I stabbed her in the eye, her eye closed, it must have been a nerve or something."

Sutcliffe ran back to his car and drove away.

As he was making his escape, an Iranian student, Amir Hussain, was walking up Alma Road when he spotted a cream raffia handbag on the pavement.

He took it back to Lupton, where he also lived. He couldn't find a staff member to hand it to, so he took it to his own flat in H Block, which he shared with four male students.

They discussed it briefly and, not knowing what else to do with it, left it on the kitchen table until the morning when they planned to hand it in.

But one of the flatmates was a 49-year-old mature student called Tony Gosden who was a former chief inspector in the Hong Kong police. He wasn't happy about the handbag, and before he went to bed he had a closer look and noticed three small splatters of blood. It was also apparent that nothing had been stolen from the bag – a Barclaycard with the name Jacqueline Hill was still inside it.

Tony knew his stuff – "In an inquiry like this, the first few minutes are vital. The longer you wait, the colder the trail gets" – and he alerted other flatmates. One of them, Paul Sampson, called 999 at 12.03am and two uniformed constables were sent to check it out. A sergeant back at the police station glanced at the message form on which the call details had been written – "Found handbag covered in blood" – and remarked: "This will be the Ripper's 13th victim" before continuing with whatever he was doing.

The two officers arrived at Lupton at 12.12am, but right from the off the students felt they were disinterested.

"I kept saying: 'What about the blood?' And I kept thinking that somewhere there might be a young girl bleeding but breathing," said Paul.

One of the officers tried but failed to find a member of staff. They completed a lost property form, had a cup of coffee and went to search the area near to where the bag was found. Their search of the opposite side of the road to where Jacqueline lay lasted approximately four minutes before they received a call about a burglary and left.

A furious row would later erupt around this curtailed search and whether it presented a missed opportunity to save Jacqueline's life, although when asked if he thought she might still be alive, Sutcliffe said matter-of-factly: "No, I don't think so."

Their subsequent incident report failed to mention the blood staining on the bag, so it was logged as a lost property matter.

The following morning at ten minutes past ten, as the cold, grey day dragged itself past a late dawn, a manager of one of the shops in the Arndale centre walked up the car park ramp and glanced over the edge to the scrubland below where he saw a woman lying on her back, 30 yards from where Amir had found the bag.

Initially, the police thought a second maniac was on the loose, the same one who had attacked Dr Bandara and Margo Walls.

The officer in charge of Jacqueline's investigation, Detective Superintendent Alf Finlay, said at the first press conference: "There is no evidence to link this death with the so-called Yorkshire Ripper."

Around the same time, Prof Gee was coming to a wholly different conclusion.

During the post-mortem, he discovered the tell-tale, crescent-shaped wounds to the head and a stab wound to the chest, which quickly persuaded the police to change their minds.

"No woman is safe while he is at large," said George Oldfield, who was by now back at work after his lengthy convalescence following his heart attack and who was delivering a depressingly familiar warning to the public.

Unable to give up on the personal approach which had come to seriously hamper the inquiry, Oldfield added: "He is an intelligent individual and very crafty, and I have never underestimated him."

The reaction from the public was immediate, intense and furious.

There had been student marches and calls for action following Barbara's murder in Bradford, but the anger now stepped up a level.

A campaign group called Women Against Violence Against Women organised a march in Leeds on the weekend after Jacqueline was murdered. Around 500 protestors marched through the city centre where a group of around 70 – described as "militant feminists" in a police memo – stormed the Odeon cinema where the controversial, erotically-charged thriller *Dressed to Kill,* starring Michael Caine, was playing. They threw red paint over the screen in protest at what they saw as its exploitative tone.

Up to 50 police officers struggled to keep control as the marchers moved towards the university and chanted outside the BBC studios. They tried to invade a pub and the university refectory where Iron Maiden were playing and banged on car windows demanding to know of male drivers: "Where were you on Monday night?"

Jacqueline's boyfriend was another struggling to contain his anger.

"I am shattered, angry and sick. It makes me want to hit someone," said Ian.

Leeds was a city gripped by fear. Women were terrified of walking the streets alone, boyfriends and husbands insisted on accompanying their wives and girlfriends if they went anywhere at night, and areas began to resemble ghost towns as female customers abandoned pubs and restaurants. If they did go out, they were invariably armed with rape alarms.

There were fresh demands to call in Scotland Yard, but Chief Constable Ronald Gregory still refused to bow to the pressure.

He did, though, agree to the changes at the top of the investigation which had been advised by Lawrence Byford, Her Majesty's Inspector of Constabulary, following a two-day visit to the force to assess the progress of the inquiry. The most notable was the decision to relieve George Oldfield of his command of the Ripper Inquiry. He was five years in, tired and recovering from a major heart attack. He was considered to have run out of steam.

Privately, Byford considered one of the biggest challenges facing the inquiry had been Oldfield himself, with his "lack of personality and pedestrian manner" becoming more marked as it dragged on.

Det Chief Supt Jim Hobson was promoted to replace him and given the temporary rank of Assistant Chief Constable.

Another change, again on Mr Byford's suggestion, was the introduction of a hand-picked "Super Squad" of four senior officers considered to be among the best police minds in the country.

They would provide a critical oversight of the investigation and suggest improvements and were assisted by a fifth team member, the Director of the Home Office Central Research Establishment at Aldermaston, after Byford insisted that the "highest scientific expertise" was needed.

Their work laid bare just how out of control the investigation had become. One glaring example being that they were unable to even ascertain something as simple as how many photofits had been produced of potential suspects and which of these had been released to the public.

Concerns about West Yorkshire's inability to solve the case had by now reached the highest levels. Exactly a week after Jacqueline's body was found, the Prime Minister, Margaret Thatcher, raised the case during a meeting with the Home Secretary, Willie Whitelaw, in the presence of the Cabinet Secretary and Permanent Secretary of the Home Office.

She was furious the killer remained at large. She pointed out that the police had "totally failed" to stop the murders, which "constitute the most appalling kind of violence against women".

Thatcher, whose own daughter Carol was 27 at the time, made it clear that this was more than just a criminal investigation, it had become a matter of public confidence in the police service.

"So vexed was the Prime Minister by yet another murder … [she] announced her intention of going to Leeds that weekend to take personal charge of the investigation. Nobody but her, she thought, really cared about the fate of these wretched women. Certainly no man could care enough," said her biographer Hugo Young.

Peter Sutcliffe wasn't a fan of the Iron Lady even before he got to hear about her wanting to help the efforts to arrest him.

"She made it hard for the unions, for the working man. All the working man has got is his union, to back them up, because it's the only defence they've got, and she destroyed the unions.

"She interfered and asked for the Met to come up and help the Yorkshire detectives. She couldn't have done any more, they did everything possible and they made so many mistakes."

Whitelaw couldn't fail to agree with Thatcher, but he gently reminded her that the Chief Constable was operationally independent. She couldn't order him to do anything. All they could do was make suggestions, which is what Mr Byford had spent the last few days doing.

While Britain's biggest ever manhunt was becoming intensely political, the mother of the latest victim cared about only one thing.

"I want to ask everyone, not just in Leeds, but all over the country to help us find the person who killed my daughter," said Doreen Hill.

The two officers' failure to fully investigate the discovery of Jacqueline's blood-stained handbag on the night of the attack led to bitter criticism of the West Yorkshire force. The public was fast losing confidence in the force's ability to protect them.

The officers were censured at an internal disciplinary investigation – police-speak for a slap on the wrist – and the sergeant who made the comment about it being the Ripper's 13th victim was also admonished for failing to act further on his suspicions.

The constables expressed sincere regret at their failure to conduct a proper search and the disciplinary process concluded that had they done so, they would have almost certainly found

Jacqueline. The injuries she had suffered were so severe she would likely have been dead by the time they started their brief, flawed search. But it is impossible to know for certain.

A week after Peter Sutcliffe had murdered his 13th victim, his old friend Trevor Birdsall finally decided to act and wrote an anonymous letter to the police detailing his suspicions that Sutcliffe might be the Ripper.

He had long harboured these suspicions but, of course, for years now everyone knew that the Ripper had a Wearside accent.

What pushed him on to act was a newspaper report about the latest murder in Headingley, which included the description of a car police wanted to trace. He was struck by how closely it tallied with Sutcliffe's dark brown Rover 3500, the car his old mate had given him a lift in not long ago when they had met up for the first time in a while.

"I parked up outside my house on Garden Lane in my Rover," remembered Sutcliffe. "He pulled up right behind me in his car. He started talking and asking me things, as if he was trying to confirm his suspicions of me."

Birdsall's letter was given priority level number one, the highest level, and an action form was filled in for Sutcliffe to be interviewed.

Thanks to the overloaded system, the form sat in a wire tray and was never acted upon. It was never even looked at again until after Sutcliffe's arrest.

Unaware of this problem, but concerned that his letter wouldn't be enough to spur the police into action, Birdsall and his girlfriend called into the main police station in Bradford at 10.10pm on Wednesday, November 26.

Among other things, he told an officer of the incident back in August 1975 when he and Sutcliffe were on a night out in Halifax and his friend had vanished for a short time (the night he attacked Olive Smelt).

The report of this interview was filed into the system – and was never found again, even after Sutcliffe's arrest.

Birdsall later convinced himself that his approach to the police had persuaded them to launch a covert surveillance operation, tracking Sutcliffe's every move until the moment was right to pounce.

The truth of how the long sequence of murders was brought to an end is far more mundane and routine.

CHAPTER 23

CONFESSION

On the evening of Friday, January 2, two uniformed officers headed out of Hammerton Road police station in Sheffield on a 10-6 night shift.

Sgt Bob Ring and PC Robert Hydes were both married fathers of two. Ring was 47 and had been a police officer in Sheffield for 26 years, joining up after completing his National Service as a signalman with the army in Hong Kong.

Hydes, 31, was a later starter. His first career was, like many others in Steel City, in engineering. He made machine tools for the aircraft and automotive industries before switching careers because he felt the police offered better long-term prospects.

He joined in February 1980, just ten months before this latest night shift with his more experienced colleague, having spent the previous month on attachment to CID to learn the plainclothes ropes. His stint there included a shift in the force intelligence unit, where he was able to read the file on the Yorkshire Ripper.

At 10.20pm, following the traditional start of shift briefing, he was behind the wheel of a patrol car as he and Ring headed out into the night. The city was still recovering from New Year's Eve just two nights before. Surely this would be a quiet one.

* * *

At 4pm that day, Peter Sutcliffe walked out of his house telling Sonia he was off to sort out his sister Jane's Mini, the sporty little red number that Sutcliffe himself used to own before she bought it off him.

He delivered it to her on November 9, four days after attacking Theresa Sykes, but it broke down on her first long journey and Peter had fixed it for her.

Now, two days after New Year's Eve, he told Sonia it had broken down again. But instead of heading towards Bingley to see Jane and her erratic car, he was heading south, towards Sheffield.

* * *

Sgt Ring recognised that part of his role, sitting alongside an inexperienced colleague, was a mentoring one. It was important for Hydes to gain experience in all aspects of the job, so he asked him if he had ever compiled the necessary paperwork to prosecute a prostitute for soliciting.

"No," replied Hydes.

"Well, let's go and find one," said Ring.

* * *

A few days earlier, Sutcliffe's tax disc on his Rover had run out.

"My insurance was running out at the same time," he said. "I wasn't going to re-tax my car and insure it, I was going to trade it in for a big van that we could work with the pottery and the art stuff."

Refusing to shell out to tax a car he was about to trade in, he drove to a scrapyard at Mirfield, near Dewsbury, where he found a number plate with the registration HVY 679N that had fallen off a Skoda. The other one of the pair was still attached to the car, but he quickly removed it and drove home, where he used black tape to attach it to his own car, covering the genuine registration of FHY 400K.

"In those days, the plates had a black rim around the edge, so it looked okay. I went to work with them on."

Now, on January 2, he was driving his Rover with the false plates in place through Bradford. When he got to the M606, the short motorway which links the city to the M62, he would later tell police that he had spotted a couple of hitch-hikers.

"I gave three people a lift to Rotherham and Sheffield from Bradford. They offered me £10 to take them home, so I did," he said.

As the clock ticked around towards 10pm and now on his own, he drove through the dark, Sheffield streets in the direction of Havelock Square. Just like Chapeltown in Leeds and Manningham in Bradford, it was a formerly grand area which had hit hard times. It became known as an area of high unemployment, drug abuse and crime and, by January 1981, as the place to pick up one of the city's street prostitutes.

Sutcliffe pulled over to the kerb and had a brief discussion with a 19-year-old called Denise. She looked into his dark eyes as she told him the price. There was something about those eyes she didn't like, and she made her excuses.

* * *

Sgt Ring and PC Hydes drove through the streets to Havelock Square, keeping an eye out. There were no obvious targets to allow the rookie cop to make his first soliciting bust, so his sergeant suggested they head to one of the spots where the women take their punters, such as Melbourne Avenue, which sits above the fee-paying Sheffield High School for Girls.

It's a public road which feels private. Grand mansions that were formerly private homes have been converted into business premises which sit back from the street with pillared entrances guarding long driveways.

Number three was known as Light Trades House, a former family home standing high and proud which was now the headquarters of the Federation of British Engineers' Tool Manufacturers, an organisation that represented smaller firms in the supply chain for the steel industry on which Sheffield owed much of its past prosperity.

Late at night, the driveway leading up to Light Trades House was dark and deserted, the perfect location for another kind of work.

* * *

A couple of minutes after Denise had turned him down, the man with the dark eyes in the Rover was back. This time it was her friend, 24-year-old Olivia Reivers, who approached his car. She had been making ends meet in this way for the past four years and had two young mouths to feed back home. Her friend's concerns about this punter were not going to stop Olivia earning another much-needed tenner. She opened the passenger door, climbed in and directed him to the quiet, dark road behind the girls' school.

When they reached the entrance to Light Trades House, Sutcliffe reversed up the drive, something other punters never did. Parking his car pointing towards the gate meant they had no privacy if someone else pulled into the drive. It made for a quick getaway, though.

He handed over the tenner, appearing edgy and nervous, which wasn't uncommon among the married clients, but what was unusual was that he talked about his wife a lot more than most.

"He seemed worried about her," said Olivia. "He told me there had been a couple of miscarriages and that seemed to make him sad."

They were interrupted briefly when another car turned into the same driveway.

"They must have seen us there as it reversed out and drove away," said Sutcliffe.

After a while, they got down to business, or at least they tried to.

"I tried to warm him up, but there was no response, he was cold as ice," said Olivia.

She spent around ten minutes trying to arouse him to no avail.

He fastened his trousers and started talking again, chatting away until the inside of the Rover suddenly exploded in an onslaught of blinding light.

"Oh, crikey," thought Sutcliffe.

Another vehicle had pulled into the drive and illuminated their car, picking out every detail so whoever was in front of them would be able to clearly see a man sitting in the front seat and a woman next to him.

"Leave it to me," Sutcliffe urgently whispered to her, suddenly having another reason to be nervous and edgy, "you're my girlfriend."

* * *

As Hydes turned into the dark driveway of Light Trades House, his headlights picked out a parked car facing them with a man in the driving seat, a woman next to him.

It didn't need a star detective to realise the rookie was about to get his first solicitation collar.

"We parked in front of the Rover car," said Hydes. "I got out and approached the driver and asked for his details."

"John Williams, 65 Dorchester Road, Canklow, Rotherham," replied Peter Sutcliffe, of Garden Lane, Bradford.

"Who's she?" the sergeant asked him, indicating to the woman in the passenger seat.

"My girlfriend," replied Sutcliffe, a story which survived just one more question when he was asked her name and confessed he didn't know.

"Who are you trying to kid?" replied Ring. "I haven't fallen off a Christmas tree."

The officers radioed in to check the plates on the Rover. They came back as belonging to a Skoda, registered owner a Mr Aslam Khan.

Ring walked back to the Rover and removed the keys and peeled the tax disc off the window.

"They said: 'This tax disc doesn't belong to the car.' I said: 'It does, it's the number plates that are wrong, not the tax disc.' I told them, but they try and take credit for things which they don't deserve. And they were too stupid to realise that they were all black tape around the edges of the number plates where they were taped on, stupid buggers."

The "stupid" buggers weren't anything of the sort. They arrested both Sutcliffe and Olivia on suspicion of theft of the number plates.

No-one at this stage knew the true identity of the driver of the Rover, least of all Olivia. It was only later she came to realise that for those few minutes she was the luckiest woman on the planet.

"I suppose she was relieved to get away with her life," said Sutcliffe.

If the police had not pulled into the driveway on a routine check, would he have killed her?

"Oh yeah, yeah, most likely yeah… that was my mission, that was my purpose."

As they were placing Olivia in the patrol car, Sutcliffe told the officers he was desperate to spend a penny.

He had an ulterior motive and as the officers were putting the woman into their car, Sutcliffe reached under his seat and grabbed the hammer and knife that were in their usual hiding place and walked towards the darkened entrance to the building.

"I was going to throw them over the wall because there was some woods nearby, but I didn't because I thought it might make a noise. So I put the implements below a bush. They didn't hear anything."

After placing the weapons on the ground behind a small oil storage tank, he walked back to where the officers were.

He had successfully hidden two items that could implicate him in something far more serious than the theft of number plates, but it wasn't all good news for Sutcliffe. His jacket on the back seat of the Rover contained a second knife in a pocket. He knew he had to get rid of it somehow. He still had the mission to protect.

* * *

The officers drove the pair to Hammerton Road station, where they were placed in separate interview rooms. Olivia was well known to the police and knew it was pointless telling them anything other than the truth. She was soon allowed home, although the man was a different issue.

His manner was beginning to ring alarm bells.

"He was very agitated and apprehensive," said Hydes, "even when we were talking about the simplest of things. I got the impression he wanted to get out of the police station as quickly as possible."

A photofit issued after an earlier Ripper attack was on the wall. It bore a close resemblance to the man they had in, who by now had given his name as Peter William Sutcliffe and had also confessed to stealing the number plates. The likeness was commented upon by a vice cop, who was one of two officers assigned to collect Sutcliffe's car from Light Trades House. They were well versed in punters' behaviour and found it odd that he had parked facing the road. No-one ever did that.

Back at the station, Sutcliffe asked to use the toilet and, once inside, locked the door, took the knife from his jacket pocket and hid it in the cistern.

"If they'd have had any sense, they'd have realised that I'd already relieved myself before I came to the station," he said. "But they were too slow to realise that I went to the toilet again and put it in the flushing bowl. They searched me, but I'd already hidden that in a toilet."

Once Sutcliffe had admitted stealing the number plates, the police had to decide whether to charge him for that minor offence, which would have involved releasing him to appear at Dewsbury magistrates' court at a later date, or to keep questioning him thanks to the general unease that was building around this agitated suspect.

Ring phoned Dewsbury police station, which covered the area where the number plates had been stolen, and relayed the basic facts.

Around 1am, he also phoned the Ripper Incident Room in Leeds. Every officer across Yorkshire knew that the incident room must be informed about any man arrested in connection with red light activity.

A detective sergeant called Rob Bennett picked up the phone at Millgarth and Ring briefly explained they had a man arrested in the company of a prostitute who had given a false name, had a gap in his front teeth, lived in Bradford and had a Yorkshire accent. Definitely not a Wearside one.

DS Bennett told Ring he would check the card index and get back to him. For once, the much maligned system actually did its job. Bennett found Sutcliffe's card and saw that he had been interviewed previously.

The card entry stated that Sutcliffe had been cleared on the basis of his handwriting, but to his eternal credit, Bennett didn't let that sway him. He considered handwriting too flimsy a reason for elimination and decided to dig further. He pulled up other paperwork relating to Sutcliffe's interviews and discovered that he was a long-distance lorry driver, which had long been considered a possible occupation for the killer. Most importantly, he saw that Sutcliffe had never been positively alibied for any of the attacks.

Bennett called Hammerton Road and said he should be held in custody for further investigation.

By now, Sutcliffe was fast asleep in a cell as arrangements were made for three officers to head down from West Yorkshire to collect him and his Rover car.

They arrived early the next morning and at 7.40am left Hammerton Road for Dewsbury with their man and his car, one driving the Rover, the other following in the police car and the third in the back handcuffed to the suspect.

No-one was punching the air at this stage thinking the Ripper was in custody. This was simply the latest in a very long line of potential suspects who had to be checked out.

Following his brief sleep, Sutcliffe was calmer and as the convoy headed north the car enthusiast in him couldn't help but briefly ignore his plight and watch with pride as his powerful Rover car started to pull away in front of them, leaving the police car trailing as the officer driving it grumbled.

"They couldn't catch up," he said. "I was in the police car behind and he said: 'What's that idiot doing? I'm flat out and he's leaving me behind'."

They arrived at Dewsbury police station at 8.55am and Sutcliffe was logged in at 8.59am.

He was taken to a holding cell while his wife was informed by telephone that her husband was at the police station being interviewed about stolen number plates.

Sutcliffe knew he was in for a long day of questioning, but he had no intention of helping the police.

"I couldn't tell them about the mission," he said, "I had to tell them lies to cover it up. I couldn't tell anybody, Sonia didn't know, my mother didn't know, nobody from the family, nobody knew. It was between me and God."

Did nobody close to him suspect him of any links to the Ripper attacks, even at this late stage?

"No, only Trevor Birdsall suspected because he'd been with me a couple of times."

* * *

Detective Sergeant Des O'Boyle was only 32, but he was already an experienced Ripper squad detective. He had worked on the most recent survivor attack, Theresa Sykes, had interviewed countless witnesses and potential suspects, and had also been involved in the Wearside Jack end of things.

He was interviewing suspects at the rate of one a day, so his weary response of "Who is it this time?" when his boss phoned him to pop over to Dewsbury and interview the 'Ripper' could be forgiven. But everyone had to be treated as if he was the one, so he collected the necessary paperwork and read through it as his colleague, Detective Constable Rod Hill, drove them to Dewsbury.

The first thing they did when they arrived was to search Sutcliffe's Rover, where they found three screwdrivers in the glove compartment. They then went inside to interview him. It was just after 3pm.

"I was immediately struck by his eyes," said O'Boyle. "They were the most piercing, black staring eyes I've ever seen."

Hill took notes as O'Boyle asked the questions (police interviews were not routinely tape recorded in 1981), taking it slowly to build up a rapport, gently establishing the basic facts around his work, home and social life.

Sutcliffe appeared calm as he admitted things weren't great at home. There had been quarrels recently, although not too bad – "me and Sonia were too cautious and worried of upsetting each other to argue" – and there were money worries due to his impending job loss thanks to his drink-driving arrest.

When asked about their sex life, he insisted they had been having "normal sex". When asked how that could be given the rows, he replied: "We forget about rows when we go to bed."

After more than two hours, there was little to raise any suspicion. O'Boyle went to see Chief Superintendent John Clark, who was in charge at Dewsbury, and told him: "We don't think it's the man."

In all the millions of words written about the Yorkshire Ripper case, Clark's name barely gets a mention, but he is undoubtedly one of the unspoken heroes. He was not satisfied with this assessment of O'Boyle's. There had been something about this suspect which

CONFESSION

he felt warranted further inquiry. He relayed that to O'Boyle while also telling his custody suite officers to detain Sutcliffe for longer.

After discussions with the incident room, the two detectives went back to speak to Sutcliffe again, with the instructions to press harder. As they did, O'Boyle's suspicions began to grow.

Sutcliffe was weary of the never ending questions, but there was no way he was ready to confess. He had lied to dodge some questions and there were gaps in his story, but they hadn't cornered him yet.

"I had to tell them lies to cover it up," he said later. "I couldn't tell them about the mission. I told them anything, really, just to shut them up."

By 8.45pm they were done for the night. O'Boyle needed to go over the notes and discuss the day's events with senior officers. Sutcliffe had earlier agreed to give a sample of blood and hair which showed he was blood group B, but was not a secretor. The killer of Joan Harrison and the man who sent the letters and tape had both been secretors, meaning Sutcliffe didn't kill Harrison and he wasn't Wearside Jack. The significance of the revelation that he wasn't responsible for the letters and tape, which had come to dominate the inquiry, was yet to sink in.

Sutcliffe was taken back to his cell. As he was settling down for his second night's sleep in custody, Sgt Ring was reporting for duty at Sheffield's Hammerton road station. After the 10pm parade, the duty inspector told him the man they arrested the previous night was still in custody at Dewsbury.

Ring had had a sleepless night and an unsettled day. There was one aspect of last night's collar which didn't sit right with him, and now he learned the man was still being questioned which only served to heighten his sense of unease. Twenty-four hours was a long time to hold a number plate thief.

Without telling anyone else where he was going, he drove back to Light Trades House.

245

Ever since the arrest he had been questioning whether they were right to let the suspect spend a penny – and what had he been doing in those few moments?

Armed with his powerful police issue torch he retraced Sutcliffe's steps, shone the bright circle of light around on the ground and behind the small oil storage tank, poking through a pile of damp leaves, he saw the head of a hammer.

He radioed the station and asked for Hydes and an inspector to join him. It was 11pm.

When the other officers got there, Ring wanted to stress-test his discovery. He knew it was potentially world-shifting, but it couldn't be, could it?

"Is it the handyman's?" he asked his colleagues of the hammer.

Hydes's torch had picked out another implement lying close by the hammer.

"The hammer might belong to the handyman, but who does the knife belong to?"

At 11.05pm, a call was made from Sheffield to the Incident Room at Millgarth where the duty inspector was Detective Inspector John Boyle, not to be confused with O'Boyle.

He listened patiently, put the phone down, and then called O'Boyle at home and asked for a rundown of the day's events.

O'Boyle said their suspicions were at a decent level, but there was no one crucial piece of evidence which said Sutcliffe was the Ripper.

It was Boyle's turn to talk and he quickly explained what the Sheffield uniforms had found when they returned to the scene.

O'Boyle could barely contain his excitement.

"Yes," he yelled down the phone. "We've got him," making such a noise his wife came to check what all the commotion was about.

Holland was informed and ordered the Sheffield scene be secured and for Boyle and O'Boyle to head there straightaway.

When the officers arrived, there was an inevitable butting of horns with their uniformed South Yorkshire colleagues. The unspoken accusation hung in the air from West Yorkshire that South Yorkshire had screwed up. Letting a suspect wander off to hide vital evidence was the height of unprofessionalism.

For their part, the South Yorkshire lads felt the detectives were rude and ungrateful. After all, they had provided the crucial breakthrough, even if it was 24 hours on.

An uneasy peace eventually broke out and the two detectives headed off to speak to Olivia Reivers.

* * *

On Sunday morning, Dick Holland and a number of other detectives drove to Garden Lane to search the house and transport Sonia to the police station.

Holland asked her about his movements on Bonfire Night, the night Theresa Sykes had been attacked. Clark's had already confirmed that Sutcliffe had clocked off at 5.03pm that day, but Sonia, unaware of this, said they had to cancel going to a party because Peter said he had to work late.

Holland, in possession of the knife and hammer found at the arrest scene, searched the house and in the kitchen found a knife block with one missing. The knife he held in his hand in an evidence bag fitted perfectly. He began to feel the first small waves of excitement.

At Dewsbury, a different set of detectives from the previous day were getting ready to speak to Sutcliffe in the basement interview room, Detective Inspector Boyle and Detective Sergeant Peter Smith.

The discovery of the weapons in Sheffield (the other knife Sutcliffe had hidden in the toilet would not be found for another four days) placed them in a much stronger position than their colleagues the previous day.

Boyle pressed him hard on why he had travelled to Sheffield and his movements on Bonfire Night. The detectives kept after him and Sutcliffe kept pushing back until, eventually, all the fight went out of him.

"I just wanted to get it over with… I was tired… I was fed up of it all. They had an idea, they had their suspicions, but they didn't have proof until I told them."

Boyle kept going – the false plates, the kerb crawling, Bonfire Night, his bogus stories to explain his car being in red light areas. The lies, all of the lies. They could only mean one thing.

Sutcliffe was in turmoil.

"It was all weighing on my mind and it was a lot of pressure I was under…"

But it wasn't just the pressure being piled on by the police that he was talking about, it was the years of pressure he claimed to have faced by having to obey the voices and commit the attacks.

"Yeah, yeah, yeah… more pressure than they [the police] were putting on me, a lot more pressure," he said.

He still tried to dodge and wriggle, a last-ditch attempt to avoid the inevitable as Boyle kept after him.

"Do you understand what I am saying?" the officer said. "I think you are in serious trouble."

The pressure, external and internal, suddenly became too much. It was 15 years since he first claimed to have heard the voices in Bingley cemetery. He had spent nearly half of his life keeping them and the mission and all of the attacks hidden from the outside world, but in an instant he decided to bare his soul.

"It was a relief. I just got fed up, and I said, 'I know what this is all leading up to.'"

Boyle wanted him to say it.

"Leading up to what?" asked the detective.

"I said. 'That guy they call the Yorkshire Ripper.'"

"What about the Yorkshire Ripper?"

"Oh… well… it's me."

And just like that, it was all over.

"I was glad to be caught as I thought all that pressure would be taken off me. I did hope I wouldn't have to kill again.

CONFESSION

"I decided to just tell them everything. I'd had enough, I weighed up all the things I'd lose, a great wife, my house, my job, everything, thinking I'd never see it all ever again.

"You should have seen the look on their faces, you'd have thought all their Christmases had come at once."

He was read his rights, declined a lawyer and made only one request of the police.

"Don't go telling her, knocking, banging on the door and telling her… just say I'm in custody and I'd like to see her," he told the officers.

They agreed and kept their word. Sonia, who by now was at Dewsbury station, was taken into the CID office to find her husband sitting quietly, looking tired and drawn.

She still didn't know the exact reason why he was there and wanted to know from him what this was all about.

"What on earth is going on, Peter?" she asked.

"It's me, love" he told his wife, "I'm the Yorkshire Ripper."

CHAPTER 24

WEEDY WIMP

Events moved both quickly and slowly after Sutcliffe confessed.

The world ground to a halt for Sonia as she struggled to comprehend what he was saying.

"She looked really stunned, poor lass. I really felt sorry for her," he said.

When she was finally able to speak, she said: "What on earth did you do that for, Peter? Even a sparrow has a right to live."

Beyond his initial concern for Sonia, Sutcliffe's only other concerns, typically, were for himself.

"I was glad to be caught as I thought all that pressure would be taken off me. I did hope I wouldn't have to kill again in order to save them from eternal damnation.

"It was a relief for me really, I know I was facing a long time inside or whatever, but it was a relief to get it off my chest."

He began giving his official statement which would take up the next 15 hours and 45 minutes with a break for sleep part of the way through.

Holland felt a huge sense of relief, but when he took his first look at the face of the man he had devoted almost the last half decade of his life hunting he was underwhelmed.

"I thought he looked a weedy wimp," he said. "He was quietly spoken, almost effeminate in his speech and manner, he didn't give the impression in any way of being the overpowering evil man."

Oldfield was at home having his Sunday dinner with his family. He was no longer in charge of the inquiry, but Holland rang him to say: "We've got the bugger."

Oldfield then called the Chief Constable, Ronald Gregory, who was also at home, reading in his lounge.

"Fasten your seat belt," Oldfield told him, "we have got him."

Gregory replaced the receiver and allowed himself a moment. He closed his eyes as the enormity of the phone call sank in before driving over to Dewsbury.

Word quickly reached the incident room, where there was elation at the development. It also swiftly reached the media, and the force began receiving calls from as far afield as Australia and America.

Sutcliffe was talking freely in the interviews, but he wasn't being totally truthful because he still felt compelled to keep his true motivation a secret.

"I couldn't tell them about the mission, so when they were asking me questions, I had to tell them lies to cover it up."

One example of these lies was an incident he related to police and repeated at his trial.

Following the confrontation with Sonia over the Italian and his attempted revenge with a prostitute, losing a fiver in the process, he said he saw the woman a few days later in a pub.

He demanded his money back, only to suffer more humiliation when she loudly rebuffed him within earshot of everyone in the pub.

"I felt humiliated, outraged and embarrassed," he told his trial, claiming it triggered a need for revenge against prostitutes. A few weeks later, he staged his first attack with the sock full of pebbles.

The pub confrontation has long been thought of as a critical step on the path leading up to the attacks.

But speaking in 2014 from Broadmoor, he revealed he invented it to keep his true motivation from the police – the voices from God.

"I told the police that so they wouldn't get a hint about the mission. I told them a lot of stuff that wasn't true to mislead them because I thought they were getting near to finding out about the mission."

He treasured the voices – they were his and they made him feel "very special" – and he was not willing to give them up.

"I thought it was a miracle. Because God was in charge, he was conducting everything and I knew everything would be all right. He misled the police several times and I just knew it was a miracle happening every time.

"You can't argue with God. I firmly believed 100% that it was God giving me the instructions to do those things, and I believed it was the right thing. He was protecting the mission and he kept saying to me, look after the mission, don't tell anybody or anything, between you and your creator, so I told nobody.

"I done some bad crimes. I didn't think they were crimes at the time, I thought I was doing the right thing, you see. I was deluded, but I didn't know that, I thought it was a miracle."

Senior officers didn't care less about the intricacies of his motivation at this stage. They were just itching to go public with the news of his arrest after years of stinging criticism for failing to catch the Ripper.

Doyle and Smith were under pressure to complete Sutcliffe's statement as soon as possible, but he had an incredible recall of detail for each attack – something which he retained until the end of his life – and there was a huge amount to get through.

He insisted he had nothing to do with Joan Harrison in Preston in 1975 and if it wasn't self-evident to everyone by now thanks to his accent, he confirmed he hadn't sent the letters and tape.

Gregory had sent a cadet to buy a bottle of whisky and when DS O'Boyle stuck his head around the door of the second floor conference room to confirm the suspect's detailed confession meant the arrested man was indeed the Yorkshire Ripper, the cheers of delight rang out.

"They were all laughing and joking," said Sutcliffe. "They were all celebrating and half of them were drunk. Oldfield, he was drunk as a skunk, his face was as red as a cherry. Bright red face, veins sticking out all over it. I thought to myself, 'He hasn't got long to go'."

It was decided to hold a press conference even though the suspect was still being interviewed, and at 9.15pm Gregory walked into a room at Dewsbury police station crowded with around 100 journalists.

He was accompanied by Oldfield and Hobson and the trio looked like they had just won the lottery, which, in policing terms, they had.

They sat down in low brown armchairs. Gregory read a brief statement detailing the basic facts that a man – he did not name Sutcliffe – had been detained in Sheffield in connection with the theft of number plates.

Following further inquiries, he said, he was now being "questioned in relation to the Yorkshire Ripper murders".

He went on: "It is anticipated that he will appear before the court in Dewsbury tomorrow."

He then added, in a comment which erased any doubt over whether they had the right man or not: "I can tell you that we are absolutely delighted with developments at this stage... really delighted."

He glanced to his right and looked at Oldfield, who was stretched back in his chair, his gaze directed upwards, silently lost in his thoughts, and said: "George is delighted as well."

"Is it fair then to say," said one of the reporters, "that the general hunt of the so-called Yorkshire Ripper is now being wound down?"

After years of barbed comments about the failures of his men to catch the Ripper, Gregory couldn't help himself.

He turned to the journalist, pointed at him and triumphantly declared: "Right."

It sounded like it should have been accompanied by an exclamation mark.

Up in the North East, Detective Inspector David Zackrisson, the Northumbria officer who had expressed the strongest doubts about the letters and tape, received a phone call from a West Yorkshire colleague to inform him of the arrest.

"He said: 'They've got him, the Ripper'... he said: 'Is there something you want to ask, Dave?' I said: 'Yes – where does he come from?' He said: 'Well not bloody Sunderland, I can tell you... it's Yorkshire', and do you know, I could have cried."

Sutcliffe's lengthy statement continued until 4.30pm on Monday. At 4.41pm, in the Detective Sergeants' Office at Dewsbury Police station, he was formally charged with the murder of Jacqueline Hill and the theft of the number plates.

It was pitch black outside Dewsbury magistrates' court, where a vengeful mob had gathered. Five years of pent-up fury was being vented and if they could have got to him, they would have ripped him limb from limb.

A hundred officers were in attendance to hold them back as Sutcliffe was driven to the side entrance in a police van with coins and stones bouncing off the vehicle. The crowd roared when Sutcliffe emerged with a blanket over his head, handcuffed to Des O'Boyle. Six uniformed officers gathered around them as the 100-strong wall of their colleagues held back the baying crowds.

Shouts of "die yer bastard, die," rang out.

Sonia and her dad Bohdan were in court and as Sutcliffe was brought in at 4.55pm his wife turned round to look at him, then patted him on the hand and whispered something that no-one else could hear.

The continuing chants of "die yer bastard" wafted into the courtroom as the court clerk Dean Gardner twice announced Sutcliffe's name with no response.

He looked to the dock and asked: "Which one of you is Peter William Sutcliffe?"

Boyle, who hadn't shaved in days, replied: "It's him, not me."

The clerk then said to the defendant: "You did in Leeds, West Yorkshire, between November 16, 1980 and November 19, 1980, murder Jacqueline Hill against the peace, contrary to the common law."

The hearing lasted just eight minutes and Sutcliffe had spoken just three times. He answered 'yes' when asked if he understood the charges, 'no' he did not want reporting restrictions lifted and 'no' he did not object to being remanded.

He was being charged with just one of the murders for now, the rest would follow. He was remanded in custody, but before he was taken to prison the police took him back to Garden Lane one last time to identify clothes he had worn during the attacks and also any tools or knives he had used.

"I did actually think it'd probably be the last time I'd set foot in my own home. It was quite a sad feeling, and I still didn't know for sure how long Sonia would stay by my side."

There was one strange aspect of his arrest which was never revealed until many years later.

When Sutcliffe arrived at Dewsbury, he was not searched properly. It was only done at the end of his long interview, before he was taken to court.

As he undressed, Des O'Boyle checked his clothes. In the pocket of his coat, he found Sutcliffe's underpants.

He then removed his trousers and the officer saw that he was naked underneath apart from a strange garment, a pair of leggings fashioned from a silk, V-neck sweater, the sleeves being used for his legs, with the v-neck area providing an open area around his genitals. Padding had been stitched into where his knees would be. The implication was clear – they were designed to allow Sutcliffe to easily kneel over his victim after he had felled her and masturbate.

O'Boyle was dumbfounded. He queried what they were, and Sutcliffe simply replied that they were leggings.

They were placed in evidence bags, but what happened to them then was every bit as strange. No mention of them was made in the formal interview record, Sutcliffe was not questioned about them again and the prosecution lawyers at his trial were never made aware of them, much to their later fury. They would have been a compelling piece of evidence to show to the jury.

Following the court case, the police exhibits officer, Detective Constable Alan Foster, was told to dispose of various items of Sutcliffe's property in an incinerator, but retained possession of the leggings thinking they may be useful in any future investigation into Sutcliffe for other attacks.

He took them home and stored them in his loft.

The puzzle of why they never featured in the trial has never been satisfactorily answered, but the potential importance of them was dismissed by Sutcliffe who claimed a more innocent explanation.

"The winters were really freezing the last time when I were out there, '81, just before my arrest, that's why I had them leggings. It was that bloody cold outside loading the trailer. It was bloody freezing.

"They were just ordinary leg warmers, winter woollies that I wore when it was freezing cold. There was nothing strange about them. It was obvious they were to keep you warm."

His arrest was like a bomb going off in his own family, the shock-waves of which they would never fully escape for the rest of their lives.

They gathered at his sister Maureen's house after hearing the news, convinced it was a mistake until a police officer arrived to tell them he had confessed. The only positive anyone could think of was that his devoted mother wasn't around.

"I just thank God she didn't live to see what happened because it would have killed her," said his dad John.

Sutcliffe's youngest brother Carl wanted to hear it from his own mouth.

"I saw him in prison and he was his same relaxed, normal self. I said: 'Is this really you, Peter? You're the Ripper?' He said: 'I'm afraid so, our kid'.

"He looked a bit apologetic but didn't say sorry. I asked: 'Why?' And all he said was: 'Just cleaning up the streets, our kid, just cleaning up'."

CHAPTER 25

TRIAL SHOCK

Peter Sutcliffe's home for the next 16 weeks was Armley, now officially known as Her Majesty's Prison Leeds, but still just Armley to everyone in Leeds.

He was placed under round the clock watch, with everyone determined he wouldn't take the coward's way out before his trial.

Sonia began visiting regularly, often with a list of items to discuss as a team of prison officers looked on and took notes. A daily log of Sutcliffe's physical and mental condition was also kept in the book.

On January 8, six days after his arrest, Prison Officer John Leach was in charge of the note-taking as part of his 11-hour shift when Sutcliffe told Sonia he was facing 30 years in prison unless he could convince everyone that he was mad.

"Sonia was really upset, she was on a visit and I said it loudly in front of the staff and everybody, I just said it to cheer her up a bit, I said: 'Oh never mind I might only do 10 years in a loony bin.'

"I said that if the psychiatrists found in my favour, that I might get out in 10 years."

Was this the first step in a master plan to avoid a life sentence in a tough, high security prison? He claimed not.

"I only said it to cheer her up and they took it literally. One of the staff wrote it down in his dirty little notebook and they used it in court. All I was doing was trying to ease her mind and make it not seem too bad.

"I wouldn't say that out loud in front of them anyway if I was serious. Everything was taken out of context.

"I wasn't trying to whisper. I said it out loud because you should have seen the state Sonia was in when she came to visit me. She was wretched, absolutely washed out and distraught. I had to say something to try and lift her spirits a little bit because she looked gone to me."

It was while at Armley that he gave his first hint of the mission to another person.

During sessions with psychiatrist Dr Daphne Sasieni, who was based at the prison, he began to talk about what he claimed had been his motivation for the attacks.

It wasn't a smooth process, though. During one of their sessions, he got upset and angry and threatened her, causing her to call for help.

"She was a very clever lady. But she was questioning me and saying: 'There's something a bit strange about this, we'll have to talk about it later.'

"She said something that upset me, so I said, before you could ring the buzzer and bring the staff in, I could get that pen and jab it into your eye straight into your brain and you'd be dead. So she pressed the buzzer, and they didn't come and she panicked, it had disconnected somehow or other. She was really frightened to death because she wasn't getting any assistance.

"I wouldn't have done anything to her. I just stated something to her because she was saying things that upset me so I thought I'll upset you. They didn't come, and she got up and ran to the door terrified and said: 'Where were you?'"

Sadly, Dr Sasieni was unable to question him further as she died suddenly a short time later.

"She went on holiday and died suddenly before she could come back to pursue it further," said Sutcliffe, who was left thinking it may have been linked to their row.

"It must have shocked her so much that she died of a brain haemorrhage. She went on holiday the next day for two weeks and a day later she died straight away. She was terrified."

Sutcliffe's trial was due to begin in the famous Court Number One at the Old Bailey on April 29 when the Attorney General himself, Sir Michael Havers QC, would take charge of the prosecution. Harry Ognall, considered one of the most able trial lawyers in the north, would be his junior.

The stained oak-panelled courtroom has been the scene of some of the most dramatic legal moments of the 20th Century.

The Kray Twins, Ruth Ellis (the last woman to be hanged in the UK in 1955), William Joyce (better known as the World War Two Nazi propagandist Lord Haw-Haw) and Dr Hawley Harvey Crippen have all stood in the same dock that Sutcliffe was placed in that Wednesday morning when he was brought up from the cells.

Sonia took her seat next to her mother Maria. At the back of the courtroom were Doreen Hill and Jacqueline's fiancé Ian Tanfield, David Leach, the father of Barbara, and Olive Smelt and Anna Rogulskyj, all on the same row.

The public gallery was packed with 34 people, some of whom had queued through the night to secure their place, and there wasn't a spare seat to be had on the lawyers' benches. The press bench was packed with reporters from all over the world.

They all watched intently as Sutcliffe, accompanied by four prison guards, entered the dock at 11.01 wearing a light grey suit and pale blue shirt, no tie – "I didn't want a tie on, it was too hot".

As he settled himself in the dock, Sutcliffe failed to conjure a single thought for any of his victims or their families.

Despite being surrounded by police officers, lawyers, members of the public and relatives of the women he attacked, he only had thoughts for one person.

"Thinking of Sonia… hoping she'd be all right, that's all that bothered me, nothing else. Must have been a nightmare for her, poor lass."

The judge was Mr Justice Boreham, a 62-year-old former grammar school boy who for the previous six years had been based in the north as a presiding judge on the North-East circuit, meaning he was keenly aware of the terrible toll the Yorkshire Ripper's activities had taken on northern communities.

As the parties settled themselves, no-one realised that he was about to preside over a day of "drama and confusion".

The court clerk put the 20 charges to the defendant. In between them was a table laden with seven ball-pein hammers, a claw hammer, several knives and eight screwdrivers, each with their own yellow evidence tag.

Sutcliffe wasn't happy at the persuasive visual impact they were likely to have on the jury.

"They took all the tools out of my garage and put them on a table and I hadn't used them as weapons. There was only about two or three that I'd used. Even the judge was waving the weapons about saying, imagine attacking somebody with this. Obviously the crimes have been committed with weapons, any fool knew that."

Sutcliffe pleaded guilty to each of the attempted murders and "not guilty to murder, but guilty to manslaughter on the grounds of diminished responsibility".

Sir Michael – father of the actor, Nigel Havers – got to his feet to outline the prosecution case.

The defence of diminished responsibility is an exception to the rule in criminal cases that it is the prosecution's job to prove a case, not the defendant's to prove his innocence. It is a partial defence to murder in that it does not absolve a defendant of all responsibility but rather reduces the level of their culpability, from murder to manslaughter. It is the defence's role to satisfy the jury it has been met. As it only applies to murder, Sutcliffe was only able to plead the defence in relation to the 13 murder charges and not the seven attempted murder charges, which he admitted.

To successfully plead diminished responsibility, he had to show he was suffering from an abnormality of mind (which can arise from a condition of arrested or retarded development, from an inherent cause or be induced by disease or injury) which must have substantially impaired his mental responsibility for the killing.

So his lawyers had to prove he wasn't fully responsible for his actions because he was unable to appreciate that what he was doing was right or wrong, or was unable to exercise self-control to stop himself because of an abnormality of the mind (in his case, the mental illness of paranoid schizophrenia).

Trying to prove this case was lead defence barrister James Chadwin QC, a Glaswegian whose "rotund figure, battered wig and penchant for cheroots" led legal observers to consider that he bore more than a passing resemblance to John Mortimer's Horace Rumpole.

As Sir Michael got to his feet and began to speak, it became apparent that the defence would have very little work to do.

Four psychiatrists had been instructed to assess Sutcliffe – two for the prosecution, two for the defence – and the Attorney General explained that all four were of the same opinion. He was suffering from paranoid schizophrenia, which amounted to an abnormality of the mind as required by the diminished responsibility defence.

The Crown would, therefore, accept Sutcliffe's not guilty pleas to murder, but guilty to manslaughter due to diminished responsibility.

The judge placed his fountain pen down and in a considered, polite manner, shocked the packed courtroom.

He explained that he had "grave anxieties" about the prosecution's stance and asked of Sir Michael: "Where is the evidence which gives the doctors the factual basis for these pleas?"

Sir Michael explained that he had met with the doctors and discussed their diagnoses in detail and was satisfied with them. His learned friends on the other side of the courtroom were also happy with their opinions.

But not all of the learned friends in court were happy. Ognall was a sceptic and said later: "I think I felt differently because I came from Yorkshire and was more aware of the enormity of the reign of terror this man had imposed."

Before the case, he had told Havers of the doubts he had over Sutcliffe's claim that he was "God's instrument". He simply didn't believe it and was confident the claims would not stand up to scrutiny in front of a jury.

Havers rejected his argument and pressed on with his own plan, which would save the victims the anguish of a long, drawn-out trial.

But he was struggling to persuade the judge, who came back at him as if Sir Michael had answered the wrong question.

Regardless of whether he and his learned friends were happy, the judge wanted to know: "What's the supporting evidence?"

The judge said he had "grave anxieties" about Sutcliffe's pleas and asked Havers to explain why he was accepting them.

It took Havers 94 minutes to outline in detail the psychiatric evidence and Sutcliffe's own testimony that he was acting on the instructions of God, but the judge still wasn't satisfied.

There was also the matter of the public interest. Huge swathes of the country had lived in a state of fear for many years, and he felt the millions of people in those areas had an interest in the case being tried by a jury.

Speaking for just four minutes, the judge gave his ruling. He highlighted the weakness at the heart of the medical case – the defendant's diagnosis rested purely on what the defendant had chosen to tell the doctors – and that it was in conflict with his first version of events given to police after his arrest.

He said it was a "matter which ought to be tested", the public interest demanded it. There would be a trial.

Neither set of lawyers had anticipated such a decision, and both said they needed time to prepare for a full trial. The judge gave them six days.

This presented the prosecution with a dilemma. After arguing that Sutcliffe was guilty of manslaughter due to diminished responsibility, Havers now had to flip 180 degrees and present a similarly convincing argument that he was guilty of murder.

Sutcliffe was furious.

"The doctors were all unanimous, and so was the Attorney General. He agreed with the doctors that it was schizophrenia I was suffering from and there wouldn't be a trial.

"The judge said: 'Oh, we'll see about that – bring a jury in to decide'. It's never happened in British legal history where the doctors have all been unanimous and yet the judge has overturned them. He was biased that judge. The whole thing was a medical issue and he should never have done that."

Six days later, on Tuesday, May 5, (the Monday was a Bank Holiday) lawyers, detectives, grieving relatives and members of the public – this time including the Arsenal goalkeeper Pat Jennings – once again gathered in Court Number One at the Old Bailey.

Sutcliffe took a weird satisfaction in how many people turned up.

"It was a big court and it was packed. Pat Jennings was there, the footballer and other footballers were there, a lot of people I recognised that I didn't actually know because there were the sports profiles and stuff like that."

Havers opened the case for the prosecution. For the first time, the public learned that Sutcliffe was claiming to have been acting on the orders of God as part of a divine mission to clear the streets of prostitutes.

They also learned he had been interviewed a barely believable nine times by police investigating Ripper killings before his arrest.

Havers revealed that Sutcliffe had a best friend, Trevor Birdsall, who had suspected he might be the Ripper.

Doreen Hill, the mother of the Ripper's last victim, slowly shook her head when she heard that.

The Attorney General warned the jury of the gruesome nature of some of the crime scene photographs they would have to look at. At one stage, a man in the public gallery fainted. It seemed like the trial was destined to be conducted amid an air of high drama throughout.

Havers explained to the six men and six women of the jury that their task was to decide the question at the heart of the case – whether the doctors were correct and he had committed the killings due to a mental illness, or whether their diagnoses were simply wrong.

"You will have to consider whether the doctors might, in fact, have been deceived. Whether he is the sort to pull the wool over their eyes or whether – another possibility – the doctors are entirely wrong," he said.

At one stage Havers infuriated many when he continued the theme which had run throughout the police investigation – that the lives of some victims were apparently worth more than others.

"There had been 20 homicidal attacks of women aged between 16 and 47," he told the jury, "some prostitutes, some of easy virtue, and you may think, saddest of all, the last six were all of totally unblemished reputation."

His remarks led to protests outside court, yet more drama for a case which was hardly lacking in it already.

He ended by summarising the challenge that lay ahead for the jury.

"You have to decide whether, as a callous, clever murderer, he deliberately set out to create a cock-and-bull story to avoid conviction for murder."

Sonia wasn't in court to hear any of this. She left shortly before the proceedings began when the defence made a last-minute decision to keep her in reserve as a potential witness to give evidence on behalf of her husband. (Witnesses are not allowed to sit through other evidence to ensure their own testimony is not influenced by anything else they have heard).

After Havers finished his opening, the prosecution kicked off its case by Ognall reading the 35-page report compiled by the lead psychiatrist Dr Hugo Milne. He had interviewed Sutcliffe on 11 occasions over 12 weeks and, as all four doctors involved in the case were of the same opinion, the other three were happy for Dr Milne to take the lead.

The jurors were told that it was only during the seventh meeting that Sutcliffe finally revealed his mission to kill prostitutes to Dr Milne, and it was the eighth before he disclosed that he had heard voices at the grave of Bronislaw Zapolski in 1966.

The doctor had also spoken to Sonia, who had been described by her husband in his interviews as over-excited, highly strung, unstable and obsessed by cleanliness.

After the report was read to the jury, the prosecution called a number of witnesses who had been friends with Sutcliffe, including Trevor Birdsall. He became ill in the witness box and had to be given a chair as he revealed he had harboured suspicions of his friend stretching back more than a decade. He said those concerns vanished when the letters and tape persuaded the entire country that the killer had a Wearside accent.

The Barker brothers – David and Ronald – gave evidence and told how they would tour red light areas with Sutcliffe on nights out.

Ronald kept a diary, which he read from in court and which included entries detailing nights out with Sutcliffe just hours before he committed attacks, including on June 25, 1977, when he dropped them at home in Bradford before driving to Leeds to murder Jayne MacDonald.

When asked if he had ever thought of Sutcliffe as an aggressive man, Ronald replied: "No, it never entered my head. I have never seen anything that struck me as an aggressive attitude towards women. In fact, he was rather quiet, you could even say he was slightly shy."

After the prosecution case ended, the defence got ready to call its witnesses.

In the end, Sonia's anticipated appearance never happened.

"They asked me if I'd go in the witness box. I said, yeah," said Sutcliffe later. "They said, can we get Sonia in the box as well? And I saw the way they were lying and cheating and saying all sorts of nasty stuff, so I said, no I don't want her in the box, I'm not having her subject to their abuse.

"She wanted to give evidence on my behalf, but I wouldn't let her."

Sutcliffe took the stand at 11.52am on Monday, May 11. The courtroom was transfixed, but being the centre of attention didn't bother him. He wasn't nervous or apprehensive as he took the stand.

"I felt I had to go in the box to put my side of it because none of them were putting my side of it."

As he gave evidence he was calm, assured and articulate to a degree which surprised many.

But the matter-of-fact way in which he relayed the most gruesome details of the murders shocked everyone.

Occasionally sipping water from a white mug, he told of how he heard God's voice for the first time in Bingley cemetery and felt that it was "very wonderful".

He said God had told him that prostitutes were the "scum of the earth" and it was his job to "get rid of them", and how he didn't look forward to killing and went through "absolute turmoil" before each attack but, ultimately, it was "all intended by God".

The following day – day six of the trial – it was the job of Havers to cross-examine Sutcliffe.

Havers tried to build the case that the true motivation was sexual, based on how some of the wounds were inflicted.

Sutcliffe denied and parried. At one point, he claimed he was not aware that he had stabbed Josephine Whittaker in the vagina.

To make his point, Havers walked to the evidence table. There were gasps from the jury as he took hold of the 10in-long rusty Phillips screwdriver which had been sharpened to a point and raised it into the air.

"To put the stab wounds in the vagina with no injury to the lips of the vagina is unusual. How did you do it?" asked the Attorney General.

"By moving it around," replied Sutcliffe, although he continued to deny the injuries indicated a sexual motive.

Havers pressed on – why had he inflicted injuries on so many women's breasts?

"I thought it was the best place to stab them and kill them."

But why the vagina?

"It was an obvious place."

And the breasts?

"It was close to the heart."

His combination of admissions, denials and God-based deflections was infuriating and meant Havers struggled to pin him down. Sutcliffe had an answer for most things, and when he didn't, he had the perfect get out – blame God.

In another quirk of the case, Sutcliffe disagreed with not only the prosecution case but also his own defence. He still considered himself to be on the mission at the time of the trial and therefore didn't think he was mentally ill.

"They were saying I was mentally ill, the doctors should be listened to, I was saying no, there's nothing wrong with me, I'm not mentally ill."

So there were three versions for the jury to consider – he was a sexually motivated killer (prosecution), he was mentally ill (defence), it was down to God (the defendant).

Sutcliffe's version may have been self-evidently the product of mental illness, but whether he was making it up as the prosecution claimed or genuinely believed it due to his illness as the defence said, it did mean that he was an assured witness, with many observers feeling he was enjoying his time in the spotlight.

After Sutcliffe, it was the turn of the psychiatrists.

Dr Terence Kay, a forensic psychiatrist from Leeds, and Malcolm McCulloch, the medical director of Park Lane hospital in Liverpool, which later became Ashworth, had been retained as prosecution witnesses.

The Bradford-based psychiatrist Dr Milne and Dr Pat McGrath, the last ever Medical Superintendent at Broadmoor Hospital before the position was abolished, were to appear for the defence.

Once the judge had made the ruling that the case would go to trial, Drs Kay and McCulloch were dismissed as prosecution witnesses and told to make themselves available to the defence.

Dr McGrath, who was due to retire in a matter of months, was on a pre-arranged holiday at the time of the trial, so he never appeared.

Dr Milne was the first to take the stand. He said Sutcliffe was "extremely dangerous" but was not a sadistic sexual psychopath.

He said that he showed classic symptoms, which he was convinced were not simulated, including visual and auditory hallucinations and had exhibited signs of psychotic detachment and grandiose ideas.

As he finished this walk through by his own side's barrister, Dr Milne had no way of knowing what was about to hit him during cross-examination by the prosecution.

With them both being based in Yorkshire, Ognall and Dr Milne had met many times before in court. They liked and respected each other, but there would be no old pals' act from Ognall.

The ordeal Dr Milne was about to endure would infuriate the doctors to the extent that they considered it an "attack".

It was remarked later that it felt like the medical experts, and forensic psychiatry as a whole, were on trial rather than Sutcliffe.

Ognall had spent many hours pondering what his first question should be, knowing the importance of a strong start.

He settled on this: "Of everything that Sutcliffe told you about his reasons for killing these women, was there any single thing you did not accept?"

If the doctor said yes, it instantly undermined his entire case. He would be agreeing that Sutcliffe had lied to him, therefore how could he trust everything else he had told him?

If he said no, Ognall was convinced that he could identify aspects of Sutcliffe's testimony which were clearly untrue, which also destroyed the claim of a "divine mission".

Dr Milne opted for "no". He had accepted everything that Sutcliffe had told him.

Ognall then set about attempting to dismantle the medical diagnosis in the hope of proving Sutcliffe was a sexually motivated murderer.

For long periods of time, Dr Milne refused to concede there was any sexual element.

But Ognall kept pushing, with the exchange, at times, becoming angry as Ognall demanded of the doctor: "I will have an answer."

He focused on specific aspects of the attacks, such as the injuries Josephine Whitaker suffered.

"Would you agree that the most fiendish cruelty was most deliberately done for sexual satisfaction?" Ognall asked Dr Milne, who admitted: "It could have been sexual."

Pressing home his advantage, Ognall asked the doctor whether, based on this evidence, did Sutcliffe deceive him by claiming there was no sexual element?

Dr Milne replied: "Yes."

He also focussed on the way that Sutcliffe had moved Emily Jackson's body by placing a piece of wood between her legs and said there were sexual elements to the Rytka, Jordan, Hill and Smelt attacks.

How could all of that evidence, taken together, not indicate a sexually-motivated killer?

Dr Milne insisted he did not consider that Sutcliffe was primarily a sexual killer.

Ognall: "I put it to you Dr Milne, that this man was not a tortured soul, being told by God 'you must kill'. He's a man who craves for it, like an addict for their next shot of heroin."

Milne: "He never, ever wanted to be seen as a sexual killer."

Ognall: "No – because if he puts himself forward as a sexual killer, then the divine mission goes out of the window. That's why, isn't it, doctor?"

Milne: "It could be."

Ognall: "If the jury decides that Sutcliffe knew full well that his last six victims were not prostitutes, then the divine mission to kill prostitutes lies in smithereens?"

Milne: "I agree."

Ognall: "Then it becomes murder?"

Milne: "Yes."

Sutcliffe was furious with the doctor for abandoning his original position to one that appeared to support the notion that he was a sexually-motivated killer.

"He was a coward," said Sutcliffe. "He was agreeing because they tried getting him into a corner and make him look silly, and all he was interested in was not looking silly."

The psychiatrist's concession of a sexual element to some attacks and acceptance that Sutcliffe was capable of lying was damaging to the defence. But he refused to budge from his initial diagnosis, stressing that lying was not inconsistent with paranoid schizophrenia.

Ognall turned to practical elements of Sutcliffe's behaviour to show he was cunning and deceitful, just like any other criminal.

More than half the attacks had taken place on a Friday and Saturday night when Sonia was at work at the care home.

"If Sutcliffe was no more than the helpless and hapless victim of God's will, why did God confine himself so much to those two evenings, when his wife was away at work? Why did God only direct him on Fridays and Saturdays?"

Dr Milne said he did not believe that Sutcliffe only had the urge to kill at weekends, more that he was able to exert some self-control, which was consistent with the disease.

Ognall then came up with one of his most memorable lines when he noted that for a time Sutcliffe had been in London when Sonia was at college and travelled extensively for work, but there were no attacks in the capital or the south.

"Is this God only a Yorkshire God?" Ognall asked.

Years later, while in Frankland, Sutcliffe said he did hear the voice when he was away from Yorkshire, but it advised him to wait until he was back in the White Rose county before conducting another attack.

He said: "It used to say: 'Wait until you get back, you know what you've got to do, bear that in mind, be prepared, not now, wait, you don't know the area to make your escape.'"

After Dr Milne left the witness box, the next two doctors were called to give evidence. Their ordeals were briefer but also at times uncomfortable. Dr Malcolm McCulloch was accused by Ognall of showing "apparent indifference" when he admitted he hadn't even studied the details of the prosecution case (which included Sutcliffe's police confession) until the day before the trial started. Havers later said of this: "What sort of expert is that, who forms a view without knowing all the facts?"

Yorkshire-based Dr Terence Kay, whose day job involved examining patients at Armley and Wakefield prisons, said the only possible alternative to the diagnosis of paranoid schizo-phrenia would be if Sutcliffe was a psychopath and sexual sadist. He said he had studied sadistic killers and had seen no evidence that Sutcliffe was one.

The defence case was over, with the doctors left furious at their treatment. More than a decade later, Dr McCulloch commented that the trial had been "so unusual and unsatisfactory from the psychiatrists' point of view, that feelings and interest still run high".

Dr Milne also harboured resentment over his treatment for a long time, according to Sutcliffe.

"He came to see me at Broadmoor years later," said Sutcliffe. "He was writing a book, I don't know whatever happened to the book, but he died a couple of years after that. He told me he came to see me because he wanted to write a book and straighten things out because it hadn't gone right at the trial, and he was very upset and disappointed."

Both sides delivered their closing speeches and the judge summed up the evidence, stressing the importance of the debate over Sutcliffe hearing the voice in Bingley cemetery.

The psychiatrists put huge weight behind this experience, yet the prosecution highlighted its obvious weakness – it rested solely on Sutcliffe's own telling of it, with no independent corroboration that what he was saying was true and accurate.

"I do not wish to appear at all flippant," the judge said to the jury, "but this is rather like you claiming to have swum the Channel. When a friend doubts your word, you take him and show him the Channel. The fact that it is there doesn't prove anything, does it? The doctors, however, claim that it does prove something."

He told the jury there were three crucial questions to answer.

Firstly, was the defendant suffering from an abnormality of the mind when he committed each killing? Secondly, if he was, did that abnormality arise from a mental illness?

Lastly, did the abnormality impair his judgment to the extent that he was not responsible for his actions?

The second two could only be answered by medical evidence, not the jurors themselves.

They had to concentrate on the first question to reach a verdict and to help them they had to consider three matters of fact. Did Sutcliffe hear voices at Bingley cemetery which he perceived to be from God (referred to as his primary schizophrenic experience)? Even the medical experts agreed that if this was not true, his entire case collapsed.

Secondly, was Sutcliffe deluded into thinking he had a divine mission to "exterminate" prostitutes (not just women in general)? Lastly, did Sutcliffe genuinely believe at the time of each attack that his victim was a prostitute? It didn't matter what he thought before or after, it only mattered what he was thinking at the time of the actual attack.

The jury of six men and six women were sent out to consider their verdicts at 10.21am on Friday, May 22.

CHAPTER 26

DEBUNKING MYTHS

As the jurors are filing out of the courtroom to begin their deliberations, it is perhaps the most suitable juncture of the entire Peter Sutcliffe story to consider the crucial questions – how and why did he become a serial killer?

To make their minds up, the jury had the benefit of expert opinions from psychiatrists, the prosecution case and Sutcliffe's court testimony as well as his police confession.

What they didn't have, which we now have, was the years of further testimony from the killer himself when he no longer had any need to lie, including his response to theories offered by doctors, lawyers, police officers, politicians and other commentators on what turned Peter Sutcliffe into the Yorkshire Ripper.

The theories are many and varied. They include the Freudian – a deep love for his mother and a hatred of his father – and the radical feminist – he was the product of a violent patriarchy where contempt for women and violence directed at them was the norm.

There was the theory that he didn't have anything against prostitutes in particular but was simply projecting the resentment he felt towards 'fallen women' in general or women who had failed him onto them as they were the most accessible group of victims.

There was also the theory that he was secretly gay, or had a strong feminine side to his personality which he hated and feared to the extent that he tried to kill it by proxy, again by targeting society's most accessible victims.

There were the two theories his trial focussed on – the act of killing sexually aroused him, or he was compelled to kill due to a severe mental illness.

Or, instead of a mental illness, was he a psychopath, like so many other serial killers?

Simplest of all in one sense, was he just plain evil?

Lastly, there were the many Sonia-based theories. Did his tortured mind think of her as a 'prostitute' after the incident with the Italian, which developed into a desire to punish all prostitutes. Or did his home life with her strict rules drive him to it because he felt emasculated by her dominant role and killing was a way of re-exerting his masculinity? Or was his true desire to kill Sonia, for whatever reason, but, unable to bring himself to do so, he did the next best thing and killed other women.

* * *

What did Sutcliffe think of all of these theories?

Firstly, was he gay?

Coming to terms with being gay in the tough mill town of Bingley in the 1950s and '60s would have been undoubtedly a crushing experience. Homosexuality wasn't even legal in Sutcliffe's formative years, and the macho community he grew up in meant coming out was all but impossible. Homosexual acts between two consenting men who were 21 or over were not legal until 1967, ironically the year that Sutcliffe turned 21.

Struggling with your sexuality in a household driven by strong male stereotypes like his dad John and brother Mick might trigger an extreme psychological reaction that could be reflected either outward or inward.

When his dad was asked whether Peter might have been gay, he was horrified by the very idea. He gave the impression he would have been more appalled to learn his son was gay than the Yorkshire Ripper.

"All my boys are boys and all my girls are girls and there's nothing in between with any of them," he said. "Peter was just a quiet little lad, that's all. He didn't have any sort of... affectations."

Sutcliffe claimed to have a normal sex life with Sonia, but there was evidence from men and women who knew him before he met her to suggest that on the rare occasions he engaged in sexual activity with girls he seemed disinterested.

There was also an incident on a lads' trip to his grandfather's caravan in Arnside on the south coast of Cumbria with a friend.

The other man later claimed that during a conversation about sex, Sutcliffe lost his temper, grabbed a knife and cut him in his genital area.

Sutcliffe also exhibited an unusually puritanical side to his character for a Bingley lorry driver. In an era when it was common-place for the mills, engineering firms and truck depots where he worked to have a Pirelli calendar or similar showing scantily clad women on the wall, Sutcliffe baulked at such material.

When discussing his arrest and the police search of his house, he was at pains to point out the material they *didn't* find.

"They even went through all our love letters I sent to Sonia when she was at college in London, read through all of them, didn't find a thing. No naughty books or naughty pictures in the house or nothing. There were nothing like that, no dirty books, I never read them, never had no time for them, I rejected them when people tried to show me them, I wouldn't look. I said it's perverted this, like spying through a keyhole. They didn't find anything because there was nothing to find."

His fellow truckers were an earthy bunch who were far more likely to openly discuss and swap such magazines than to be ashamed of being found in possession of them, as Sutcliffe appeared to be.

Taken all together, does this raise a question mark over his sexuality?

"Speculation and lies," is how he described such stories, adding: "I've never been like that in my life. Even as a kid, I was never any way like that. I've never been effeminate in the least."

Of the camping incident, he claimed it was just not true. While discussing it much later when he was in Frankland, Sutcliffe insisted the man had suffered the injury through an industrial accident.

"No such thing, we never had any kind of problem between each other. He just made that up for a story. He worked at a dripping factory in Bingley and there was big melters that you lifted the lid up and threw the meat in there to make the dripping you see, and boil it up and melt it all, and it came down on his prick. He had to go to hospital."

That might be the case but, interestingly, Sutcliffe didn't stop there. He went further by throwing his own accusation at the man in question.

"He was a bit funny that way, a bit queer, a bit… He married and had kids, but he was a bit funny like that, a bit queer, he'll get these ideas."

What about Sutcliffe himself? Did he engage in sex with other men, either before his arrest or after? He said not, expressing a distaste for men on long-term sentences who, denied female company, sought physical comfort with each other.

"I wouldn't lower myself to be depraved like that. It doesn't affect everybody, certainly won't affect me."

Four years after he arrived at Frankland he said: "It disgusts me that it goes on in here. A lot of these people are queers, they call one of them Gorgeous George and he's as ugly as the back of a fireback.

"I hate queers, I think they're disgusting. Sodom and Gomorrah, that's sodomy they practice. The Bible tells you about that, warns you about that sort of thing, to despise that sort of behaviour. God himself hates it.

"I don't like homosexuals at all, they're just a bunch of perverts. God made Adam and Eve, not Adam and Steve, it's a disgusting practice."

To emphasise the point, he told of a time in Broadmoor when an opportunity did arise, with another of Britain's most notorious criminals.

"Ronnie Kray once made advances, but I told him to piss off. One side of him I didn't like, the queer side of him. I was in my underpants and washing my hair at the sink one day, and he stood there leering at me, I thought bloody hell, piss off Ronnie. He was as bent as a nine-bob note. Ron was always on the hunt for somebody, he had young lads fawning after him because they were frightened of him. He went for them."

If there was little direct evidence that Sutcliffe was gay, there was plenty that he was the product of an abusive childhood at the hands of his father, who treated his own wife, Sutcliffe's mother, appallingly.

Was Sutcliffe's exposure to this behaviour enough to spark a deep-rooted view of women that might combine with other factors later in life and explain his offending?

Or did the way his father treated him lead to low self-esteem, a character trait common in many serial killers?

Perhaps, but, inexcusable as it was, John Sutcliffe's conduct was hardly exceptional for that era and the Sutcliffe household was far from unique in the tough, post-war working class housing estates.

Many other children had similar upbringings and didn't turn into serial killers, and Peter wasn't even the primary target of his father's abuse.

"He used to beat me brothers up when they were little. He never beat me up, he hit me with a belt a few times, but never beat me up with his fists and his feet," he said.

And, despite the abuse and abandonment issues, Sutcliffe's view of those early days, looking back from his twilight years, was mostly positive as he dismissed out of hand the idea that his family played any role in the murders.

"It was nothing to do with the family whatsoever. I had a good childhood, I was happy."

So if he rejected the idea that the blame for his crimes lay at the feet of his father, what about his mother?

They were particularly close, but could the strength of that bond have been the problem? Could it have given way to a sense of disappointment and resentment when he realised she wasn't as perfect as he wanted to believe?

A hugely significant family event was when her infidelity was exposed at the hotel confrontation arranged by John.

Did that incident foster a belief that women would always let him down and were, therefore, deserving of punishment?

His anger over the hotel showdown was, though, directed not at his mother for betraying the family but at his father for driving her into the arms of another man.

"My mother was such a good soul, she'd never stepped out of line, but he drove her to it in the end out of desperation."

Sutcliffe was close to the women in his family, but what about his view of women generally? Were the murders the result of an all-consuming hatred he developed for all women, whatever the origins of that hatred might be?

Not so, according to him.

"I didn't hate women, I loved women. I'm no misogynist or anything like that," he said.

Anyone who might have accused him of such?

"They're just typical silly statements people come out with. To fit the image, if it fits the image, use it."

When he said 'the image', he meant that of a woman-hating serial killer based on the premise that if a man kills women repeatedly, then he must hate women.

It's hard to interpret his actions as anything other than a

deep-seated hatred of women, however complex the origin of that might be, but as far as Sutcliffe was concerned it was a "false image".

Sonia plays a central role in many theories of why he murdered.

After all, it was a bitter row with Sonia over the Italian which triggered the very first attack.

Bob Taylor, who was a young detective constable on the Ripper investigation and later rose to the rank of Detective Chief Superintendent, speculated: "When he killed, was it murder by proxy? His compulsive personality became focused on women, but why? Was he killing Sonia over and over again?"

Others wondered whether the suffocating home environment and Sonia's obsessive cleaning regime tipped him over the edge.

Sutcliffe dismissed all of the Sonia-based theories out of hand, citing her ongoing support for him since his arrest as the reason that undermined them.

"Sonia was the only one to be at the trial, braving all the hostility. She must have loved me more than I ever realised, bless her heart."

Their support for each other long after Sutcliffe's conviction proves their bond was as strong as it was complex. Whether it had any role at all in sending him down the path to murder, it's difficult to see how it was the main or even only motivator in sending him out onto the darkened streets to smash 22 women over the head with a hammer.

In many ways, the most complicated theory is the one aired by the prosecution at his trial – that he was a sex killer.

It was hotly disputed at the Old Bailey, where the Crown insisted the attacks were clearly sexual, the defence would only concede a small number of largely irrelevant aspects were and Sutcliffe denied any of it was sexual.

The repeated thrusting of a blade into the same wound, even if it is in the abdomen away from the genital area, is seen by some experts as clearly sexual.

The American serial killer expert Robert Keppel, who helped investigate the Ted Bundy murders, is clear about this point.

"Knives are fearsome and unyielding, and their phallic nature as weapons supersedes any harm the predator can inflict with his penis. Knives are therefore sexual weapons psychologically as well as weapons of combat."

Then there were the strange leggings that Sutcliffe was found to be wearing when he was arrested.

Were they designed with a sex motive in mind? Did he masturbate at the scene of his crimes?

"What a load of rubbish," was Sutcliffe's response, claiming the lack of his DNA at the crime scenes showed he didn't perform such acts. "They never had my DNA. They had to ask me when they interviewed me, so I gladly gave them it because I know it wouldn't make any difference."

If sex was the true, central motivation, then it would be expected to be present in some form in all the attacks, but the evidence from one of the prosecution's own witnesses undermines this.

At the moment of his arrest he was with Olivia Reivers and, by his own admission, was getting ready to kill her. Yet the supposed sex killer was in a noticeably unaroused state, according to Olivia.

How could he be a sexually-motivated killer, given her testimony? And yet, how could he not be, given the elements of some of the other attacks?

Throughout his life, Sutcliffe was desperate not to be seen as a sex attacker.

In relation to stabbing through the same entry wound, he rejected the contention that it was sexual, instead citing a more sickening, yet pragmatic explanation.

"I didn't enjoy stabbing them, so when it was in, I just moved it about to kill them, moving it in different directions."

Similarly, the raising of the upper clothing to expose the breasts had nothing to do with sexual gratification, he said, but was for practical reasons.

"They said it was a sex act, to stab them in the chest. That was ridiculous. How else do you stab somebody?

"That's where you stab to kill. I'm not going to stab their little fingers, am I?"

Most of his contribution to this aspect of the debate, though, focuses on his desperate desire to not be seen as a sex attacker rather than an exploration of his motives.

He would quickly rise to anger when anyone suggested he had been a sexual predator.

"I'm not at all, I never have been. I was trying to stamp that sort of thing out when I was on my mission. It's hurtful.

"All they seem to do is try to make me out like I'm some kind of a sex maniac and it couldn't be further from the truth."

Despite his stance, the evidence suggests there was a sexual element, but it wasn't the only element.

This is not an uncommon feature among serial killers. Research has shown that sexual motivation is more prevalent than any other explanation for serial murder, but not all serial killers overtly express the sexual element and among those killers who do admit to it, it's often not the only element.

Eric Hickey, a former professor in the criminology department at California State University and an FBI consultant, conducted a study of 399 serial killers, a piece of research that is used to help educate criminal investigators all over the world.

He found that sexual motivation was the most common explanation, with 46% of the killers he surveyed stating it as a reason, but only 9% gave it as the *sole* reason. Killers often admitted they enjoyed killing but rarely killed for enjoyment only, and the sexual element was often only a vehicle to achieve their ultimate goal to degrade the victim or to exert power or control over them.

Another expert working in this area is Steven A Egger, the professor of Criminal justice at the University of Illinois and project director of the Homicide Assessment and Lead Tracking

System (HALT) for the state of New York, the first statewide computerised system to track and identify serial murderers.

His findings are similar to Hickey's in that he argues that "although the sexual component is frequently present in a serial murder, it is not the central motivating factor for the killer, but an instrument used to dominate, control and destroy the victim".

If a sexual element was present in Sutcliffe's crimes, but it was not the only element, what other motivating factors were at play?

He was a peculiarly self-absorbed character, both in relation to life's trivial issues when chatting to family or friends on the phone during his incarceration but also in connection to the major, defining moments of his life, the attacks.

He internalised every thought, rarely looking outward to consider how his actions might affect others, only ever being concerned about their effect on him or, the only two notable exceptions, his mother and Sonia.

"When I got home [after an attack] it wasn't on my mind, it was easy to get into bed and go to sleep," he said. "I never thought about the victims. My only thought was, could this murder be the one to lead the police to capturing me or getting close? That was my only concern. I had no trouble at all sleeping.

"Once I had done my kill, it was as if I had satisfied the voice. Once I had done the kill, the voice vanished."

This self-absorption leads to the next possibility – was he a psychopath?

The word 'psychopath' is now outdated in medical and legal circles. Someone who in earlier times would have been termed a psychopath would now be described as having an anti-social personality disorder.

Personality disorders differ from mental illness in that they are inherent and untreatable with medication. Extensive talking therapy may shave off the harder edges of the disorder, but the essential core nature of it, which is as much part of their personality as another's generosity, say, or gregariousness, will always be there.

People with personality disorders possess an outwardly normal shell which hides a deeply abnormal personality. A range of factors are used to clinically identify a psychopath which include, but are not limited to, narcissism, high self-esteem, propensity to violence, callousness, lack of empathy, manipulative, pathological liars, impulsivity and lacking in behavioural controls.

Psychopaths are not mentally ill but do lack a sense of moral guilt and an inability to control their impulse for instant gratification.

Various theories exist as to what causes personality disorders with genetic and environmental factors potential contenders, as is a traumatic head injury. Sutcliffe suffered such an injury when he crashed his motorbike after the fight at the pub.

So was Sutcliffe a psychopath?

All the evidence and medical opinion suggests not. Psychopaths are motivated by an all-consuming fantasy world, which is as addictive to them as heroin to a junkie.

They thrive on subjecting their victims to a high degree of suffering and a significant part of their enjoyment of a murder is not just controlling the victim, but witnessing the terrifying effect that the control has on them.

Ian Brady, who along with Myra Hindley was responsible for the Moors Murders, the killing of five children in Manchester between 1963 and 1965, was a classic example of a psychopath. The victims were sexually assaulted and tortured as Brady tape-recorded part of the horrific ordeal.

It goes without saying that Sutcliffe's victims all suffered an agonising and terrible ordeal. But, appalling and repellent though his actions were, he did not seek to prolong their suffering to afford himself further gratification in the same way Brady did. Whatever satisfaction Sutcliffe derived from murder, it was the lead up to it and the act itself which provided it, not the extended suffering of the victim once she was in his clutches.

Brady was also deeply narcissistic. His letters from the psychiatric hospital where he served his sentence were peppered with withering comments about how pathetic and useless the rest of the world was, and how only he knew the answer to life's many questions.

He had a towering ego with an overbearing sense of superiority.

Although Sutcliffe was a self-absorbed character, he didn't exhibit anywhere near the same degree of narcissism. Sutcliffe was more akin to the boring bloke at the bar who steers every conversation to somehow always be about him, rather than the sneering superiority of Brady.

Neither did psychiatrists find any evidence of a hidden, all-consuming fantasy life. His insistence that the police found no "naughty books" or any similar material in his house appears to support this.

A psychopath's fantasy can be about far more than sex, of course. He may, for example, possess an extensive fantasy of bringing an end to mankind by staging a High School shooting. But as well as Sutcliffe's insistence on the ordinariness of his sex life, there was no other suggestion of any well-developed fantasies in any area of his life.

Asked whether he ever considered himself a psychopath, he said: "No, no, no. Psychopaths got a love of hurting people, it's in their nature. They said you can't treat a psychopath. I've never been labelled a psychopath.

"Never tortured anybody to make them suffer. It was all over in a second, those attacks. They were knocked unconscious, so they didn't know what was happening."

If an antisocial personality disorder can be discounted, was he insane by way of a mental illness, namely the paranoid schizo-phrenia which the medical experts at his trial diagnosed?

Schizophrenia is a brain disorder which is treatable but not curable.

It was first identified as a mental illness in 1887 by a German psychiatrist, Dr Emile Kraepelin, and the term itself was coined just over 20 years later by a Swiss expert, Eugen Bleuler. It comes from the Greek *schizein*, meaning to split, and *phren*, meaning mind, although it has been suggested that 'shattered mind' might be more appropriate than 'split' given the wide-ranging effects the condition can have on a person. A "decreased ability to know what is real" is another way it has been described.

More than a century on from those early milestones, huge advances have been made to understand the condition, but in many ways it also remains shrouded in mystery. There is no cure, no biological or genetic test to identify whether someone has it, and the exact cause remains unknown. There are ongoing debates over whether it is actually a disorder in itself, or should be viewed as an umbrella term for a range of different conditions. In some countries it is no longer even called schizophrenia. Japan replaced it with "integration disorder" in 2002 as it was felt "schizophrenia" carried too much stigma. Following this change, the number of people seeking treatment increased. In South Korea, it is now known as "attunement disorder".

The only way to diagnose schizophrenia is for experienced practitioners to interview and observe. The diagnosis is, therefore, based on what the patient says and how they act, something which troubled the judge at Sutcliffe's trial.

Sufferers experience one or more of a range of symptoms including hallucinations, which can be auditory (hearing voices) or visual (seeing something that isn't there), and delusions (they believe a powerful group such as the CIA is targeting them). The patient experiences these symptoms during a psychotic episode which will be temporary, but will return.

Possible causes include family genetic history or environmental factors such as physical or psychological trauma an unborn baby suffers in the womb, or emotional stress as a young person.

Sutcliffe did have a family history of mental illness, although he didn't put a lot of store by it.

"Yes, an aunt and uncle of ours suffered mental illness for years, but they died many years ago. They were from opposite sides of the family."

They had both been found at various times wandering around exhibiting strange behaviour, but no detailed information about their conditions was known.

Traumatic brain injury has also been floated as a possible cause, with no conclusive proof either way.

It is often assumed that serial killers must be mentally ill – how can they not be, given the horrific suffering they inflict on others? But researchers point out how few serial killers exhibit psychotic behaviour in their everyday lives.

One American study which examined the psychiatric assessments of nearly 2,000 people arrested for homicide between 1964 and 1973 found that only 1% were considered to be psychotic, a finding supported by other research.

Others highlighted how so many killers – and this includes Sutcliffe – appear normal in every aspect of their lives, apart from when they are killing. The only time they appear insane are when they are committing insane acts.

As Sutcliffe's dad John said: "He certainly had some kind of madness in his mind, though I never once saw any sign of it."

Elliott Leyton, a former president of the Canadian Sociology and Anthropology Association who has been termed the 'father of serial killer research', has said: "No matter how hard our psychiatrists search, they are unable to discover much mental disease among our captured multiple murders (except in the nature of their acts)."

Hickey also touches on this area and says: "Serial killers are rarely found to be suffering from psychotic states."

Paranoid schizophrenia was so rare in the 399 serial killers he studied, it doesn't even feature in his book's index.

A puzzling aspect of Sutcliffe's case is that not one person has ever reported witnessing him exhibit seriously abnormal behaviour in his everyday life. His schoolmates and early work colleagues may have thought him a bit odd, and girls in his teenage years talked of an intensely shy boy, but no-one ever talked of any behaviour that appeared to come from psychotic episodes. If Sutcliffe was insane, the only time he exhibited this insanity was in the few minutes he was attacking women.

The psychiatrists who examined him dealt with this conundrum with a diagnosis of encapsulated schizophrenia, a form of the disease in which the rest of the personality remains intact, meaning he was capable of murder during the brief psychotic episodes while appearing sane and normal the rest of the time.

Sutcliffe backed this view: "Doing those terrible things was only a small part of my life, most of the time I was normal."

There was plenty of scepticism of this view from non-medical people involved in his case, but the psychiatry world remained as one in its support of his original diagnosis.

Yet the world of psychiatry is one of shifting sands and ongoing research coupled with society's changing attitudes means the official list of disorders will never be set in stone. Homosexuality, for example, was officially listed as a sociopathic personality disturbance in America until 1973, six years after it was decriminalised in the UK.

The two manuals which classify mental illnesses for practitioners and researchers around the world have, in recent times, changed the way schizophrenia is classified.

Previously the condition had been divided into a number of different sub-types, including the paranoid schizophrenia sub-type which Sutcliffe was diagnosed with.

This division had come to be seen as an unhelpful and imprecise tool when it came to diagnosing a patient, with the sub-types increasingly thought of as varying symptoms of the same disorder rather than distinct disorders in themselves.

By the early 2010s, paranoid schizophrenia was hardly ever referred to in medical research.

So if Sutcliffe was assessed now, he wouldn't be diagnosed as suffering from paranoid schizophrenia.

That's not to say he wouldn't be diagnosed with schizophrenia or a similar but distinct psychotic disorder. Given the faith the medical world showed in his 1981 diagnosis, that would almost certainly be the case.

But the shifting definition of schizophrenia and different ways it is viewed by experts around the world underlines how inexact a science it is to try and evaluate what was going on in Peter Sutcliffe's mind.

To reinforce that difficulty, many of the non-medical experts involved in the Yorkshire Ripper case never did agree with psychiatry's version of Sutcliffe's thought process.

They felt his claims of hearing voices from God didn't stand up to scrutiny when placed next to the practical aspects of some of his attacks. Believe what he does, not what he says, was their view.

As the barrister Harry Ognall said at the trial when doubting the idea that Sutcliffe was simply a pawn of a Lord who only ever seemed to direct him to attack within the boundaries of West Yorkshire, save for the two Manchester exceptions: "Is this God only a Yorkshire God?"

Ognall's difficulty with the medical view was based not only on the manner in which Sutcliffe inflicted some of the wounds, but the cunning and calculated ways in which he tried to evade arrest, just like any criminal does.

For example, his extensive efforts to retrieve the Jordan £5 note. He spent over a week thinking about how to recover the vital piece of evidence, then spent hours driving to Manchester to look for it, mutilating her body in an uncontrollable fury when he failed to locate it and then heading home. Can all of those actions be laid at the door of a mental illness? If not, then other factors must be at play as well.

The final component in the complicated equation of what made Sutcliffe tick is, simply, was he evil?

Just as with schizophrenia, there is no scientific test to determine whether someone is evil or not. It can't be measured and therefore doesn't feature in the scientific world, but outside the laboratory it is a term which is used often and is reserved for people who have committed the very worst acts.

But, for all that it is a commonly used term, does evil even exist as an explanation of why people do bad things? Is evilness their motivating factor rather than being ill, or a psychopath? And if it does exist, how bad does bad have to be to amount to evil?

One researcher defined it as "individuals who appear to have progressed past worldly temptations, have become devils unto themselves, completely without guilt, remorse or compassion for their victims."

Another stressed that it is a process which includes the principle of agency or choice. There are countless decisions to be made to do the right thing or the wrong thing on a path between being all good and all bad. The more wrong decisions a person makes, the further along the path towards evil it takes them.

Yet another definition is that evil people are "people of the lie", constantly engaged in self-deception and the deception of others. As such, evilness may not be defined by laws, but it can be defined by our view of the "consistency of their sins".

All the major religions believe in evil and they have billions of followers, which is a pretty strong consensus to support its existence.

Even one of the medical experts called at Sutcliffe's trial, Dr Pat McGrath, the medical superintendent at Broadmoor for 24 years, believed in it.

While in charge at Broadmoor, he refused to allow Moors Murderer Ian Brady to be admitted, saying he was one of only two men he had ever met who were not sick, but evil, and therefore beyond help.

Sutcliffe knew what it meant to be evil, but claimed it didn't apply to him.

"I know I'm not at all in any way shape or form, in fact I thought I was doing good work, God's work. I've never been evil in my life. I've always been a God-fearing person.

"I've never had any evil intent, I always thought I was doing something good, inspired by God. I know it was wrong, but I thought it was the right thing to do, getting messages from God and all that, and it couldn't be wrong."

But in terms of considering whether Sutcliffe was evil, sometimes it's the little details which speak the loudest.

Many years after his arrest, following decades of treatment with anti-psychotic medication, countless therapy sessions and a long time to reflect on what he had done, Sutcliffe's comments about his victims and the suffering he inflicted on them, published here for the first time, help reveal his true nature.

These comments were offered unprompted in quiet, one-to-one conversations held away from the ears of doctors or Broadmoor staff. They weren't made as part of any process that could have benefited him, so there was no reason for him to lie. These comments, therefore, reveal more of himself than even he realised.

He referred to one of the women he attacked as "ugly" and said of another that "she had a horrible smell about her".

These weren't work colleagues he was being cruel about or anonymous women he had seen in a pub or passed in the street. They were women whose lives he had taken or destroyed.

He talked about one victim with a complete lack of empathy for the desperate situation she found herself in, which had not been helped by his acts.

"After I attacked her, she was in the paper arrested for prostitution a month later. She wasn't seriously injured. She was arrested for soliciting, it was in the papers, caught soliciting a month after being attacked."

He claimed the women who survived his attacks were publicity seekers.

"They love it, the publicity, they seek it," he said.

He also described a relative of a murder victim as a "publicity seeker", threw the same insult at someone who had found one of his victim's bodies and claimed he had done all of his victims a favour by making them part of "an exclusive club".

When discussing his second to last non-fatal attack on the Singaporean doctor Upadhya Bandara and it was pointed out that her first name was difficult to pronounce, he said: "Think of someone letting go of a balloon, UP-IN-DE-AIR".

He laughed as he said it.

And when talking about Margaret Thatcher's dissatisfaction with the police's inability to catch him and her threat to travel to Yorkshire to sort it all out herself, Sutcliffe said: "If she did come up to Yorkshire, she could have been one of my victims."

Again he laughed. It wasn't a serious threat to cause harm to the former Prime Minister. It was said in a way which is arguably even more sinister and telling. He was using his crimes as a basis for comedy. That's pretty evil.

At different times, Sutcliffe rejected every theory about why he became the Yorkshire Ripper.

But towards the end of his life, after decades spent in top security accommodation with plenty of time to ponder what he had done and why, what was his opinion of the reasons behind his transformation into a serial killer?

"I was suffering from an illness which caused hallucinations which were so realistic that I misinterpreted what was happening to me," he said.

"Mental illness can be a deciding factor in a person's actions, as they will tend to act out of character.

"I didn't want to do what I did, I was being controlled by my illness, but the tragedy is I didn't think I was ill, I just believed I was caught up in a miracle, so when things happened to thwart the police I simply believed it was divine intervention and thought no more of it.

"It's played down or even ignored by society, they only want to see people as being bad.

"It was only a short, brief period in my life, the events only took a short time, a matter of two or three minutes and I was gone."

And yet, even when claiming his actions were the result of something beyond his control, he still found himself unable to express full remorse.

"I've got deep regrets, I wish it'd never happened, but what can you do? You can't turn the clocks back and you can't have the knowledge then that you have now."

Such limited regret that he did express was always qualified and inevitably led quickly back to how his actions had had a devastating effect not on others, but on himself.

"Personally, I felt deeply traumatised not believing my mind was my own when I was suffering from the hallucinations – as I now know them to have been. It took me over 12 years inside before I gained any insight into my illness, and even then it was after I'd been put on anti-psychotic injections, which at first I strongly opposed.

"The brain is a very complex and fragile thing, and no-one should sit in judgement unless they are properly qualified in matters relating to mental illness – or if someone in your family has suffered from some such affliction. Only then can you speak from personal experience."

He held on to the diagnosis of paranoid schizophrenia like a drowning man clings to a piece of driftwood, using it to absolve himself of all responsibility. It wasn't him that committed those unthinkable acts, it was his illness. And if he could also toss a chunk of the culpability fate's way, then all the better for leaving him with no blame to deal with.

The mental illness diagnosis allowed him to pack away his terrible deeds into a box that he could shut tight and place in the furthest corner of his mind. Having done that, he came to view his murders as if they were not his to own.

That allowed him to achieve a sense of peace denied to his victims and their families, which was underlined by the indignant way he reacted if anyone ever labelled him as bad or evil.

"'Oh what a bad guy he is and all that' and I'm not, they don't focus on the illness.

"It was a serious mental illness that I had all them years. And I accepted it. I've come to terms with it that it wasn't God. And that's the only reason it permitted me to go ahead with it, believing it was a miracle from God, you see. I don't believe that now, my whole outlook and everything has changed drastically.

"It's no use beating your head against a wall though because there's little you can do to put matters right – just make your peace with God."

He may have been desperate to believe that everything was down to one simple cause – his mental illness – but perhaps a truer, more complete view of the forces at work in transforming him into a serial killer came from his own mouth in a brief throwaway remark he made when discussing whether he had been ill or a sexual predator.

"Nobody's one-dimensional," he said.

The police investigation into his crimes was the most expensive and complex the country had ever seen. Some of the most able and qualified lawyers and medical professionals in the country tried to make sense of why he had killed, and why so many times.

They couldn't agree and nearly half a century on with the benefit of huge advances in forensic psychiatry and every related discipline, we still don't know, precisely and definitively, what makes a serial killer.

The jury couldn't make their minds up either.

CHAPTER 27

BEHIND BARS

Judges always ask jurors to reach the most desirable result possible – a unanimous verdict whereby all of them agree that the defendant is either guilty or not guilty.

That's not always possible so, when the judge is content they have exhausted every possible route to unanimity, he will offer them a majority verdict, which is 10-2 on a jury of 12.

At 3.28pm, just over five hours after the Sutcliffe jury was sent out, they returned to inform the judge that unanimity was proving impossible.

The judge offered them the option of returning a majority verdict and, as is often the case, this fresh alternative option quickly unpicked the deadlock and at 4.15pm everyone who was eagerly waiting in the corridor watched as the usher unlocked the court doors. There was a verdict.

The foreman of the jury took six minutes to deliver the 13 verdicts in turn – guilty of murder on all counts.

The jury had rejected the medical evidence that Sutcliffe was mentally ill and instead sided with the prosecution – he was a calculated, sexually-motivated killer who had lied about the voices and the mission. He was bad, not mad.

On his feet and surrounded by five security guards, Sutcliffe had listened impassively as the verdicts were read out. When the foreman finished, he sat down. Sutcliffe made to follow him, but two of the guards prevented him from doing so. He had just lost the right to do the simplest of tasks without the permission of someone in authority.

Mr Justice Boreham said it was difficult to find the words to adequately describe the depravity of Sutcliffe's crimes before telling him: "I have no doubt you are a very dangerous man indeed. The sentence for murder is laid down by the law and is immutable. It is a sentence that you be imprisoned for life."

He recommended that Sutcliffe should serve at least 30 years before he could be considered for release. He also passed seven life sentences for the attempted murder charges which Sutcliffe had admitted.

The journalists rushed to file copy, conscious that the clock was marching towards deadline. The police officers and prosecution lawyers celebrated the jury verdict, the defence psychiatrists licked their wounds, and Sutcliffe was placed in a prison van and taken to Brixton prison. Eleven days later, he was transferred to Parkhurst on the Isle of Wight.

"I came back from court to Brixton and collected my things. They took me in the van to Parkhurst on my birthday, second of June. I thought, that's typical, they done it on purpose.

"I've been in several prisons on this sentence. Armley, Brixton, Wormwood Scrubs, Isle of Wight and then up to Broadmoor. The worst place I think was Wormwood Scrubs. There were cockroaches all over the place. Used to have to look out for them in your food. Brixton was another manky-hole."

The prison van which took him to Parkhurst drove from London to Portsmouth and then onto a ferry for the 45-minute crossing.

"I didn't see anything, the van had no windows in it. They didn't have people carriers then. It drove downwards into the ferry, so even if it had windows you couldn't have seen anything. I had handcuffs on as well."

His arrival at the top security prison went smoothly with little negative reaction from other inmates, at least to begin with.

"We all had our own cells. I had an 'A' sign [on the cell door]. A big 'A' for category 'A' prisoner, the most dangerous. I wasn't in solitary or anything, I was mixing every day.

"We had cardboard furniture in case we hit anybody with a chair or something. Cardboard table, cardboard chair, only the bed wasn't cardboard.

"The only association we had was two half-hour sessions of exercise per day outside and a two-hour film show at night from around 6pm to around 8pm.Then we were banged up for the night.

"I was never segregated, they just left me to get on with it.

"It's a tough nick, one of the toughest. Two prisoners in the cells either side of me hung themselves. Everybody thought it'd be me next, but it wasn't to be. It's the easy way out. It's a lot harder to do a long, many-year sentence.

"The earliest part of a long sentence is the hardest and the most likely time for a person to contemplate suicide. It's really bad and not even knowing if you're gonna ever get out or stay in the rest of your life.

"But who'd rather do life than have a lethal injection? Doing life's a hell of a tough thing when you're doing 30-40 years inside or whatever until the end of your life, it's a hell of a burden. Often you think to yourself, it'll be a lot better if you'd have just been done away with in the first place.

"You have to be strong to carry on. Sonia was visiting me every month and I felt loved – as well as hated – so I kept going.

"My first Christmas inside was in Parkhurst. It seemed really strange having Christmas dinner on my own in my cell for the first time. That's where the prisoners always ate as they didn't have a dining area. They brought all meals round to your cell on a trolley."

Shortly after the trial, Sonia had announced her intention to stand by her husband regardless of the verdict.

"I shall go on visiting him wherever he is," she said.

She kept her word and began making the journey from Bradford to Parkhurst every month, staying on the island so she could make repeated visits to him, lumping together her entire month's allocation across a few days.

"They had a special place where visitors could stay," said Sutcliffe. "It was only about a fiver a night. She'd visit for three days on the trot and she used to come every month. You could have three visits a month, she had all three one after another in the same week."

While he was at Parkhurst, Sutcliffe met a number of other notorious inmates, including Reggie Kray who was doing a life sentence for the murder of Jack 'The Hat' McVitie in 1967.

"I knew Reggie in Parkhurst, he was in the next cell to me for quite a while. He only weighed about 11 stone, very slim, about 5ft 8in, everybody pictures them as being big fellas, but they weren't, just ordinary. I was on the same wing as Reg for two years and we got along okay."

Like most prisoners, Sutcliffe only had respect for the Krays, which is more than he displayed for another high-profile inmate he had met briefly during his time in Wormwood Scrubs before his trial.

"Ian Brady seems to actually enjoy people's suffering, but then that's the trademark of a psychopath," he said.

"I played a game of chess with him. I played Brady two or three times, but he wouldn't play me in the end because I beat him.

"Not that I was friends with him, but he was an acquaintance, you get acquainted with all sorts of people.

"He brought the meals round to the cells on a trolley, he had an air of… like he thought he was… like a snob, like very important."

A number of years later, a newspaper article revealed Brady's claims to be the most notorious criminal in the country, dismissing Sutcliffe because "he's had 34 mentions in the press this year. I've had 144" and adding: "Why do you think I'm still top of the ratings after 40 years?"

Sutcliffe was furious.

"He's such an idiot is the man, such a loose cannon, saying he's a much bigger criminal than me and all that, who wants to hear that rubbish? Pathetic. You wouldn't think somebody would be proud of what they'd done, would you? I can't understand him, he's just a psychopath, an idiot, full of himself, and he's shallow, very shallow and stupid, he's not intelligent really in the real sense of the word. Thinks he's the bee's knees.

"It shows how his mind works, doesn't it? He's sick in the head, he's proud of what he's done.

"He basks in the publicity. He loves it, he says he were more popular than the original Jack the Ripper. He's wrong in the head, he's mentally ill the man, he might not even realise it himself, but he is. I mean, look at the things he comes out with. He equated killing kids with a triviality. He's mentally ill to say things like that.

"He loves the publicity. Unlike myself, I hate it, but he seems to thrive on it. He even gets jealous if I seem to get more publicity than him, which is very weird."

Yet, despite his dismissal of Brady's league table of criminals, Sutcliffe couldn't stop himself making a bid for top spot.

"I'm a lot more high profile than anybody else."

While in Parkhurst, Sutcliffe also met a well-known prison visitor who would become a close friend.

"I first met Jimmy Savile in 1981 at Parkhurst.

"He did a lot of charity and marathon running and stuff. And he used to come round the prison at Parkhurst. He came in chatting to me, asking how I was, did I miss Yorkshire?"

Sutcliffe was a keen painter, something which Savile quickly focused on.

"He said: 'I wonder if I could ask you a favour? Would you do a portrait of me for Stoke Mandeville Hospital?' I said: 'Yeah, all right.' So I did a big picture of him, a really big one, in his tracksuit, and he's supposed to have hung it up there.

"I used to enjoy art at school, but I never really got into it seriously until I began copying all the great masters' works when I was in Parkhurst.

"I was self-taught and it really did help to pass the time."

As Sutcliffe was settling in at Parkhurst, with a failed appeal against his conviction behind him, the recriminations over the way the police conducted the Ripper investigation were in full swing.

The West Yorkshire force came in for bitter criticism for failing to apprehend him earlier and a wide-ranging inquiry was launched into their investigation, led by Lawrence Byford, HM Chief Inspector of Constabulary.

Sir Lawrence, who was knighted two years after the report was published, made it clear that the investigation had cost lives by its failure to apprehend Sutcliffe earlier. A large part of the criticism was directed at the Oldfield-driven obsession with the tape and letters which derailed the investigation.

His recommendations also heralded huge changes in the way that major investigations in the future would be conducted, with computers soon replacing the paper-led approach.

There was a huge interest in the report, including among the wider public, but there wasn't deemed to be enough public interest to actually make it public.

The report was unveiled in the House of Commons by the Home Secretary Willie Whitelaw on January 19, 1982, but the full report was not published.

There was no national security interest at stake and it did not pose a threat to any individual or any ongoing criminal investigation (one section dealing with other possible attacks could have been redacted), yet only a summary was publicly released.

Politicians and the public – especially in Yorkshire – were baffled and furious. There had been serious errors in the inquiry and the people who had suffered most from them were those in Yorkshire, yet they were denied the chance to read the report exposing those failings.

A number of Yorkshire MPs pleaded in the House of Commons for Whitelaw to release the full report, and he claimed: "I am anxious to be as forthcoming as possible."

But not forthcoming enough. It would be another 24 years before the report was released and then only after the Tony Blair government introduced the Freedom of Information Act to improve the public's right of access to official documents.

Down on the Isle of Wight, the man who had been responsible for the need for the report felt he had enjoyed a smooth transition to prison life, but by early 1983 he had become a relative recluse.

He spent most of his time alone on F2 wing in the jail's hospital, a unit reserved for inmates under psychiatric observation. There were ongoing efforts to have him transferred to a secure hospital and Sutcliffe's recollections of that period suggested his mental health was deteriorating, although as ever, his memories were self-serving and aimed at reducing his own culpability for his actions.

"I don't have any nightmares," he said. "In the past I've had... they weren't nightmares, they were actual visual things that happened to me. That's when I was hallucinating, you see.

"Like when one of the victims came back at night, floating above my bed in Parkhurst, and she said she understands why I had to do what I did and God's explained it to her and all that.

"It was my second victim, Emily Jackson, who came back to me in my cell. God told her she shouldn't have led the type of life she had been living, she told me that God had explained to her why I'd killed her, and it was okay.

"It was when I was wide awake, really upset me, though before she finished speaking she changed into my mother. Really shook me up that.

"Her body floating in the air and changing into my mother, and then my mother's voice came.

"She told me that she never knew what I'd been doing to all those women as she'd died before my arrest, but the spirits have told her everything."

Was this a way of him subconsciously trying to cope with what he had done or justify it in some way?

"It could have been, I suppose," Sutcliffe said before yet again trying to make the case that he wasn't wholly bad, despite the awful deeds he had done. "I wasn't like that all the time, those terrible things I done were only a small part of my life, I was just like anyone else doing normal things most of the time.

"It wasn't me who was doing it, I was doing it under an influence of what I thought was God's voice, I was totally detached from real life."

In Parkhurst, Sutcliffe had developed a habit of censoring newspapers before other inmates could read them by either scribbling out reports he didn't like or cutting them out. He had grown to hate the media and constantly moaned how newspapers and television documentaries were biased against him.

This self-appointed role as prison censor infuriated other inmates, and when he scribbled over an article about a recent prison siege he upset the wrong man.

Jimmy Costello had earned his criminal spurs on the tough streets of Glasgow's housing estates in the 1960s when violent, knife-wielding gangs such as the notorious Tongs ruled the roost.

He was serving ten years for firearms offences when, on Monday, January 10, 1983, he smashed a glass coffee jar and thrust it twice into Sutcliffe's face when he took exception to yet another bout of censorship, nearly blinding him. He suffered a five-inch cut across the left side of his face which raked across his eyelid, narrowly missing his eyeball and leaving him needing 30 stitches.

Costello was sentenced to another five years and was later moved to Broadmoor while doctors continued their efforts to also have Sutcliffe transferred to a similar establishment.

Twice, in 1982 and 1983, psychiatrists recommended to the Home Secretary that he should be transferred from prison. On both occasions, their recommendations were rejected. It was felt that his condition did not merit it and, so soon after the trial, the public interest continued to outweigh such a move.

As these discussions were taking place, Sutcliffe said he was told by the voices that his mission was finally over.

"That happened in '83, in Parkhurst. It's only when I was told that the mission was over, and I wouldn't have to do anything like that again, I told the doctor. That mission was only a small part of my life. I was pleased to hear it was over. I still had the voices for years later, telling me good and bad things."

Did he have any involvement in the process relating to whether he stayed in prison or was moved to hospital?

"No, I never tried to get moved anywhere, other people tried to have me moved."

That move finally came when the Government relented in March, 1984. The then Home Secretary, Leon Brittan, was persuaded by the medical professionals that Sutcliffe's condition had deteriorated to such an extent that a transfer to hospital under the Mental Health Act 1983 was now necessary.

Brittan didn't want to make such a high-profile decision without keeping the Prime Minister fully informed, especially after her previous interest in the case when Sutcliffe was still at large.

He sent Thatcher a note dated March 22, 1984, outlining his plans and including a copy of the statement he intended to make to the House on the day that the transfer would take place, timed for after Sutcliffe had arrived at Broadmoor.

He made it clear that the medical reports left him in no doubt that Sutcliffe should be transferred so he could receive treatment (in prison, medication could only be administered with consent and Sutcliffe wasn't consenting).

Without treatment, Brittan said, he could represent a "grave danger to prison staff and other people who come into contact with him".

He added: "At this stage there is no means of knowing whether he will have to remain in hospital indefinitely or whether he will recover his mental health sufficiently to allow him to be sent back to prison to continue his sentence."

He planned to announce the move in the House with a written reply to an arranged question from a fellow Tory MP, which would start: "I have received recent reports from which I am satisfied that Sutcliffe's mental condition has seriously deteriorated and that he is now suffering from a grave form of mental illness."

Thatcher, always one for detail, responded with a short, barely legible note scribbled at the top of his memo saying: "Do you need the word 'grave'?"

David Barclay, Thatcher's Private Secretary, spoke to staff in the Home Office to clarify this issue. They explained that the word helped explain to the public that his condition had worsened since the trial and the law requires that the Home Secretary must be satisfied that the mental condition an inmate is suffering from is "grave" before he can authorise a hospital transfer.

Barclay finished his briefing note to Thatcher by asking: "Content, in the light of this explanation, for the present wording to stand?"

Thatcher gave the green light. She wrote on Barclay's memo: "Yes. MT." The handwriting still wasn't very clear, but no doubt Barclay could read it well enough.

Brittan delivered the news of the transfer on March 27, 1984.

"He did me a favour there did Leon Brittan," said Sutcliffe, delighted now he was finally in a hospital rather than a top-security prison.

"They only decided to transfer me from Parkhurst because the doctors didn't give up. They kept pressurising Leon Brittan to move me as they were angry at what happened in court with such a blatantly biased judge."

It was another remarkable chapter in the wrangle between the medical and legal worlds, with the jury's rejection of unanimous medical opinion being considered unusual enough for it to be discussed in legal circles for years to come.

A few hours before Brittan's written answer was published, Sutcliffe was asleep in his cell at Parkhurst. It was early and still dark outside. He was woken by a noise outside his cell window and the sound of guards approaching.

"I didn't even know I was going. I heard a lot of commotion outside my window in the yard, that's the first thing I knew that I was going. There's no preparing or nothing. They just came and took me. I heard heavy footsteps coming towards my cell, doors slamming, and then they got closer, came into the block and coming nearer and nearer to my cell and I thought 'Oh hey up, they're coming for me'.

"The door burst open and the screws said: 'Come on, you're being moved, so get dressed.'

"I put a few clothes on and left everything, they said they'd send it on. I didn't even know where I was going. I thought I might be going to Ashworth, I didn't know I was going to Broadmoor.

"I was taken outside, it was still dark, and put into the prison van. We had a police escort down to the ferry and when we got to the mainland we got a police escort to Broadmoor."

The van had darkened windows, meaning Sutcliffe got a limited view on the 90-minute journey from Portsmouth to Berkshire, complete with police escort. But he was able to peer through the windscreen to observe the entrance of Broadmoor when the convoy finally arrived at the hospital.

"I could see it through the glass at the front, I could see the entrance with the clock above it.

"I was seeing this place as my home for the rest of my life."

He was taken to Glastonbury Ward within the Somerset House building, where he was checked in by staff before being taken for a bath.

"They take you into the bathroom, stripped down completely and get into the bath. You have a bath, wash your hair, there's about 10 of them stood round you grinning and talking, you feel like you're in a goldfish bowl.

"I was locked in with just my pyjamas for three days before being allowed to join the community in the dayroom.

"It was very strict in those days and you just had to sit in your chair. If you wanted to use the toilet you had to raise your hand and ask permission."

Once settled in, he was given access to some of the vast number of letters which had been sent to him while he was at Parkhurst but had not yet been given due to the rules on the number of letters inmates can receive while in prison.

"In Parkhurst, we were only allowed three letters per week. When I was being transferred, there were three large hessian sacks full of letters to me, letters I wasn't allowed in Parkhurst. When I arrived at Broadmoor they said to me, pick one bag, which I did. They then said, 'now you're here, you can write to as many people as you like'. I decided to pick so many of the most recent ones, it was overwhelming after being allowed only three letters per week."

What he also found overwhelming was the morning and night-time routines.

"When you used to get up in the morning, you used to come out of your room in the nude, stand in the corridor and wait till they came and unlocked your locker that was fastened to the wall at the other side of the corridor with your clothes in. You had to leave your pyjamas inside your cell, and everybody's stood in the corridor bollock-naked waiting to get dressed. It was really weird. A queer's paradise. And the same time at night, you had to get all your clothes off, stood in the corridor, put them all in the cupboard. They came and locked the cupboards and then they opened your doors, so you had to stand there bollock-naked till they came and open your doors to let you in at night and then you put your pyjamas on. It was terrible. It was meant to humiliate people.

"And you used to have to wear a shirt and tie at your meal times. It's all changed now, though. Some things have changed for the better, some have changed for the worse."

Sutcliffe arrived at Broadmoor at a critical time, one of the most notorious periods in its history, when there was an unprecedented focus on some of the highest profile offenders the country had ever known.

CHAPTER 28

BROADMOOR

Broadmoor opened in 1863 as an asylum for the criminally insane with the first residents being 95 women, many of whom had killed their own children, most likely while in the grip of undiagnosed and untreated postnatal depression.

The following year, five blocks to house men were opened alongside the solitary women's block.

The sprawling campus in the village of Crowthorne, Berkshire, was the only facility of its kind in the UK, until Rampton opened in Nottinghamshire in 1912 to cater for disturbed people in the Midlands and the north, and it quickly established a unique place in the nation's psyche.

It was imbued with a sense of Gothic horror, the sinister asylum where the most crazed and terrifying criminals were locked away. The foreboding red brick architecture, including the iconic main gate and clock tower, only served to strengthen the public's view of the place. If it was a movie, dark skies would be spitting out thunder and lightning.

A series of incidents helped cement this view, the most notorious of which came in 1952 when John Straffen escaped and murdered a five-year-old girl while on the run.

The old Victorian buildings were replaced in 2019 with a purpose-built hospital, the latest in a long line of changes since 1984 when Sutcliffe arrived. The naked morning and evening parades, for example, have long been scrapped.

Although it retains the status of a category B prison, Broadmoor is a hospital not a prison and is run by the West London NHS Trust, not the Ministry of Justice.

Around 70% of the patients (which can total 210, all men – the women's block having been closed in 2005) end up there following a criminal conviction, but once there they are 'patients' not 'inmates', they reside in 'bedrooms' not 'cells' and are being 'treated' not 'punished'.

When Sutcliffe arrived, there was an unrelenting focus on high-profile patients such as Ronnie Kray. The 1980s had kicked off with a child killer escaping and then three weeks later a man serving time for killing a friend with a grappling hook also made good his escape.

A couple of years before the decade began, two patients barricaded themselves in a room with a third, who they subjected to nine hours of torture.

They hog-tied him with the cord from a record player, partially skinned him and then strangled him to death before parading him in front of the door spyhole so the guards could see what had been achieved in the time they had been unable to gain entry.

Treatment at Broadmoor comes in the form of medication and a range of therapies including art and craft, and cooking. Various talking therapies, such as cognitive behaviour therapy, are also employed.

The main goal is for patients to achieve 'insight', which means an acknowledgement that something is wrong with them, the staff are trying to help them and if they co-operate they may improve.

Sutcliffe struggled for years to achieve this insight. He accepted he was no longer on the mission before he went to Broadmoor, but he was a long way from accepting that he was mentally ill.

"It was a message from God two years after my trial when I was told I'd never have to kill again and the mission was over. It was nothing to do with treatment as I never had any treatment while I was in prison."

He refused to take anti-psychotic medication for almost a decade. In 1993 staff began forcibly medicating him following a ruling by the Mental Health Commission. Following this, he developed a more favourable view of therapy and began to engage in that side of treatment.

One common side effect of the medication – some of which is taken in tablet form and swallowed with a cup of water which Sutcliffe called "Bingley Vodka" – is increased appetite. Another is increased lethargy, which in turn leads to decreased interest in exercise.

Also, food in general takes on a revered status due to most other worldly pleasures being denied the patients. The weekly visit to Broadmoor's food shop where patients can stock up on fattening snacks like sweets, crisps and biscuits is a highlight of most of their lives.

All of this means that obesity is a major issue in Broadmoor, along with the Type 2 diabetes it can be a cause of. Up to 25% of Broadmoor patients have diabetes, compared to 5.9% in the population as a whole.

Sutcliffe was no different. Thanks to his love of food, his weight ballooned while in Broadmoor and, like so many of the other patients, he developed diabetes.

He attended cookery lessons with the Occupational Therapist, and his voice brimmed with pride when he told how he had been chosen to demonstrate how to make Yorkshire puddings.

The social side of life at Broadmoor also illustrates how it is a hospital not a prison, and at times barbecues were arranged for the patients, which Sutcliffe loved attending.

After one, he said: "It was really enjoyable. The food was brilliant and plentiful. There was loads of those jumbo sausages and burgers left over as we only had five patients as guests and the usual O/T's [Occupational Therapists] and psychologists there for the free grub. There was everything you could possibly think of to go with the meat and lots to drink plus different gateaux."

At a Christmas party one year, Sutcliffe surpassed himself when he managed to eat three meals.

"I had the steak and the chips and onion rings and mushrooms, then I had sausage and mash with peas and thick gravy and then I had a chicken curry with rice and peas. A big gateau with ice cream."

It was no surprise that his weight was heading towards 20st.

Eating is such a cherished hobby among Broadmoor patients that food items and soft drinks take on a value which outweighs their actual monetary worth, leading to huge dramas if anything goes missing.

One day Sutcliffe discovered two, two-litre bottles of cola belonging to him and another patient had vanished from a fridge which was usually locked with only staff members holding keys. He was incandescent.

"Talk about sneaky, we've got a tea leaf on the ward, stole two bottles of diet coke. It's diabolical stealing our stuff."

Although it's not a prison, Broadmoor keeps to strict routines.

"I get up at 7:15," said Sutcliffe, "then the medicines at half past, breakfast's at 7:45, last person's usually finished by 8:10, and then it's the community meeting, the plan of the day meeting at 8:15, which don't usually start till 20 past, that goes on 20 minutes or so-so, then it's getting on for 9 o'clock."

The contents of a bedroom are also strictly controlled.

"We can have a bed, a wardrobe, a large chest of drawers, a table or small cabinet, a TV, a VCR, a music centre, posters (on one wall only) 30 items of clothing plus in addition 12 pairs of socks, 12 pairs of boxer shorts, 12 CDs plus 12 tapes and five videos, 12 books, 12 magazines, two drinking mugs and a teaspoon, plus a chair and, of course, your bedding and a pair of very thick curtains as there are bright lights outside the windows at night."

It may not be a prison, but there were still bars on Sutcliffe's windows, and during his early years at the hospital he found himself staring at them as an audacious plan began forming in his mind.

If he could acquire a hacksaw blade and spend the night sawing through the bars, then eventually he might be able to make it out into the grounds and scale the perimeter wall.

It was an escape plot straight out of a Hollywood movie and in-keeping with the best scripts, he didn't just involve any old fellow patient to help him achieve his aims. He went for the top drawer – Ronnie Kray.

He met Ronnie – the twin brother of Reggie, who Sutcliffe got to know at Parkhurst – shortly after arriving at Broadmoor.

Just like his brother, Ronnie was doing life for murder after he shot dead George Cornell in the Blind Beggar pub in Whitechapel in 1966 and, just like Sutcliffe, he had been diagnosed with paranoid schizophrenia. After a spell in prison, he was transferred to Broadmoor in 1979.

Broadmoor gossip had it that they didn't get on, which was not so according to Sutcliffe, who also rebuffed the idea that Ronnie hated him so much that he previously arranged for a prisoner in Parkhurst to attack him when he was there.

"I read it in a newspaper, I think it said that Ronnie had put a contract out on me, but when I met him I pulled him about it and he totally denied any such thing. If it was true, he must have been scared to admit it, but I believed him and we got on okay.

"I used to cut his hair and we used to sit and chat. Ronnie couldn't stand his hair being long; he always had to have it short and looking smart.

"I'm a Laird of Camster in Scotland. [A friend] bought me some land up there, I've got a certificate and everything and a photograph of the land. Ronnie wanted to buy it off me. He thought he was gonna get out… he didn't know he was gonna drop dead.

"He always thought people were talking about him, but he always trusted me, and he trusted me to cut his hair and we got on all right."

Ronnie had a reputation of being a sharp dresser, appearing in the visiting room in a striking suit with monogrammed handkerchief and cufflinks. But Sutcliffe revealed that was just for public show, and his dress sense on the ward left something to be desired.

"He dressed like a tramp on the ward. Scruffy old jeans and scruffy shirt, not dressed up at all. He only wore [suits] to show off to impress people, but when he came back to the ward he was a bit of a slob."

It was no surprise Ronnie made an effort to look his best for visits, given the list of celebs who went to see him, which included Richard Burton, Barbara Windsor and Debbie Harry.

"I seen Roger Daltrey and lots of people come to visit Ron," said Sutcliffe, who also revealed that drama was never far away when Ronnie was about.

"I remember when he came back with all blood on his suit from a visit where his visitor had punched him in the face. Ronnie was a bit trusting, he thought everybody who wanted to visit him were a good friend and he hadn't seen this bloke for donkeys years, and he had a grudge against Ronnie and he punched him on the visit. They had to drag him out."

The twins have been immortalised in numerous films and television shows over the years, including the 1990 movie *The Krays,* when they were played by the pop star brothers Gary and Martin Kemp.

"Them two Kemp brothers came to visit Ronnie and Reggie many times and discussed everything, got to know their personalities, so they could portray them as near as possible.

"So Ronnie was happy with that and so was Reggie, they thought they'd done a pretty good job on it.

"He didn't like his mother portrayed as cursing like that. But they were fairly happy with the outcome of the film."

Did Ronnie's reputation mean he got special treatment in Broadmoor?

"No, he was treated the same as everyone, it's just what people put in books for his public image. One time his job was to clean the toilets. A member of staff went into a cubicle and took a look, shouting out to Ron. He said: 'Ron, did you clean the toilets?' To which Ron shouted back that he had. With that, the member of staff said: 'Well, get fucking back and clean the shit off properly.' Ron went back and cleaned the toilet. After that, Ron packed that job in. It was a voluntary job to earn a little bit of extra money."

The idea that Ronnie and Sutcliffe didn't get on is further undermined by the revelation that the Kray twin helped him acquire the hacksaw blade which he intended to use to achieve his freedom.

"It came from a friend of Ronnie Kray's who was a patient in Broadmoor," explained Sutcliffe.

Had it been smuggled in from outside?

"It could have been brought in, as security wasn't that good back then, but inside Broadmoor we had workshops, that's where I think it came from. I just know Ronnie Kray was involved in getting us the blade."

The blade was snapped in half and a friend of Sutcliffe's, who intended to escape with him, took the other section to get to work on the bars in his own room.

"I nearly managed to cut through one of the bars in my cell window," Sutcliffe said proudly.

After progressing the escape attempt each night, he hid the blade during the day behind a skirting board.

Sonia has previously been reported to have had knowledge of what he was up to, but he insisted that was not the case.

"Sonia had nothing to do with it," he said.

The escape attempt came to an abrupt end when, without warning, he was moved to another room.

"For some reason I was moved to another cell, nothing to do with what I'd been trying to do.

"After a while, that cell was being decorated and it was noticed that the bar on the window had been nearly cut through. Because it had been a while since I'd done it, it had turned rusty so no connection was made to me."

Ronnie Kray died in 1995 after collapsing with a heart attack on a corridor in Broadmoor aged 61. Sutcliffe revealed that it was Kenneth Erskine, the Stockwell Strangler who was convicted of seven murders in 1988, who raised the alarm.

Erskine was also one of the patients who came to Sutcliffe's rescue when he was attacked in 1996, the second attempt on his life since his trial.

Paul Wilson, who had been sent to Broadmoor following a conviction for robbery, tried to strangle Sutcliffe in his bedroom using a flex from a pair of stereo headphones.

The incident was largely hushed up at the time, but Erskine was one of those said to have gone to Sutcliffe's aid. Seven months after the attack it was reported that the Crown Prosecution Service had advised that Wilson should not be charged due to a lack of evidence.

Wilson was thought to have launched the assault because he resented being locked up with sex offenders. Sutcliffe didn't like to talk about the incident beyond repeating his mantra that he was not a sex offender.

Thirteen months after that incident Sutcliffe was targeted again and, just like in Parkhurst, the attacker went for his eyes.

Ian Kay, 29, had been sent to Broadmoor after he was diagnosed with an abnormal personality disorder following his conviction for the murder of a Woolworths assistant manager during a shop raid.

On March 19, 1997, Kay asked another patient on Henley Ward to turn his music up loud and then grabbed a pen which he used to stab Sutcliffe in both eyes in a sustained attack, although he insisted he fought back.

"I only grabbed his head as he was behind me, I flung him over my shoulder in front of me, I thought about stamping on his head and kicking it, but I decided not to, he then ran off.

"I'm not sure whether it was his pen or one of mine, as I was facing the opposite direction when it happened, not that it made much difference whose pen it might have been."

Following the incident, Sutcliffe was left blind in his left eye.

Kay admitted attempted murder and was ordered by a judge to be detained under the Mental Health Act.

These incidents may suggest that Sutcliffe was without friends during his time at Broadmoor, but that wasn't the case.

He became friendly with a number of patients, but one of his most cherished friendships was the one that had started at Parkhurst and then strengthened after he arrived at Broadmoor – Jimmy Savile.

Utilising his unique combination of charm, bravado and deceitful cunning, Savile had bizarrely managed to wheedle his way into a position of authority at Broadmoor.

He became its unofficial entertainment manager, had his own car park space and an apartment in the grounds. He was also given his own set of keys which afforded him unfettered access to wards, enabling him to abuse a number of patients at will.

During this time, he was becoming ever more friendly with Sutcliffe.

"When people had visits, he used to come round to the visiting hall for a chat," said Sutcliffe. "I always used to have a good chat when he used to sit down at the table with us and I used to introduce him to my visitors. He had his funny little sayings, 'now then, now then', all them sort of things.

"Let the train take the strain, his adverts for British Rail. Done them for free. He was very generous, anything to help out because British Rail were in a bit of a crisis at the time.

"I used to sit for ages chatting with him. Lovely fella. Always had a good laugh with him.

"He was totally non-judgemental. He said: 'Nobody's famous or special, everybody's just people.' That was his outlook and that's why he mixed with people at the top and prisoners and all sorts of people."

Sutcliffe never suspected that Savile – later exposed as one of the country's worst ever sex offenders – was anything other than a decent Leeds bloke, or that his main motivation in mixing with people in places like Broadmoor was to abuse them.

Others had their suspicions, but they never amounted to anything until after Savile's death in October 2011, aged 84, an event which upset Sutcliffe.

"A sad loss. Poor old Jimmy, he had a good send-off didn't he, a gold coffin, went round Leeds where he used to live and all the people lining the streets."

Savile was buried in Scarborough and, in keeping with his quirkiness, he left instructions for his coffin to be placed at an angle looking out to sea.

"That's right, facing out to sea," said Sutcliffe. "Of course, he couldn't see because he's below ground. So it didn't make sense, just daftness really. He had a sense of humour."

The rumours of abuse which had swirled around Savile during his lifetime began gaining greater traction after his death.

Almost a year later, ITV broadcast an investigation into the allegations which blew the case wide open. Within three weeks, the Metropolitan Police were pursuing 400 lines of inquiry from 300 victims across the UK as the BBC admitted it was engulfed in a "tsunami of filth".

Fifteen months after Savile died, the Metropolitan Police revealed the full, shocking extent of his abuse which stretched over 54 years and took in at least 450 victims at multiple sites across the country.

He had assaulted victims in NHS hospitals, a private hospice, on BBC premises and in schools.

They even included a terminally ill child, attacked by Savile during a visit to London's Great Ormond Street Hospital.

Metropolitan Police Commander Peter Spindler perfectly summed up how Savile's celebrity status and unique personality had enabled him to get away with it for so long.

"He groomed a nation," he said.

It was a barely believable litany of abuse, yet his loyal friend the Yorkshire Ripper refused to believe it.

Sutcliffe dismissed the allegations as a "witch hunt" and said he was "incensed at all the bad publicity Jimmy Savile was getting now that he's dead… and he can't defend himself."

While he was in Broadmoor, Sutcliffe was informed that his father had passed away, aged 81. Despite his feelings of hatred towards his dad earlier in his life, his death in the summer of 2004 still moved him.

He wasn't allowed to attend the funeral, but he was taken on a day trip to visit the spot where the ashes had been scattered in Arnside on the southern tip of Cumbria six months later. It was where the Sutcliffe family had spent many holidays over the years and where his grandfather had a caravan.

"It was very windy, such a freezing wind coming in off the sea, but I was allowed to walk around without handcuffs, so I walked along the beach for a distance and stopped at the spot where my brother Carl had scattered Dad's ashes.

"I brought two pebbles back from the beach as a keepsake.

"The guys noted that I was quiet and reflective on the journey back from Cumbria, but I was thinking of Dad and recalling many incidents from the past. I really needed closure and the trip out did provide that.

"I was very upset at not being able to attend Dad's funeral after being denied the chance to see him before he died.

"Over the past 10 years, I have become very close to Dad. I was able to speak to him on the telephone at the cancer hospice a few days before he died, and he said the staff were kind and gave him anything he wanted. He knew he had just days to live."

It was also while Sutcliffe was in Broadmoor that the intriguing mystery at the heart of his case was finally solved.

On the morning of October 19, 2005, journalists from across the north raced to Flodden Road, a street of semi-detached houses on the Ford estate in Sunderland.

Wearside Jack, the man who had successfully diverted the biggest criminal inquiry the country had ever known, was about to be unveiled.

But anyone anticipating a twisted genius being responsible for such a successful hoax was about to experience a Wizard of Oz moment.

When the curtain was yanked back, there was no towering intellect behind it, rather a pathetic drunk who had slipped so far down the slippery slope that he was unable to give any sort of detailed explanation for his actions of nearly three decades earlier.

John Humble was 49 and lived with his brother in a rundown, two-bedroomed council house. Most days, he could be seen shuffling to the local shop to buy a two-litre bottle of Ace Cider for £1.99.

He was so drunk on the day he was arrested that when he woke the next day in a cell he had to be reminded that he had been arrested and was now in a police station in Leeds, almost 100 miles from his home.

The police had finally caught up with him thanks to a cold case review of the hoaxer case, during which DNA from the letters was matched with a sample Humble had given when he was arrested for drink-driving in 2001.

It was a slam dunk case and within 48 hours of his arrest he was charged, but the question everyone wanted answering – why? – proved frustratingly elusive.

All Humble himself could offer, on the back of many years of heavy drinking, was that he had been out of work at the time and bored. It was a "prank – just a bit of fun", he claimed.

His family later revealed he had an obsession with both the 19th Century Jack the Ripper case and the Yorkshire Ripper, and the hoax may have been a misguided act of revenge.

As a youngster growing up on Sunderland's Hylton Lane estate (not far from where the experts thought Wearside Jack hailed from) he began getting into trouble with the police. In 1975 he was convicted of assaulting an off-duty officer and sent to a notorious juvenile detention centre in County Durham where he suffered physical abuse and possibly worse.

He was released with a burning sense of hatred of the police, which would soon combine with his growing obsession with the Yorkshire Ripper case.

Following his arrest in 2005 he admitted to four charges of perverting justice and on March 21, 2006, at Leeds crown court was sentenced to eight years in prison.

He was released in 2009 and moved to South Shields, a few miles north of Sunderland, where he lived under a different name. He died in July 2019, aged 63.

After Humble sent the inquiry spinning out of control by posting the cassette tape, Sutcliffe murdered three more women.

While he was in Broadmoor he finally admitted two further, non-fatal attacks which had not been included in his trial.

They are the only further attacks he has ever confessed to, and it was all thanks to the dogged efforts of Keith Hellawell, the Jaguar-driving senior West Yorkshire officer who would later become Chief Constable of the force before being appointed Drugs Tsar under Tony Blair's Labour government in 1998.

Following Sutcliffe's arrest, forces around the country had pestered West Yorkshire to be allowed to interview him to establish if he was responsible for unsolved murders in their areas.

By then, West Yorkshire was reeling under criticism on multiple fronts for their Ripper investigation, including for the relatively short period of time they had spent interviewing him after his arrest.

If other forces were allowed access to him and he admitted to other killings West Yorkshire had missed in those early interviews, it would be another embarrassing blow.

So Hellawell, then a chief superintendent, was tasked with leading an investigation into other potential attacks. He compiled a list of 78 unsolved murders and attempted murders potentially committed by Sutcliffe stretching back to 1966. That was whittled down to the ten most likely, which were looked at in greater detail.

Hellawell visited Sutcliffe on numerous occasions at Parkhurst and Broadmoor until, in 1992, his relentless pursuit paid off when he received a message that Sutcliffe wanted to see him in Broadmoor.

"I called for him to come, I said I've something to tell you that's come up in my memory."

He admitted to attacking Tracy Browne in 1975 and, although his memory was hazier in relation to Ann Rooney, he accepted he attacked her as well, in 1979.

Suspicions remained that he was responsible for other attacks, and in 2017 West Yorkshire officers visited him in relation to 17 non-fatal assaults.

He insisted he was not responsible for any of the attacks.

"There isn't any, I admitted everything, there's not a single one more or anything that I've done.

"The police have already interviewed me about all these cases and they're quite satisfied I couldn't have been in the area, and there was absolutely no evidence to point to me of any of these things. It's just nothing to do with me, these cases."

On a couple of occasions he hinted there might have been another one or possibly two further attacks he had committed. But in the same breath he said he couldn't remember the details and then rejected the suggestion there were any more.

"Might be an odd one attack... I don't know, there might have been one or two," he said.

Yet his constant self-regard raises a question mark over this assertion.

Sutcliffe rarely cared about how his actions affected others, so he was unlikely to consider relatives of victims from any unsolved crimes he was guilty of.

"I'll have to ask the police if they plan to prosecute me if I recall anything because that means I'll be dropping myself in it if I remembered anything, wouldn't I?" he said quietly one day in Frankland, leaving the unspoken thought on the table that if there were any other attacks he wouldn't have admitted to them.

In February 2018, West Yorkshire Police announced he would not be charged with any further attacks. The Crown Prosecution Service had already made the decision in 1992 that he would not be charged with the Browne and Rooney attacks. It was considered that as he was already serving life imprisonment, there was no public interest in pursuing another trial for further attacks.

In 2010 a ruling was made at the High Court in London to change his sentence to a full life term.

The judge at his original trial had recommended that he serve a minimum term of 30 years before being allowed to apply for parole, but a legally-binding tariff had never actually been set.

Sutcliffe, now known officially by his mother's maiden name of Coonan after changing it to avoid attention when he opened a bank account, had been resigned to the outcome.

But he still railed against what he viewed as a biased judiciary, media and public who had it in for him.

Blind as to why anybody would have a negative view of his situation, he said: "There's always somebody in there trying to throw a spanner in, especially in my case because of all the publicity, that's what ruins the case. They don't take your circumstances into account, they don't look at it properly, they only base it on what you did in the beginning. They ignore the rest of things, it's all wrong, really.

"I haven't done anything wrong all the time I've been inside. And yet they slap a whole life tariff on me. That's pure spite."

He also remained angry at the never-ending headlines revealing more offending by his old friend Savile.

He was most incensed at the allegations that Savile had committed crimes at Broadmoor and convinced himself that his old pal's status as a keyholder meant he couldn't have been guilty.

"What a load of rubbish. He had the keys to the place. All this nonsense about him interfering with patients, it's gobbledygook. He wouldn't do that in Broadmoor, he wouldn't do it anyway, I know that. He was a highly popular man, he ran over 80 marathons for charity, who else would do that? I think that shortened his life, wearing himself out like that. He had a good heart, and he was very generous with his charities. As far as I'm concerned, he was a nice fellow was Jimmy, very generous."

The continuing investigation to identify the full extent of Savile's offending involved thousands of people receiving questionnaires to ask if they had ever been abused by him, including Sutcliffe.

"I got a questionnaire through the post saying you knew Jimmy Savile, would you like to be interviewed and see if you can list any wrongdoings? I'm not having 'owt to do with that. They're trying to use him as a scapegoat so they can dig more dirt. That's what's been going on all along. I don't believe half of it. Nobody's sticking up for Jimmy."

The weight of revelations eventually became so overwhelming that even Sutcliffe conceded at least some of it was true. But he still couldn't accept the full extent of it.

"Admittedly he must have done a few wrong things, but it's just ridiculous the stuff that they're throwing at him, I mean he's dead as well. They're just having a witch hunt."

Just as he refused to accept complete culpability for what he did himself, he never did acknowledge Savile's full wrongdoing.

The death of his close friend meant Sutcliffe had lost one of the reliable pillars of support in his life. But another remained as loyal as ever. His ex-wife Sonia.

CHAPTER 29

SONIA AND I

From the moment that her husband was arrested on suspicion of being the Yorkshire Ripper, Sonia Sutcliffe became a target.

She was a target not only of arsonists and burglars, but also of those who held the view that "she must have known".

A few days after the Old Bailey trial started, while Sonia was in London supporting her husband, their house in Garden Lane was attacked with a firebomb being thrown through the living room window. Around £1,000 worth of damage was caused to the furniture in the front room, but that was far from the end of it.

The house was repeatedly burgled, at least nine times in the first five years after the trial.

As well as the physical attacks, she could never escape the air of suspicion held by many that she must have had some idea that her husband was responsible for the murders, something that Sutcliffe always insisted was not the case.

"I was never covered in blood, people used to say Sonia must know something because of all the blood, but there wasn't any. She's perfectly as white as snow. It's just stupid people speculating. She never saw anything out of the ordinary. Time I came in, she was in bed. When I was out late, because I'd be playing snooker with the lads next door, the Barkers, and I'd drop them off and then go on the mission. And when I was long distance away I used to ring her at night saying 'Oh, I can't make it back, I haven't got enough driving hours left, so I can't make it back. I'll be having an overnight, so lock up and go to bed', so she wasn't worrying about me."

There was never any evidence or hint that Sonia had any knowledge of his crimes, yet the gossip and threats never ceased. Many years after Sutcliffe's conviction, Sonia was still on the receiving end of poison pen letters.

"She's had threatening letters," said Sutcliffe, "anonymous of course, the cowardly bastards.

"When she's being threatened, she has to face it all. She is subject to this rubbish. They're terrorising her and these people haven't the slightest empathy and they know she's been perfectly behaved all the time. She put up with a lot bless her, she's a good lass."

Sonia later married again after she and Sutcliffe finally divorced, but she remained supportive of her former husband. That was one of the reasons for the continuing air of suspicion. People couldn't fathom it. Many women finding themselves in a similar position wouldn't think twice of heading straight for the door and then the divorce courts.

Not Sonia. Her support for her first husband never ceased.

"She stuck with me for many, many years, before she even thought of a separation. All credit to her and then even after that when I suggested she find somebody else, she still keeps coming to see me. She really must have loved me a lot. Most women would have just washed their hands of somebody, but she knew me so well, my personality and that, she couldn't let go.

"No one could have asked for a better, more loyal wife than Sonia was to me and as a friend she still is as loyal and yes, I am very proud of her. She's an angel."

She even agreed to become Sutcliffe's next of kin again after his sister Anne, who had held that position for a number of years, died in 2005.

Once she had reconciled herself to the length of the sentence he had been given, she had some practical matters to deal with.

"She didn't know what to do with all my clothes. I had a nice white suit and she kept that for a long time, then eventually she gave it to a charity shop."

Knowing he wouldn't be coming out for a very long time, if ever, Sutcliffe suggested they should divorce so she could find someone.

She refused for many years, but finally agreed in 1994. Even then, he said, she underlined her reluctance by timing it for April Fool's Day.

"Sonia did it on the 1st of April because she didn't want to do it. Her heart wasn't in it. She had no life, we couldn't share what we used to share, we couldn't go places, we couldn't have a life together. I encouraged her to get a divorce and find somebody else. Believe me, my heart was in my boots all the time when I was telling her. I said find somebody else… I said you look young for your age, you could find somebody else easy enough. I only had her happiness in mind. They say if you love something, let it go."

Three years after their divorce was finalised, Sonia took him at his word and married a hairdresser from Bradford called Michael Woodward, who is ten years her junior.

When Sutcliffe spoke about this new relationship a sadness crept into his voice.

"I told her to find someone else… I wish I didn't now."

Not having much choice, Sutcliffe largely accepted this new relationship, although he couldn't help but have the odd dig at her new husband.

Despite this new relationship, Sonia kept visiting her ex-husband.

"She came back again and kept coming to see me."

More than three decades after the trial, when Sutcliffe had let himself go and was now an overweight, unkempt and unhealthy pensioner, he hadn't lost sight of what he first found attractive about Sonia.

"I had two lovely visits from Sonia on Friday. She visited the afternoon and the evening. She looked well, she looked beautiful

I'd say. She hasn't gained any weight at all, she's got a lover, and she was dressed nicely and she looked lovely."

Sonia's ongoing loyalty may have seemed inexplicable to many, but after so many years Sutcliffe took it for granted and was furious if the smooth running of her visits was ever interrupted.

Due to the distance she had to travel – a 400-mile round trip from Bradford to Broadmoor – she usually booked in for a double visit, one in the morning and another in the afternoon to give her the full day with him apart from the lunch break. But on a Saturday in June, 2010, things didn't go to plan.

"They said: 'Oh, you can come in the morning but not in the afternoon', and she said, 'why not?' They said the computer says no, but they wouldn't give a reason. I took it up with the staff, and they said we'll see what we can do. One rang the visitor reception. They said she can come in the night time, at six till eight. I said look, what's she gonna do from 12 till six, for six hours? She can't hang around that long, it's out of the question.

"They said, sounds reasonable, tell her to rebook for the afternoon and we'll see what we can do. So I rang her up and said ring up and rebook it, so she did, and you know what they said? Somebody else was on duty and they said, the computer says no. They repeated it and they wouldn't give a reason.

"So I had to go to the hospital advocacy, and she took it up."

The double visit was finally booked, but Sutcliffe still wasn't happy when it took place in a different room than normal.

"It was a smaller room, where there's the staff facing us, sat right up to us, so they could hear everything you were saying, not listening on purpose, but sat within earshot. I found out what the reason was. The computer had it that the patient who attacked me 13 years ago [Ian Kay], was having a visit at the same time and they thought I might go and attack him to get revenge because I haven't seen him since. But I wouldn't, I'd forgotten all about it. Thirteen years ago. Didn't mean anything to me whatsoever. They thought I'd want to get him, but I'm not a vengeful person like that, I wouldn't. But that's the way they are in this place, they don't take chances of any kind. They said they didn't want to tell Sonia because it might upset her that I might turn violent.

"I said don't be stupid, I wouldn't, I said I'm not a violent person by nature. I said, what did upset her is you telling her the computer said no twice and not giving her a reason. Anyway, it all worked out all right in the end."

Like any other long-term prisoner, Sutcliffe's mind sometimes drifted to the other life he could have had if he hadn't committed his crimes.

"Sometimes I think it's passed quick but, other times, I think it's passed slow. It just depends what sort of frame of mind I'm in, sometimes I think, it's all that time ago since I made love to Sonia and all that, it dulls your memory, say 32 years without having sex, without making love to your wife. Or anybody, nobody at all, that's a long time in that respect.

"She's a good lass. Tells me she still loves me, even though she's married again. We send birthday cards, Christmas cards and that.

"I'd love to do something simple such as a long walk in our favourite part of the countryside with Sonia in nice weather, that would do me nicely.

"I'd have retired from long-distance driving. I'd still be with Sonia, we'd still be living in the same house."

Conjugal visits aren't allowed in the UK, a rule which, unsurprisingly, doesn't have much support among prisoners, especially lifers.

"In the marriage vows it says, let no man put asunder who God has joined together," said Sutcliffe in one of his moans about the denial of physical pleasure to prisoners and their partners. "But the system does that, so they're going against the Bible. They're hypocrites because they ask you to swear on the Bible, and yet they ignore what the Bible says."

At times he felt helpless as Sonia struggled to cope with the challenges that life threw at her without him.

Following one of her day-long visits to him in early 2012 she returned to Bradford to discover their home in Garden Lane had been burgled yet again. She still owned it, although she often stayed with her husband Michael at their flat nearby.

"They'd smashed the door off the hinges, forced it in and kicked the door in. They took a lot of stuff, the bastards. It's about the fifth time she's been burgled in as many years. The last time they smashed the door in as well."

Over the course of their many meetings, the conversation at times inevitably turned to his murderous activities.

"I have explained why I did what I felt I had to do, when I've spoken to Sonia and discussed things over the years – It's the least I could do with her staying by my side all that time.

"I never told Sonia to be careful when she went out at night all those years ago because it would have made me a hypocrite if you get my drift, I knew she wasn't at risk."

Sutcliffe clung to Sonia's support as one of the few constants in his life. But she had her own life to lead with her new husband and at times the communication between them drifted, something which stressed Sutcliffe.

On one occasion in early November 2015, he said: "Still no contact with Sonia although I saw the social worker, Nicky, on Thursday and asked for her to phone Sonia for me as she hadn't answered the phone in 10 consecutive nights. Nicky did speak with Sonia, and one of the male staff later gave me a message from Nicky to say that I could phone Sonia on Friday night and she'd discuss things with me.

"So you can probably imagine how much that lifted my spirits. On Friday, Nicky came to the ward and asked me if I'd got her message? I said yes, thank you very much! – I'll phone Sonia tonight as you said in your message. Nicky said: 'No – that wasn't my message at all. Sonia said she was feeling very harassed and had been ignoring your calls. She wants to have a break and leave things until after Christmas'. So that was a blow, I can tell you.

"There's no way of knowing whether Sonia will even want to communicate after Christmas at this rate. We no longer correspond with one another [by letter], we haven't done that for years apart from birthdays and such, plus her visits of course. The main source of communication has been the telephone. Now that's a zero option. I don't know what to do."

Sutcliffe, like many other high-profile murderers, had plenty of female admirers over the years. He received numerous proposals of marriage and right to the end of his life there were women he communicated with who wanted to be more than friends, if only the criminal justice system would allow it.

But despite this female attention, he never wavered from the belief that he and Sonia were soul mates, that she was his one and only true love.

He also faithfully kept to his habit of phoning her on her birthday, which was also their wedding anniversary, although he didn't always get through.

A quarter of a century after they divorced, he said: "I've got to try and ring Sonia again because it were her birthday yesterday and our anniversary as well."

Sonia has always been an intensely private person and hated any media attention that her ongoing relationship with her ex-husband attracted. Her visits to see him became less frequent in later years, something which he put down to that attention which she was never able to shake.

"She's very secretive, very private" he said, "she won't give anything away to anybody, she won't even tell me things on the phone. She protects her privacy, she's totally unapproachable."

CHAPTER 30

HE'S GONE

Like many people receiving treatment on the NHS for mental health issues, Sutcliffe was supported by the Care Programme Approach (CPA), a framework which assesses a patient's needs and draws up a care plan to best deal with those needs.

In later years, his six-monthly CPA meetings were dominated by the debate of whether he was well enough to be transferred out of Broadmoor, an idea which horrified him.

"It'd undo all the good work they've done over the years," said Sutcliffe, a note of stress clearly sounding in his voice.

He had moaned for years about the regime at Broadmoor, but the prospect of a return to prison suddenly caused him to view the hospital in a much more favourable light.

"Everything's terrible about prison," he said. "You don't get any mental health help or anything there. More violence, more weapons, more drugs, more of everything; there, it's a lot worse than it was.

"I was seeing this place as my home for the rest of my life. I don't mind it in Broadmoor. Overall, it's done me a lot of good.

"The category A prisons, they're a pit of black despair and hopelessness. You don't get any health care like you do at Broadmoor. You don't get any friendly words from the staff in prisons, all they do is bung you your tablets if you are supposed to be on medication and that's it.

"The treatment I've had in Broadmoor has been very good. I know it's over the top security here but apart from that, the system and the medical help is very good, really. It's helped to keep my head above water all these years."

Having been the victim of a series of attacks both in prison and in Broadmoor, he was also concerned about his own safety.

"They have weapons and all that. Broadmoor's much better because nothing gets smuggled in here. It's all drugs and smuggled in phones and violence… they have no control, the staff in prisons these days, drones get sent in with drugs dropped into the prison grounds.

"And all my correspondents [pen pals] would disappear and my phone calls. It don't look good, so I'm a bit in the dumps now."

The possibility of a transfer came to dominate his thinking and, in the summer of 2015, he claimed to have suffered three serious psychotic episodes within the space of a matter of weeks, one during a visit from a friend.

"I don't want to go into detail, but it was really bad. Don't look good, does it, maybe I'm cracking up."

The process was a slow one, but his CPA meeting on Tuesday, November 24, 2015, confirmed the inevitable.

He was told that his treatment at Broadmoor had come to an end and there was no more the hospital could do for him.

Sutcliffe was appalled.

"What a disaster," he said. "The meeting could not have gone any worse. My future looks really grim now. I don't want to go back to prison. You don't get the health care like you do here."

The news triggered a further decline in his mental health until, out of the blue, he claimed the voices had suddenly returned, the first time for years he had spoken openly and regularly about them.

He also said he had begun having paranoid thoughts, most commonly that he was being poisoned.

"I've been having a terrible stomach cramps and sickness and diarrhoea, I can't help thinking somebody's trying to poison me, gradually," he said in January 2016.

"I watch them like a hawk when they're serving the food, but I can't see everything they do because they do some of it in the kitchen. I'm just wondering who's doing it because it's not natural to be sick every day.

"I've had the hallucinations again. Since last Wednesday, I've had them several times. The voice, it agrees with me that somebody's trying to do me in. They've got it in for me, one way or another they want rid of me, I'm really depressed. Last time, it told me I had to attack, to not just attack, but I had to kill, because the voice told me that there were two prostitutes sat on the other side of the visiting room. Don't look good, does it… back to the old days."

He became so convinced that the Broadmoor management were targeting him that he said he was contemplating suicide as a way out.

"I've got so many enemies here you see in the hierarchy at Broadmoor, trying to interfere with everything, stopping visits and making Sonia's phone calls so that they're listened to all the time… got it in for me in every way. If I did it myself I'd have the satisfaction of making it impossible for them, but then again they would've won. Things are getting desperate."

The staff became concerned enough to place Sutcliffe on 24-hour suicide watch and his visits were suspended. After a few days, they were satisfied that his expressed intention of taking his own life was not serious. He was taken off suicide watch and his visits were restarted, but the following month, in February, he said the voices were back and were telling him not to trust the staff, although by now he had long come to accept that the voice wasn't God.

"The messages I've been getting recently are terrible, I haven't told the staff half of it… it's just lack of trust and the voice says: 'Don't trust them, they're against you'. I know it's a symptom of the illness, but it disturbs me. I know it's not the same source as I thought it was, God's voice, I've come to terms with it.

"It's the same voice but not only that, I hear additional voices come from time to time, my Grandmother's voice and Emily

Jackson's voice [his second murder victim] and her body floating in the air and changing into my mother. All these things, it's not just the one voice, that's the controlling voice, the man's voice. It sounds really authoritative, it's compelling. I tried to block it out. I'd been having it for about three hours, and I was really angry because it was interfering with my thoughts, and I said: 'Fuck off'. I don't normally swear, but I was so fed up.

"It interferes with you all the time, it's telling you things that you got to do, instructions and you can't shut it out, you can't block your ears, it don't make any difference.

"I was in my room looking out of the window when I heard a voice, I turned around and it seemed to be coming from a wall, it was the same voice which I used to think was the voice of God, I now know it isn't and it said: 'This is a message from your brain, don't worry about what's happening with all the talk of a move back to prison, you'll be all right'. It was a bit strange as I hadn't heard any voices for about 15 years. It wasn't just one voice, it was two, the second one was my Grandmother. The other voice told me not to tell anyone about what had happened as I had a cookery class booked, and they would stop it, so I didn't say anything. I had the cookery class, ate the food and then mentioned it to one of the staff, within seconds I could see them telling another member of staff."

As Sutcliffe himself stated, he hadn't heard the voices for years. Yet as soon as the authorities were considering a move which he was distinctly unhappy with, he claimed his mental health was in rapid decline. In March, he reckoned the voice was now telling him to kill again and he speculated whether the target was Dr Kevin Murray.

The forensic psychiatrist had taken overall responsibility for Sutcliffe's care after he was made clinical director of Broadmoor in 2001, a role which continued until March 2014.

When things were going well for Sutcliffe he placed a lot of the credit at Dr Murray's door, but once the prison transfer was on the table he projected all of his negative thoughts onto him.

He came to view him as the sole architect of the plan to move him from his cushy, settled life in Broadmoor to the harsh regime of a prison. Dr Murray was now placed in the same bracket as everyone else Sutcliffe felt was against him – police, lawyers, his trial judge, the media – who were all "nasty, biased scumbags".

"Therapeutic wise, it'll be a disaster," Sutcliffe said as he railed against the prison transfer. "I don't know how Dr Murray has the gall to recommend me going back to prison when he knows my mental health's gonna badly suffer.

"I had a lot of trust in Dr Murray until he came out with this outlandish proposal, sending me back to prison."

As the stress built, he claimed the voices were getting worse.

"It's really bad, last time it told me I had to kill a very bad man, but it didn't say his name. I wonder if it's Dr Murray, it hasn't said, but I'm waiting, it'll come back again. I don't want to harm anybody."

On another occasion he said: "The voice has told me that I may have to kill a bad man. The voice has told me I have to kill my doctor."

He also spoke in more detail about how the voice had suggested he commit suicide.

"The voice said: 'Why don't you end it all, you're only living for other people, not for yourself.' I thought about it later and thought that's what Jesus said when he came to Earth, he lived for everybody else, not for himself and gave his life, his perfect life because he was free of sin, he never done anything wrong, he was a perfect man, the one and only perfect man that ever lived, and he gave that life for mankind. That's how unselfish and... it was God's will though, of course.

"It's really driving me crazy this incessant instructions and telling me what to do, to attack people and kill myself. It hasn't got as much effect [as in the 1970s] because I know that it isn't God's instructions."

He had stopped taking his anti-psychotic medicine in the middle of December 2015 (he voluntarily restarted it on Friday, March 11, 2016) which may have been the cause of this deterioration in his mental health, coupled with the stress of transferring out of Broadmoor.

Or, of course, he may have been making it all up in the hope of dodging the prison move and remaining at Broadmoor.

Was it a re-run of the events of 35 years earlier at his trial, when he was accused of pulling the wool over the eyes of the medical experts to achieve a cushier sentence in a hospital instead of a prison?

He rejected the suggestion, but said that even Dr Murray had told him he suspected it might be the case.

"Saying I only stop the medication to stop myself going back to prison, what a rubbish thing to say."

His anger towards Dr Murray reached fever pitch in July 2016 when the psychiatrist told a tribunal, the body which decides if a patient can be released from the Mental Health Act, that Sutcliffe was ready to go back to prison.

"He just ignores everybody, he's so stubborn, marches straight ahead without considering anybody or anything. He made his mind up ages ago, he just goes through everybody like a bulldozer and ignores what they say.

"They'll be putting me on suicide watch again, but I don't care. Sending me back to prison for the rest of my days, it's like another life sentence. I can't face that. They're not listening to me, they'll find out to their cost, and it'll be Dr Murray who carries the can."

His moans and claims of voices returning counted for nothing and on Wednesday, August 28, 2016, Sutcliffe, dressed in a garish blue, green and yellow boiler suit, was handcuffed and placed in a prison van.

"Sat in a shaky old ramshackle truck, with them little compartments in it and you feel every bump. You could bite your tongue off easily."

Depressed and angry, he was driven almost 300 miles north.

* * *

If evil exists, it lives here. Sitting on the edge of the beautiful cathedral city of Durham in the North East of England, Her Majesty's Prison Frankland is home to the ugliest of souls.

It is one of only eight high-security prisons in the United Kingdom and houses prisoners who have been sentenced to ten years or more – the murderers, rapists, armed robbers and terrorists. The ones who make the news.

Despite his reservations about leaving Broadmoor, Sutcliffe settled in quickly at Frankland.

Prisoner A6214DV was moved into a single cell on A Wing which holds 108 vulnerable inmates who enjoy enhanced status.

"I wouldn't go back to Broadmoor if they gave me £1m," he said shortly after arriving. "I was pleasantly surprised, as all the cons and the staff have been fine."

He became friendly with other high-profile inmates including Ian Huntley who was jailed for life for murdering the Soham schoolgirls Holly Wells and Jessica Chapman, both ten, in 2002.

"Ian's really friendly and helpful," he said.

He also got on well with Charles Taylor, the former president of Liberia who was jailed for 50 years in 2012 for war crimes including rape, murder, sexual slavery and recruiting child soldiers during a blood-thirsty campaign to fuel the 11-year civil war in neighbouring Sierra Leone which left 50,000 dead.

Due to the difficulties of Taylor's trial being held in Africa because of ethnic rivalries, it was agreed it would take place in The Hague. As part of the international effort to bring him to justice, the UK government offered to take him should he be convicted, which is how he came to spend the rest of his life on the outskirts of Durham.

Sutcliffe was only two years older than Taylor and that common bond saw them hit it off.

"Charles just let me in in front of him to do the call," said Sutcliffe cheerily on the phone one day from Frankland. "I said I wouldn't be too long. He always lets me go first.

"He was an African leader was Charles, he knew Robert Mugabe. He speaks excellent English, very polite man. You wouldn't think he was in for genocide. I like him personally, he's a nice fella. He's easy to get on with. He gives me a TV guide every week."

One inmate who Sutcliffe didn't click with was Levi Bellfield, who was jailed in 2008 for murdering two women and the attempted murder of a third.

Three years later, he was also convicted of the murder in 2002 of 13-year-old schoolgirl Milly Dowler in Walton-on-Thames, Surrey.

"He's a total scumbag," said Sutcliffe, spitting out the words whenever he spoke about Bellfield. "And when he comes to talk to me, he's as nice as nine-pence, tries to be polite and friendly. He's a two-faced get. I don't tell him anything."

Following his arrival at Frankland, Sutcliffe's health continued to deteriorate. He was now a frail, old man and the advancing years brought with them angina, an enlarged prostate and the complications of diabetes, including diabetic retinopathy which damages the blood vessels of the retina and eventually leads to blindness.

He was also increasingly lonely. After years of visits to Parkhurst and Broadmoor, Sonia didn't once go and see him while he was in Frankland. His parents were dead, as was his sister Anne, her husband Trevor, and his old friend Jimmy Savile.

He had become estranged from most of his other siblings following a row over Anne's funeral in 2005. He wanted to attend, but they knew his presence would bring a chaotic circus of attention they just didn't need. They wanted a quiet ceremony without drama and when Sutcliffe, self-absorbed as ever, kept demanding and pleading to attend they decided to cut ties, finally sick of the years of having to listen to his self-absorbed complaints during the weekly phone calls.

His closest brother Mick was the only one who remained in touch, but he had been unwell for a while and hadn't been to see Sutcliffe since the late 1990s.

At times, it must have felt that his only connection to the past were the voices.

"The voice can still be there, but because I am on the anti-psychotic medication it dulls it to a level where I can control it.

"It doesn't really tell me to do bad things now. Only on three occasion has it told me to go and punch someone since I moved to Frankland, that's because they pissed me off in some way, but I didn't do it because I've been a model prisoner and I know how to control it."

He remained committed to what had become the main support network in his life, the Jehovah's Witnesses.

Friends who had first made contact with him when he was in Parkhurst and who later became Jehovah's Witnesses encouraged him to join the church in the late 1980s when he was at Broadmoor. He credited them, along with years of medication, for helping him "see the error of my thinking", but his years of prayer, Bible lessons and counselling never led him to issue a public apology to any of his victims.

His main consideration in terms of the benefit gained from his religious conversion was, unsurprisingly, himself.

"Seeing the Jehovah's Witnesses every week, sometimes twice a week, for a long period, it's really done me good.

"It's lifted my spirits and made me rise above all the problems. What a marvellous difference it's made to my life."

During visits from the small band of friends at Frankland, he would tuck into his favourite snack, an egg and tomato sandwich on white bread washed down with a white coffee, two sweeteners.

Sutcliffe cut a rigid figure during these visits, with his face largely expressionless, a side effect of his anti-psychotic medication.

The scars down the left-hand side of his face and neck from the attack with a broken glass coffee jar in Parkhurst in 1983 were still there, but had faded over time.

His beard was more grey than black, his hair was also greying and a bald patch was pushing through. The obsessive vanity of his younger days when he spent hours grooming his hair and beard into the distinctive, sharp-edged style which made for such memorable photos was long gone. He talked about the murders less and less in his later years because he didn't like to be reminded of what he had done.

If pushed he would discuss them and when he did a strange transformation overtook him when he departed from the rigid stillness. He would lean back in his chair and take a deep breath before slowly exhaling and begin chatting about the attacks as if they were the work of someone else entirely.

He never abandoned his belief in that one narrow theory of why he became a serial killer – it was all down to his mental illness.

It meant he was content that all the horror he was responsible for was not his fault, and if it wasn't his fault, why should he spend all of his life in prison? Sutcliffe could never quite let go of the dream of one day being released. He obsessed about the trial judge's original recommendation of 30 years, even though that had long ago been turned into a full life term.

In late 2018, two years after arriving at Frankland, he said: "I mean, look at Ron and Reggie. Reggie was released after 30 years. And they got 30 year recommendation same as me. And I've done 38 now, and he was released after 30 years because his health wasn't very good."

The idea of the Yorkshire Ripper ever being released was a pipe dream.

In the spring of 2020, life in Frankland suddenly changed drastically, just as it did all around the world. The Covid-19 pandemic meant that prisoners were locked in their cells and visits were stopped as the authorities desperately tried to prevent an outbreak inside the jail. Sutcliffe became terrified of the disease and when visits restarted after lockdown restrictions were eased, he declined to have any for fear of contracting the virus.

"I'm not risking it," he said, "it'll kill you."

He became convinced he had the disease, even though repeated tests came back negative. Then, in October 2020, he developed chest pains, struggled for breath and was found to be suffering from a slow heart rate. On October 28, he was transferred to the nearby University Hospital of North Durham after an electrocardiogram (ECG) showed his heart was in full block, which means that the electrical activity that stimulates the heart was not passing through properly.

He was fitted with a pacemaker and over the next couple of days was twice tested for Covid, both of which came back negative.

On November 4, he was discharged back to Frankland and again tested for Covid. This time it was positive.

Over the next six days he made repeated to trips to and from the hospital as his oxygen levels dropped and were then stabilised.

Sonia, who was still his next of kin, was informed by a prison manager that he had Covid and on November 12 she was told that he was seriously ill. At 10.30am that day a hospital consultant relayed a message to the prison that Sutcliffe was expected to die within the next 48 hours. He continued to deteriorate and at 1.09am on Friday the 13th, he stopped breathing. At 1.45am a doctor officially declared that the Yorkshire Ripper was dead.

A few hours later, Neil Jackson woke in the bedroom of his first floor flat in Leeds. It was nearly 45 years since his mother Emily had become the second woman to be murdered by Sutcliffe, but her photograph still takes pride of place on his living room wall.

Neil, ever the devoted son, speaks to her picture every day. He says goodbye to her when he pops out, and tells her he's back when he returns. Shortly after he woke that November morning, he saw the breaking news that was dominating the morning headlines.

He allowed himself a moment for it to sink in before he turned to his mother's photograph on the wall and said: "At last, Mum, he's gone."

THE END

Acknowledgements

The Peter Sutcliffe story is a vast one and telling it in great detail would not have been possible without the amount of raw material patiently and diligently collated by Alfie James from Sutcliffe over a period of 16 years. I am hugely grateful that he entrusted me to work with him. Researching every aspect of the story to build up the fullest picture was no small task either and was achieved with the assistance of the always helpful staff at Leeds Central Library, Manchester Central Library, Bingley Library, Newcastle City Library and the British Library at Boston Spa, Wetherby.

I owe a debt of gratitude to our agent Andrew Lownie for spotting the potential in this story and thanks to everyone at Mirror Books, particularly Paul Dove, Richard Williamson and Steve Hanrahan for their help. Thanks to Adele Parks for advice on navigating the world of publishing and to Lynn Boyd-Hall for tips and suggestions on the manuscript. Last, but most certainly not least, thanks to Mandy, Leah and Jake for their love, support and encouragement over many years.

Robin Perrie

I would like to thank Mirror Books and our agent Andrew Lownie for seeing the potential in this book. I would also like to thank Robin Perrie for his continued belief in the information I had gathered together. Due to Robin's interest, I knew he was the correct person to write this book with me. Finally, I would like to thank my wife and our children for all their unwavering support. I spent many hours researching Sutcliffe's life in order to know which questions to ask in letters and phone calls and spent many more hours travelling to Broadmoor and HMP Frankland for visits. Without my family, the 16 years it took to amass all the information would have been a lot more difficult.

Alfie James